D0560914

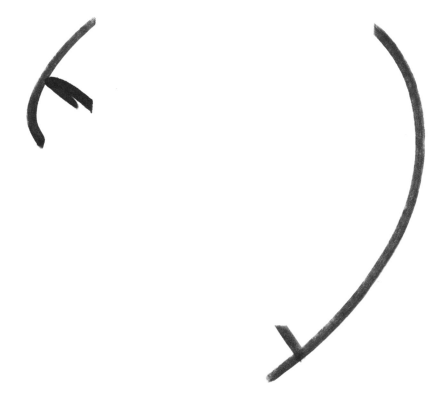

ACROSS CULTURES

Across Cultures

A GUIDE TO MULTICULTURAL LITERATURE FOR CHILDREN

✳

KATHY EAST and REBECCA L. THOMAS

Hm
Ref
55.00
4810
6/07

Children's and Young Adult Literature Reference
Catherine Barr, Series Editor

LIBRARIES
U N L I M I T E D
A Member of the Greenwood Publishing Group

Westport, Conn. London

Library of Congress Cataloging-in-Publication Data

East, Kathy.
  Across cultures : a guide to multicultural literature for children / by Kathy
East and Rebecca L. Thomas.
      p. cm. — (Children's and young adult literature reference)
  Includes bibliographical references and indexes.
  ISBN-13: 978-1-59158-336-3 (alk. paper)
  1. Children's literature, American—Bibliography. 2. Children's literature,
English—Bibliography. 3. Multiculturalism—Juvenile literature—Bibliogra-
phy. 4. Pluralism (Social sciences)—Juvenile literature—Bibliography. 5.
Identity (Psychology)—Juvenile literature—Bibliography. 6. Difference (Psy-
chology)—Juvenile literature—Bibliography. 7. Children—Books and read-
ing—United States. 8. Reading promotion—United States. I. Thomas,
Rebecca L. II. Title.
  Z1037.E19   2007
  011.62—dc22   2007013573

British Library Cataloguing in Publication Data is available.

Library of Congress Catalog Card Number: 2007013573
ISBN: 978-1-59158-336-3

First published in 2007

Libraries Unlimited, 88 Post Road West, Westport, CT 06881
A Member of the Greenwood Publishing Group, Inc.
www.lu.com

Printed in the United States of America

The paper used in this book complies with the
Permanent Paper Standard issued by the National
Information Standards Organization (Z39.48–1984).

10 9 8 7 6 5 4 3 2 1

Contents

Preface

WHEN WE BEGAN TALKING ABOUT WRITING THIS BOOK, we wanted to build on the 30-plus years each of us has worked with children—Kathy in a public library and me in school libraries. Both of us have been involved in promoting books that present diverse experiences. Kathy has represented the American Library Association (ALA) at the International Federation of Library Associations and Institutions (IFLA). I have worked on many minority achievement initiatives in Shaker Heights and participated in the work of the Minority Student Achievement Network (MSAN). Both of us teach college courses in literature for children and adolescents. We have attended conferences and even been speakers about using books with multicultural themes with children.

We began the selection process for *Across Cultures* by talking about books that we used. We realized there were many books that could be connected around themes or topics. Talking on the phone and sending email messages, we each made a list of books that we knew had to be included. We were amazed at how few of our books overlapped. Both of us knew that we wanted to use books that were highly regarded—and we have included many award-winning books. We also wanted to feature books that we had shared directly with children. This selection process could seem narrow; however, Kathy and I have served on award committees, served as reviewers, and published books about literature for children. We select the books for our libraries from all of the established reviewing sources. The books that we have included here are quality selections that have also been used by us with children.

We focused on books that deal with multicultural themes or diverse experiences. While we did not seek out books that featured white/European American characters, we did not exclude them. Especially when they fit with the topic being presented and extended the discussion of the issues in the connected books. That is why a book like *Shrinking Violet* is in with *The Name Jar*, *My Name Is Yoon*, and other books about Acceptance and Self-Image.

Another selection issue that we considered was the currency of the titles. In *Across Cultures*, the focus is on relatively recent titles that are generally available in public and school libraries. Most of the selections are from the 1990s and 2000s although there are a few books from earlier years that fit in with the topic being explored. *Across Cultures* includes 465 books suitable for use with preschoolers through children in sixth grade. It is not meant to be a comprehensive list but to serve as a starting point for activities in schools and public libraries. Many of the books in one featured area could connect with books in another; the books about Civil Rights connect with those on Protests and Migrant Workers, for example. We decided that we would keep repeated titles to a minimum; as you look at the titles in this book, you will make your own connections. We hope our book serves as a guide for book discussions, library programs, classroom activities, and reading guidance.

The 465 titles in *Across Cultures* are divided into eight chapters:

Identity, Self-Image, and Learning

Families, Friends, and Neighborhoods

Traditions—Food, Art, Poetry, Music, and Celebrations

Traditions—Folktales

Exploring the Past in Diverse Communities

Knowing Today's World

Parent-Child Book Discussion Groups

Literature Circles

The first chapters are thematic while the final chapters describe two popular strategies for involving readers with books. There are topical subgroups within the first six chapters; these are listed in the contents.

Following the main body of the book are an awards appendix and five indexes: Culture/Grade Level, Author, Title, Illustrator, and Subject/Grade Level. The Culture Index gives access by specific culture or region; for example, African, African American, Asian, and so on. When possible, a more specific culture or geographic location is appended; for example, Central American—Guatemala or African—Ghana.

Since the focus of *Across Cultures* is the element of diversity in the selected books, the culture designation indicates the main culture that is featured in the book. *The Jacket* by Andrew Clements describes the concerns that Phil, a white boy, has about his treatment of Daniel, a black student at his school. The culture designation for that book is African American as the author raises questions about racism and prejudice. Similarly, in the books about Jamaica, the focus is on Jamaica and her African American family. Some of the books in this series feature her classmates, who are from diverse backgrounds. However, since Jamaica is the focus of the series, the decision was made to designate the books as African American.

Each entry in *Across Cultures* contains the following information: author, title, illustrator (where appropriate), publisher, date, ISBN, culture, and grade level. The annotations not only describe each book but also show how it connects with some of the other books and with the topic grouping. We suggest activities and programs that would work in a school or public library setting. Often, we give examples of how the children we work with responded to the books. Along with the suggestions for using the books, there are special features such as a "Reflections" section from Kathy. When we were talking about world cultures and world literature, Kathy would remember a trip she had taken (often for ALA or IFLA) or a conference she had attended. It was a treat to hear her talk about her experiences in South Africa, Germany, Norway, and more. Including Kathy's "Reflections" on her involvement in libraries around the world and at home may provide an incentive for other librarians and teachers to take advantage of the many opportunities to travel, visit schools and libraries, and expand their understanding of the issues that face children around the world.

Preparing *Across Cultures* has been an opportunity for us to create a resource based on our experiences with children and children's literature. It allowed us to share ideas with each other, to make suggestions about books and activities, and to enjoy the process of our collaboration. Besides using our own libraries—Kathy at the Wood County District Public Library in Bowling Green, Ohio, and me at Onaway and

Lomond Elementary Schools in Shaker Heights, Ohio—we borrowed books from other area libraries, including the Cleveland Heights-University Heights Public Library and other member libraries of the CLEVNET system, and the SEO Library Consortium of member libraries across Ohio. We have been fortunate to have access to libraries with policies and personnel that are user-friendly, which made preparation of this book possible.

We would both like to thank our families and friends who encouraged us throughout the process. For Kathy, her husband Dennis provided support—and he relayed many messages from me and helped us keep on track. We also appreciate the support from our library and teaching colleagues, some of whom responded to parts of the manuscript with comments and suggestions.

Thank you also to Barbara Ittner, acquisitions editor at Libraries Unlimited, and to Catherine Barr, Christine McNaull, and Julia C. Miller for their editing, design, and production work.

—Rebecca Thomas, March 2007

CHAPTER ONE

Identity, Self-Image, and Learning

BELONGING, INDEPENDENCE, ACCEPTANCE, and individuality are some of the themes of the books in this chapter. As children have new experiences, they may feel uncertain and insecure. They want to be reassured and feel comfortable with the changes they in their lives. Even as they try to fit in, they want to know that others respect their differences and that they have their own identities.

The books in the chapter feature children who are growing and changing. At the beginning of the chapter are books for younger children—books that provide young readers with images and information they can connect with. Following these books are ones that focus on art, counting, the alphabet, and reading. At the end of the chapter are books for older readers that examine character development.

CONNECTING TO IMAGES IN BOOKS

YOUNG CHILDREN RESPOND TO IMAGES. Since many of them cannot read yet, they "see themselves" in the illustrations of books. They connect with books and reading by identifying with the visual presentation. *A Rainbow All Around Me, Shades of Black*, and many of the books by Ann Morris such as *Families* allow young children to observe the variety of colors in the world and its people. These books can be used as models to depict diverse groups of children and promote discussions about similarities and differences.

To extend the connection between the books and the readers, create a visual display using the children in your class or story group. Take photographs—you can even use the design elements and props from the featured book—and then create an exhibit that uses the words from the text with the pictures of your children. Books in the What Is . . . series, such as *What Is a Scientist?*, offer more opportunities to connect books with young children by depicting them as participants in the action. Show the children doing experiments, making predictions, and testing hypotheses. *To Be a Kid, Black All Around!*, and *These Hands* also encourage children to celebrate themselves and their accomplishments.

Two books—*Girls Hold Up This World* and *Keep Climbing, Girls*—could be paired together. After reading these books, children could make collages that depict some of their dreams for the future. The book *Kenya's Word* could also be the focus of a program with a connecting activity of making a word wall.

1 Ajmera, Maya, and John D. Ivanko ∗ *To Be a Kid*
Illus. with photographs ∗ Charlesbridge, 1999 ∗ 0-88106-841-1
MULTICULTURAL ∗ GRADES PRESCHOOL–1

A wonderful photoessay interprets what it means to be a kid in all reaches of the world. Family, school, play, and friends are among the topics included.

2 Hubbell, Patricia ∗ *Black All Around!*
Illus. by Don Tate ∗ Lee & Low, 2001 ∗ 1-58430-048-5
AFRICAN AMERICAN ∗ GRADES PRESCHOOL–1

A rhyming text celebrates the color black. As a young African American girl looks around, she sees the beauty of black: the letters on the page, the darkness of her pocket or a tunnel, the color of her parents' skin. She likes that clarinets, piano keys, beetles, ants, and the cozy night are all black.

3 Lehn, Barbara ∗ *What Is a Scientist?*
Photographs by Carol Krauss ∗ Millbrook Press, 1998 ∗ 0-7613-1272-2
MULTICULTURAL ∗ GRADES PRESCHOOL–1

Color photographs depict children from diverse backgrounds engaged in the scientific process. Vocabulary such as "investigate," "make predictions," and "observe" makes this a great book for language development. Other books in the series include *What Is a Teacher?* (2000), *What Is an Artist?* (2002), and *What Is an Athlete?* (2002).

4 Morris, Ann ∗ *Families*
Photographs by Ken Heyman ∗ HarperCollins, 2000 ∗ 0-688-17198-2
MULTICULTURAL ∗ GRADES PRESCHOOL–1

This book is part of the Around the World series, which includes *Houses and Homes* (1992) and *Hats, Hats, Hats* (1989). Each book features people from around the world with their families, homes, hats, and more.

Myles C. Pinkney and the Pinkney Family

Myles Pinkney is the youngest child of illustrator Jerry Pinkney and author Gloria Jean Pinkney. His brother Brian is an award-winning illustrator whose wife, Andrea Davis Pinkney, is an author, editor, and publisher. Myles Pinkney specializes in photography and his books capture images of children displaying a range of emotions. His wife, Sandra L. Pinkney, is the author of some of the books he illustrates.

For a study of Myles Pinkney, create a Pinkney family tree. Look at the content of the books from each member of the family and discuss the style of art. Many of the books reflect African American experiences. Jerry Pinkney uses watercolors and pencils for his pictures; Brian uses scratchboard and paint; Myles uses photography. Let the children experiment with each art medium.

Use *A Rainbow All Around Me* and *Shades of Black* to experiment with photography. Let the children discuss images that could accompany the poems and look at the photographs that are in the books. Then, with a digital camera, take pictures of kids in your class or library group—or have the kids take pictures—and create a display.

5 Pinkney, Sandra L. ✳ *A Rainbow All Around Me*
Photographs by Myles C. Pinkney ✳ Scholastic, 2002 ✳
0-439-30928-X
MULTICULTURAL ✳ GRADES PRESCHOOL–1

In a rainbow of colors and photographs of expressive, energetic children, the message of "colors all around us includes everything and everyone" is celebrated. The text is poetic and encourages language development. The focus on colors in the world promotes a reflection on the many colors of people. The book concludes with "We are the rainbow—YOU

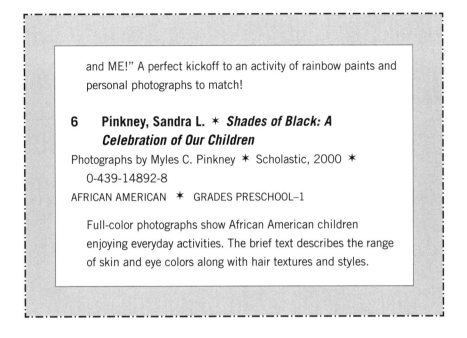

and ME!" A perfect kickoff to an activity of rainbow paints and personal photographs to match!

6   Pinkney, Sandra L. ✳ *Shades of Black: A Celebration of Our Children*
Photographs by Myles C. Pinkney ✳ Scholastic, 2000 ✳ 0-439-14892-8
AFRICAN AMERICAN ✳ GRADES PRESCHOOL–1

Full-color photographs show African American children enjoying everyday activities. The brief text describes the range of skin and eye colors along with hair textures and styles.

7 Price, Hope Lynne ✳ *These Hands*
Illus. by Bryan Collier ✳ Hyperion, 1999 ✳ 0-7868-0370-3
AFRICAN AMERICAN ✳ GRADES PRESCHOOL–1

What can your hands do? They can touch, feel, and create. They can squeeze and tickle. They can pray and clap. The poetic language of this book is accompanied by Bryan Collier's collage illustrations depicting an African American girl enjoying the creativity of her hands.

8 Richards, Beah ✳ *Keep Climbing, Girls*
Illus. by R. Gregory Christie ✳ Simon & Schuster, 2006 ✳ 1-4169-0264-3
AFRICAN AMERICAN ✳ GRADES K–2

Beah Richards was a noted poet, playwright, and actor and was active in the civil rights movement. This picture book features a poem that encourages girls to reach beyond the limitations that are often placed on them. The young girl featured here climbs a tree, going higher and higher even while she is being told to come down.

The message that "the path of life goes up and up; not down" is a powerful one for readers and could lead to a discussion about opportunities.

9 Smith, Jada Pinkett ✴ *Girls Hold Up This World*
Photographs by Donyell Kennedy-McCullough ✴ Scholastic, 2005 ✴ 0-439-08793-7
MULTICULTURAL ✴ GRADES PRESCHOOL–1

Girls (and women) from diverse cultures are described as proud, confident, disciplined, kind, generous, strong, and beautiful. Groups of children could explore words that connect with boys (many of the same words as in the book) and then build a list of words and pictures showing how "Together, we" do many things.

10 Trice, Linda ✴ *Kenya's Word*
Illus. by Pamela Johnson ✴ Charlesbridge, 2006 ✴ 1-57091-887-2
AFRICAN AMERICAN ✴ GRADES K–2

At school, Kenya sometimes daydreams and misses important information. Her teacher, Mrs. Garcia, is teaching a lesson about words. She asks the class to bring in a word about a favorite pet. Kenya is not paying attention and she brings in her pet instead—a tarantula! Mrs. Garcia helps Kenya focus and asks the class for their favorite describing word. Kenya thinks about many words and finally chooses black, which supports the concept that "black is beautiful." This book offers opportunities to discuss words and create a word wall.

CLOTHING AND CONFIDENCE

CHILDREN ENJOY WEARING "SPECIAL" CLOTHES. In *Suki's Kimono*, Suki feels that wearing her kimono helps her feel more confident on the first day of school. Jamela in *Jamela's Dress* enjoys wrapping herself in the fabric for her mother's new dress. Like Suki, Jamela experiences many emotions as she wears the fabric "dress." She is proud of the attention she receives and dismayed when she realizes she has ruined the fabric. Her confidence is restored when more fabric is purchased. *Jingle Dancer* explores the experiences of a Native American girl, Jenna, as she prepares her outfit for the powwow. Each of these books could be the focus of a program on clothing and costumes. Children can explore garments from their own heritages.

Another theme of *Jamela's Dress* is making a mistake, which is something that most children can relate to. They can also understand Suki's dilemma. She chooses to wear her kimono even though she may look different. Caring adults—a parent, a teacher, a friend—help Jamela and Suki find ways to feel good about themselves. In *Jamaica and Brianna*, the two girls argue about their boots. Jamaica's family reminds her that the boots she chose are right for her. At school, Jamaica reaches out to Brianna and their friendship is back on track.

Another clothing and confidence book is *If the Shoe Fits*. Children can identify with Rigo's problems—he does not like the brand-new shoes his mother has given him so he puts them away. Later, when he tries to wear them, they no longer fit. Readers can discuss what they would do in this situation.

Children may enjoy other books in the series about Jamaica and Jamela, which are listed here. By reading books about familiar characters, children become more confident about their reading!

11 Daly, Niki ✳ *Jamela's Dress*
Illus. by the author ✳ Farrar, Straus and Giroux, 1999 ✳ 0-374-33667-9
AFRICAN—SOUTH AFRICA ✳ GRADES K–2

Mama needs a new dress for Thelma's wedding. Jamela looks at the beautiful fabric that Mama has bought for her dress. As the fabric dries, Jamela feels the wind blow through the fabric and it wraps around her. She walks through the town in her "dress" and the fabric is ruined. Mama is disappointed in her and Jamela is disappointed in herself. But Archie, who took a picture of Jamela wrapped in the fabric, wins a prize for his photograph. He buys new fabric for Mama and the special dress for the wedding is completed in time. Mama even has enough fabric to make a dress for Jamela.

12 Havill, Juanita ✳ *Jamaica and Brianna*
Illus. by Anne Sibley O'Brien ✳ Houghton Mifflin, 1993 ✳ 0-395-64489-5
AFRICAN AMERICAN ✳ GRADES K–2

Jamaica, an African American girl, and her friend Brianna, an Asian American, hurt each other's feelings when each has to wear hand-me-down boots. They find a way to share their feelings and be friends again.

13 Smith, Cynthia Leitich ✳ *Jingle Dancer*
Illus. by Cornelius Van Wright and Ying-Hwa Hu ✳ Morrow, 2000 ✳ 0-688-16241-X
NATIVE AMERICAN—CREEK, CHIPPEWA/ANISHINABE ✳ GRADES 1–3

Jenna enjoys watching a videotape of Grandma Wolfe jingle dancing. This year, Jenna will dance at the powwow but she worries that her skirt will not have the special jingles. Jenna borrows rows of jingles from Great-aunt Sis, Mrs. Scott, Cousin Elizabeth, and Grandma Wolfe. Now her dress will have four rows of jingles. When the powwow begins, Jenna feels confident as she dances and she thinks of the heritage that she is continuing and the people who helped her. An Author's Note explores Jenna's native heritage (from the Muscogee [Creek] Nation and the Ojibway [Chippewa/Anishinabe] people). There is a description of jingle dancing and the costumes that are worn. A brief glossary is also included.

14 Soto, Gary * *If the Shoe Fits*
Illus. by Terry Widener * Putnam, 2002 * 0-399-23420-9
MEXICAN AMERICAN * GRADES 1–3

Rigo is the youngest in his family and he always ends up with hand-me-down clothes. On his birthday, his mother gives him brand-new shoes—loafers. He wears them around the neighborhood and is teased by an older boy. Rigo is upset and puts the shoes in his closet. Months later, when he decides to wear them again, they do not fit. At home that night, Rigo learns that his Uncle Celso has a new job. Rigo gives him the nearly new shoes. His uncle is delighted; he gives Rigo two coins from Mexico.

15 Uegaki, Chieri * *Suki's Kimono*
Illus. by Stéphane Jorisch * Kids Can Press, 2003 * 1-55337-084-8
JAPANESE AMERICAN * GRADES K–2

Suki wants to wear her *kimono* (robe) and *geta* (wooden clogs) for the first day of school. Her older sisters tell her she will not be "cool," but Suki does not listen. Her *obāchan* (grandmother) gave her the kimono, so Suki decides to wear it and she experiences some teasing. Suki's teacher, Mrs. Paggio, lets Suki show her kimono to the class and demonstrate a dance. Her classmates applaud her and Suki walks home knowing that it was a special day. A brief glossary explains some of the Japanese words.

More books about Jamaica and Jamela:

16 Daly, Niki * *Happy Birthday, Jamela!*
Illus. by the author * Farrar, Straus and Giroux, 2006 * 0-374-32842-0
AFRICAN—SOUTH AFRICA * GRADES K–2

Jamela likes the new dress that Mama and Gogo buy for her birthday, but she does not like the sturdy black shoes. She wants the sparkly shoes. Disappointed, Jamela decides to decorate the plain shoes with glitter and beads. Mama is angry, but an artistic merchant loves the shoes and helps Jamela decorate more pairs, which they sell, earning enough money to buy the shoes Jamela really wants.

17 Daly, Niki ✳ *What's Cooking, Jamela?*
Illus. by the author ✳ Farrar, Straus and Giroux, 2004 ✳ 0-374-35602-5
AFRICAN—SOUTH AFRICA ✳ GRADES K–2

Jamela and Mama buy a beautiful young red chicken that they will feed so it is nice and fat for Christmas dinner. Jamela names the chicken Christmas and, of course, she becomes so attached to her chicken that she will not allow it to become their Christmas dinner. Mama gives Jamela the chicken as her Christmas present. There is a glossary of terms in the book that come from several of the languages used in South Africa.

18 Daly, Niki ✳ *Where's Jamela?*
Illus. by the author ✳ Farrar, Straus and Giroux, 2004 ✳ 0-374-38324-3
AFRICAN—SOUTH AFRICA ✳ GRADES K–2

Mama gets a new job and she and Jamela must move. Jamela is not happy about this; she reluctantly helps with the packing. She crawls into a packing box and falls asleep. When the truck is loaded, she cannot be found. Everyone looks for her. Finally, Jamela wakes up and crawls out of the box. There is a big going-away celebration. When they arrive at the new house, Jamela settles into her new room. There is a glossary of terms in the book which come from several of the languages used in South Africa.

19 Havill, Juanita ✳ *Brianna, Jamaica, and the Dance of Spring*
Illus. by Anne Sibley O'Brien ✳ Houghton Mifflin, 2002 ✳ 0-618-07700-6
AFRICAN AMERICAN ✳ GRADES K–2

Brianna and Jamaica both want to be the butterfly queen in the dance class recital, but the part goes to Brianna's older sister, Nikki. Both girls are disappointed, but they continue to practice and prepare. When Nikki becomes ill, Brianna is chosen to take her place.

Then Brianna becomes ill and the performance continues without a butterfly queen dance. When Nikki and Brianna feel better, Jamaica joins them as they present a recital for their families. Brianna and her Asian American family play a larger role than Jamaica and her African American family.

20 Havill, Juanita ✻ *Jamaica and the Substitute Teacher*
Illus. by Anne Sibley O'Brien ✻ Houghton Mifflin, 1999 ✻ 0-395-90503-6
AFRICAN AMERICAN ✻ GRADES K–2

Jamaica wants to please her substitute teacher, Mrs. Duval. During a spelling test, Jamaica sees Brianna's paper and copies one of the words. She knows that she has done something wrong and she does not turn in her "perfect" paper. Mrs. Duval asks Jamaica to explain, and Jamaica shamefully confesses. Mrs. Duval understands Jamaica's desire to be perfect. She reassures her and makes her feel special.

21 Havill, Juanita ✻ *Jamaica Tag-Along*
Illus. by Anne Sibley O'Brien ✻ Houghton Mifflin, 1989 ✻ 0-395-49602-0
AFRICAN AMERICAN ✻ GRADES K–2

When Ossie goes to the park to play basketball, his sister Jamaica follows him. He and his friends tell her to stop bothering them. Later, when Jamaica is playing in the park, she is bothered by a toddler named Berto. Jamaica lets Berto play with her and then they let Ossie join them.

22 Havill, Juanita ✻ *Jamaica's Blue Marker*
Illus. by Anne Sibley O'Brien ✻ Houghton Mifflin, 1995 ✻ 0-395-572036-2
AFRICAN AMERICAN ✻ GRADES K–2

Jamaica loves to draw. During one art period at school, her teacher asks Jamaica to share her markers with Russell. Russell just makes blue scribbles on his paper and when Jamaica asks him about it, he makes blue scribbles on her drawing. Jamaica is angry and hurt. Later, she learns that Russell is moving. She wonders if he is upset about it and has been acting out. On his last day, Jamaica gives Russell her blue marker to take to his new school.

23 Havill, Juanita ✶ *Jamaica's Find*
Illus. by Anne Sibley O'Brien ✶ Houghton Mifflin, 1986 ✶ 0-395-39376-0

AFRICAN AMERICAN ✶ GRADES K–2

When Jamaica finds a stuffed toy at the park, she wants to keep it. She realizes that she should return it to the lost and found. After she returns the toy, she meets the little girl who has lost it and they become friends.

SELF-ASSURANCE THROUGH ART

HAVE YOU EVER DRAWN A PICTURE and wanted to crumple it up and throw it away? Do you compare your art projects to those around you and feel that your work is not good enough? That's how Vashti feels in *The Dot* and how Ramon feels in *Ish*. These two books, written and illustrated by Peter H. Reynolds, explore the artistic experiences of two children—their insecurities, their doubts, their critics, and finally, their successes. Vashti and Ramon find a way to feel confident; they develop a sense of self-assurance through their art. These are great books to share before beginning an art project. In one school, the art teacher uses these books to encourage students to accept their own best efforts.

Two other books feature characters who struggle to create. *Regina's Big Mistake* and *Emily's Art* describe how each main character searches for satisfaction through art projects. *Painted Dreams* features a girl in Haiti whose artistic talent and creativity help her family. *Emma's Rug* explores one child's inspiration to create.

In all of these books, the characters feel some pressure to conform but choose to be independent. They pursue their dreams and find success and fulfillment.

24 Catalanotto, Peter ✳ *Emily's Art*
Illus. by the author ✳ Atheneum, 2001 ✳ 0-689-83831-X
EUROPEAN AMERICAN ✳ GRADES 1–3

Emily, a first-grader, loves to paint and she helps her friend Kelly learn to draw butterflies. When there is an art contest, the judge dismisses Emily's picture and selects Kelly as the winner. Emily is hurt and dejected and vows never to paint again. She goes to the nurse's office to rest, and when she wakes up Kelly is there too. Kelly is upset with how her classmates are treating her. Together, Emily and Kelly help each other feel better and return to the classroom where the teacher is having a party for all of the artists.

25 Moss, Marissa ✳ *Regina's Big Mistake*
Illus. by the author ✳ Houghton Mifflin, 1990 ✳ 0-395-55330-X
AFRICAN AMERICAN ✳ GRADES K–2

Regina tries to create a picture of the rain forest but she cannot seem to get the idea in her head onto the paper. She makes a mistake and gets another sheet of paper; her teacher tells her that she cannot use any more paper now. So, Regina begins her picture. Slowly, she fills in the details. When she is almost done, her crayon wobbles and her sun is spoiled . . . or is it? She makes a moon instead and finishes her perfect picture of the rain forest at night.

26 Reynolds, Peter H. ✳ *The Dot*
Illus. by the author ✳ Candlewick, 2003 ✳ 0-7636-1961-2
MULTICULTURAL ✳ GRADES 1–4

Vashti says, "I can't draw!" Her teacher tells her to make a mark, so she jabs on the paper with a marker and makes a dot. Then she signs her name. Her teacher frames Vashti's dot picture and Vashti is inspired to explore the possibilities of making dots. Her artistic talent is admired by a young boy who expresses his desire to draw. Vashti encourages him to sign a squiggle that he has made. Vashti is depicted as a white child and the boy who admires her work is black.

27 Reynolds, Peter H. ✳ *Ish*
Illus. by the author ✳ Candlewick, 2004 ✳ 0-7636-2344X
HISPANIC AMERICAN ✳ GRADES 1–4

Ramon's love of drawing evaporates when his brother Leon laughs at him. Ramon tries to recapture his joy but he cannot, so he gives up. His sister, Marisol, has saved all of his crumpled pictures and they discuss his work. His drawing of a vase is not an exact rendering, but it is "vase-ish." The freedom of doing "ish" pictures restores his pleasure in art. He even tries "ish" writing. And he "lived ishfully ever after."

28 Say, Allen ✳ *Emma's Rug*
Illus. by the author ✳ Houghton Mifflin, 1996 ✳ 0-395-74294-3
JAPANESE AMERICAN ✳ GRADES K–3

Where does inspiration come from? For Emma, it is her rug. After she sits quietly and stares at her rug, she draws and paints. Everyone recognizes her artistic talent; she even wins a citywide art competition. Then her mother washes the rug. Emma is devastated. She believes her inspiration is gone, and she packs away her drawings and paintings; she throws away her art supplies and she throws away her rug. Sitting alone in her room, she "sees" something. Running outside, she is inspired with images. The final page is a picture of Emma—drawing again.

29 Williams, Karen Lynn ✳ *Painted Dreams*
Illus. by Catherine Stock ✳ Lothrop, Lee & Shepard, 1998 ✳ 0-688-13901-9
CARIBBEAN—HAITI ✳ GRADES 1–3

Ti Marie has a dream—to be an artist—and she draws pictures whenever she can. A mysterious neighbor, Msie Antoine, lives in a compound of houses that are brightly colored and decorated with carvings and sculptures. Ti Marie's family is too poor to buy her supplies, so she sifts through the trash from Msie Antoine. One day, Ti Marie helps her mother at the market. She notices that the wall behind their stall is large and empty and she begins to fill it with bright, colorful paintings. The people in the market come to see Ti Marie's paintings and they buy her mother's vegetables. The family realizes the importance of Ti Marie's art.

CONCEPT BOOKS: NUMBERS AND COUNTING

YOUNG CHILDREN TAKE PRIDE IN THEIR ACCOMPLISHMENTS. Learning to whistle or tie shoes, getting dressed by themselves, and going to school are important achievements. A young child develops a positive self-image by demonstrating his or her mastery of information—knowing letters and numbers, for example. Once children know how to count, they want to expand their skills. Using books that describe items from other countries introduces new information and allows children to apply their understanding of numbers.

Ten Mice for Tet, One Is a Drummer, One Leaf Rides the Wind, and *One Child, One Seed* are among the many counting books that incorporate information about other cultures. Other books, such as *Grandfather Counts*, use counting and numbers to explore immigrants' experiences as they adjust to another culture. After interacting with these books, children could create a class counting book that reflects their cultural backgrounds. This could also be an activity for a "Family Night" at a school, library, or community center.

30 Cave, Kathryn ✳ *One Child, One Seed: A South African Counting Book*
Photographs by Gisèle Wulfsohn ✳ Henry Holt, 2002 ✳ 0-8050-7204-7
AFRICAN—SOUTH AFRICA ✳ GRADES K–2

Nothando has one pumpkin seed that she plants using her two hands. Her brother and his friends weed, water, and hoe—illustrating the number three. Each new number is connected to the growth and use of the pumpkin. Finally, Nothando has one pumpkin seed to plant and the cycle begins again. This book has several themes. There is the basic counting book with a paragraph explaining the action. A sidebar provides more information about Nothando and her family and home in the Nkandla district. There are photographs of the family's house, with its walls of wood, mud, and grass. There is information about the crops and weather, the store that is a ten-minute walk from the homestead, the surrounding geography, and the meal that is made from the pumpkin. A recipe for *Isijingi* (pumpkin stew) is included and there is a map of South Africa showing the location of Nkandla.

31 Cheng, Andrea ✳ *Grandfather Counts*
Illus. by Ange Zhang ✳ Lee & Low, 2000 ✳ 1-58430-010-8
CHINESE AMERICAN ✳ GRADES 1–3

When Helen's mother's dad arrives from China, it is hard to understand him since he speaks only Chinese. Gong Gong (Grandfather) tries to speak to Helen and her siblings and is surprised and a bit disappointed that they do not know any Chinese. With no friends and no one to talk to, Gong Gong becomes withdrawn. Helen used to watch the trains go past her bedroom window, but now Gong Gong has her room and Helen must go outside to wave to the engineer. Then she realizes that her grandfather is waving too. The barriers begin to break down when Grandfather comes out to sit beside Helen and they count the cars of the train—in Chinese. Together they learn numbers—Helen in Chinese and Grandfather in English! A list of Chinese characters for words and numbers is included.

32 Hartmann, Wendy ✳ *One Sun Rises: An African Wildlife Counting Book*
Illus. by Nicolaas Maritz ✳ Dutton, 1994 ✳ 0-525-45225-7
AFRICAN ✳ GRADES PRESCHOOL–2

As one sun rises, the numbers from 2 to 10 count African animals, such as elephants, suricates, impalas, egrets, lions, and hyenas. Then, when the moon appears, the count goes from 10 to 2 with bats, frogs, crickets, owls, genets, and spiders, ending with "One sun rises over Africa." A Note describes the animals that are counted in this book.

33 Mannis, Celeste Davidson ✳ *One Leaf Rides the Wind: Counting in a Japanese Garden*
Illus. by Susan Kathleen Hartung ✳ Viking, 2002 ✳ 0-670-03525-4
ASIAN—JAPAN ✳ GRADES PRESCHOOL–1

Haiku verses present numbers from 1 to 10. Elements in a Japanese garden, including temple dogs, sandals, and koi fish, are counted. A brief note appears on each page to further explain the Japanese garden. The illustrations are in muted colors and clearly depict each item to be counted.

34 Shea, Pegi Deitz, and Cynthia Weill ✳ *Ten Mice for Tet*
Illus. by To Ngoc Trang; embroidery by Pham Viet-Dinh ✳ Chronicle, 2003 ✳ 0-8118-3496-4
ASIAN—VIETNAM ✳ GRADES PRESCHOOL–1

From 1 to 10, the mice prepare for Tet, the celebration of the new year in Vietnam. Following the illustrated pages, there is a note that explains "About Tet" and each number and phrase is given a detailed explanation. For example, "2 mice go to market" describes some of the items that would be included in a Tet celebration and highlights the importance of having flowers for luck, prosperity, and happiness. The illustrations are bright-colored embroidery and provide a clear representation of the mice to be counted.

35 Thong, Roseanne ✳ *One Is a Drummer: A Book of Numbers*
Illus. by Grace Lin ✳ Chronicle, 2004 ✳ 0-8118-3772-6
CHINESE AMERICAN ✳ GRADES PRESCHOOL–1

A Chinese American girl counts from 1 to 10. Many of the items reflect her Chinese heritage, such as dim sum and the Dragon Boat Festival. After using this book, share other books by Grace Lin including *Fortune Cookie Fortunes* and *Dim Sum for Everyone*. These books are discussed in Chapter 3.

CONCEPT BOOKS: ALPHABET

KNOWING THE ALPHABET IS ANOTHER ACCOMPLISHMENT for young children; and the alphabet also provides a framework for reports and informational text. Margaret Musgrove's classic book *Ashanti to Zulu* is an example of using the alphabet to provide a structure for information. The books featured here can provide models for projects on cultures. Children can work in groups to research different cultures and create informational alphabet books. This allows them to practice research skills as well as writing informational texts.

36 Ajmera, Maya, and Anna Rhesa Versola * *Children from Australia to Zimbabwe: A Photographic Journey Around the World*
Illus. with photographs * Charlesbridge, 1997 * 0-88106-999-X
MULTICULTURAL * GRADES 3–6

> This alphabetical tour of the world has a double-page spread about each country and its children. Maps, flags, and photos help to explain the history. A "more facts" box is also included. Other countries of the same "letter" are listed to whet the appetite for further research. This is a very attractive browsing book. (And X is for the imaginary place known as Xanadu—where you can be what you want to be!)

37 Bruchac, Joseph * *Many Nations: An Alphabet of Native America*
Illus. by Robert F. Goetzl * BridgeWater, 1997 * 0-8167-4389-4
NATIVE AMERICAN * GRADES 1–4

> Most of the letters in this alphabet book feature specific native people—Anishanabe, Blackfeet, Choctaw, Dakota, and so forth. Other letters describe items associated with native cultures, such as Eagle, Fox, and Visions. Teachers and librarians can use this book to suggest areas of further research. An Author's Note celebrates the diversity of Native Americans across the Americas.

38 Chin-Lee, Cynthia ✶ *A Is for Asia*
Illus. by Yumi Heo ✶ Orchard Books, 1997 ✶ 0-531-30011-0
ASIAN ✶ GRADES K–3

Kites, New Year, Qur'an, water buffalo, xiang qi (a Chinese game)
are among the items presented in this alphabet book. Each letter is
accompanied by a brief paragraph explaining the item and a letter
from one of the cultures. For example, xiang qi is also written in Chinese characters and yurt is written in Mongolian.

39 Chin-Lee, Cynthia, and Terri de la Peña ✶ *A Is for the Americas*
Illus. by Enrique O. Sánchez ✶ Orchard Books, 1999 ✶ 0-531-
30194-X
MULTICULTURAL ✶ GRADES 2–6

The Americas—North America, Central America, South America—
are featured in this alphabet book that covers food, sports, homes,
locations, animals, music, dance, beliefs, and more. Three additional
letters from the Spanish alphabet follow the A to Z. An Introduction
describes "The Americans and Their Languages."

40 Compestine, Ying Chang ✶ *D Is for Dragon Dance*
Illus. by YongSheng Xuan ✶ Holiday House, 2006 ✶ 0-8234-1887-1
ASIAN—CHINA ✶ GRADES PRESCHOOL–2

Celebrate Chinese New Year with this colorful alphabet book. Acrobats balance on Balls. Firecrackers and Dragon Dancers keep the Evil
Spirits away. There are Noodles, Oranges, and Steamed Dumplings
for the celebration. Z for Zodiac concludes the alphabet. Additional
information, including a recipe for New Year's Dumpling Delight,
follows the text.

41 Elya, Susan Middleton ✶ *F Is for Fiesta*
Illus. by G. Brian Karas ✶ Putnam, 2006 ✶ 0-399-24225-2
HISPANIC ✶ GRADES PRESCHOOL–3

This book opens with a glossary of the Spanish words with their pronunciation and translation into English. For example: *Abuela* (ah
Bweh lah) Grandma. An Author's Note explains the Spanish alpha-

bet. Then the alphabet book begins. Letters are presented in a rhyming text accompanied by bright, colorful illustrations. The theme for the book is celebrating a fiesta, so words like *globos* (balloons), *salsa* (sauce, music, a dance), and *velas* (candles) get you ready for a party.

42 Musgrove, Margaret ∗ *Ashanti to Zulu: African Traditions*
Illus. by Leo Dillon and Diane Dillon ∗ Dial, 1976 ∗ 0-8037-0357-0
AFRICAN ∗ GRADES 2–6

Each letter of the alphabet introduces a group of African people. Information about their customs and location is included in each brief description. This book received the 1977 Caldecott Medal.

43 Onyefulu, Ifeoma ∗ *A Is for Africa*
Illus. with photographs ∗ Dutton, 1993 ∗ 0-525-65147-0
AFRICAN ∗ GRADES K–2

The color photographs in this book invite readers to learn more about everyday life in Africa. Each letter of the alphabet correlates with an aspect of African life and culture—for example, "B is for beads a girl may wear on her head, ears or neck."

44 Tapahonso, Luci, and Eleanor Schick ∗ *Navajo ABC: A Diné Alphabet Book*
Illus. by Eleanor Schick ∗ Simon & Schuster, 1995 ∗ 0-689-80316-8
NATIVE AMERICAN—NAVAJO ∗ GRADES PRESCHOOL–3

"Arroyo," "Belt," and "Cradle Board" begin this alphabet book featuring aspects of Diné life. The illustrations depict traditional Navajo designs, such as the beautiful silver and turquoise "Necklace" and the geometric pattern of the "Rug." There is a pronunciation guide and a glossary.

ACCEPTANCE AND SELF-IMAGE

MANY BOOKS FEATURE CHARACTERS WHO FEEL DIFFERENT, lonely, and left out. Children want to be reassured that they will be accepted. They want to make friends and get along with others. Both *The Name Jar* and *My Name Is Yoon* feature a girl from Korea who feels uncomfortable about sharing her name. After reading these books, many children enjoy thinking of new names for themselves and researching the meaning of names from many cultures. *Father's Rubber Shoes* explores the need to fit in from the perspective of a Korean boy.

Being different and accepting yourself are themes in *Shrinking Violet*. *Speak English for Us, Marisol!* describes how a child who has learned English becomes responsible for the needs of many others, including adults. In *I Hate English!*, Mei Mei is reluctant to learn English, thinking she will lose her identity. *Yoko* wants to have her classmates accept her. And Alex (in *Alex and the Wednesday Chess Club*) finds a way to enjoy playing chess. All of these books celebrate children who are independent.

45 Best, Cari ∗ *Shrinking Violet*

Illus. by Giselle Potter ∗ Farrar, Straus and Giroux, 2001 ∗ 0-374-36882-1

EUROPEAN AMERICAN ∗ GRADES 1–3

Violet is very shy. She is so shy that she refuses to be a part of "Carry-the-Flag Day" at school. Most people understand, but one classmate, Irwin, enjoys teasing her. Even though Violet does not participate in many activities, she does observe and learn. She is a great mimic and can act dramatically, but she only performs for herself. When her class plans a play on the solar system, Violet is assigned to be the offstage narrator—Lady Space. On the night of the performance, she reads her part with confidence. Irwin, however, cannot find his spot on stage and everything is disrupted. Violet's creative narration saves the day.

46 Choi, Yangsook ✳ *The Name Jar*
Illus. by the author ✳ Knopf, 2001 ✳ 0-375-80613-X
KOREAN AMERICAN ✳ GRADES 2–4

Unhei has moved with her family to America, leaving her beloved grandmother in Korea. On the bus to her first day at school, kids talk to her and ask her name but are unable to say it correctly. Unhei is embarrassed by their attempts and, when she arrives at her classroom, she says she has not picked her name yet. At home, she tells her mother she wants an American name and her mother reminds her of the heritage of the name Unhei. Back at school, Unhei finds a glass jar on her desk. It is filled with names that her classmates have selected for her. Unhei does not pick an American name immediately. At the Korean grocery store, Joey, a classmate, overhears Mr. Kim call her "Unhei"; he listens carefully and repeats her name perfectly. The next day, the name jar is gone (removed by Joey in hopes Unhei would keep her Korean name) and Unhei introduces herself using her real name.

47 English, Karen ✳ *Speak English for Us, Marisol!*
Illus. by Enrique O. Sánchez ✳ Albert Whitman, 2000 ✳ 0-8075-
    7554-2
HISPANIC AMERICAN ✳ GRADES PRESCHOOL–2

Marisol wants to get right home after school. Her cat may have delivered her kittens! But Marisol's trip home is delayed by friends and family who want her to interpret for them, translating Spanish into English. Even when she finally arrives at home she must wait to see her cat while she helps her mother with the phone bill. Finally, she sees her cat and discovers that the kittens have arrived. Marisol is a child with a lot of responsibility. Her knowledge of both English and Spanish is an important asset to her community and she is proud of her accomplishments.

48 Heo, Yumi ✳ *Father's Rubber Shoes*
Illus. by the author ✳ Orchard Books, 1995 ✳ 0-531-06873-0
KOREAN AMERICAN ✳ GRADES 1–3

> Yungsu misses his friends in Korea. His family has just moved to America and Yungsu has not made any new friends. To add to his loneliness, his father is too busy working at his store to play with Yungsu. One night, Yungsu's father wakes him and explains why they have come to America. His father describes his hopes for a better future for Yungsu. The next day, Yungsu helps his mother make *bulgogi* (meat and rice wrapped in a lettuce leaf). He decides to take some to his father, who is busy at the store. On his way there, he meets Alex, a boy he knows from school. Yungsu shares some of the bulgogi and invites Alex to come for a visit. Yungsu feels happier as he continues toward his father's store.

49 Levine, Ellen ✳ *I Hate English!*
Illus. by Steve Björkman ✳ Scholastic, 1989 ✳ 0-590-42305-3
CHINESE AMERICAN ✳ GRADES PRESCHOOL–1

> Mei Mei struggles to learn English. She misses her home in Hong Kong and is uncomfortable in her new home and school in New York City. Mei Mei resents learning the language and history of this new place, fearing she will lose touch with her heritage. Her teacher helps her adjust and feel included.

50 Recorvits, Helen ✳ *My Name Is Yoon*
Illus. by Gabi Swiatkowska ✳ Farrar, Straus and Giroux, 2003 ✳
    0-374-35114-7
KOREAN AMERICAN ✳ GRADES 1–3

> Yoon, who has come from Korea, is reluctant to learn her name in English. Yoon misses her home in Korea and she likes the look of the Korean symbols for her name, which means "Shining Wisdom." At school, Yoon learns English words and, when asked to print her name on her paper, she uses different new words like "cat," "bird," and "cupcake." Her teacher accepts these offerings, smiling at Yoon and giving her time to adjust. A girl at school offers Yoon a cupcake and, as she feels more comfortable, she writes her name, "Yoon." The col-

orful illustrations capture Yoon's imaginative visions of herself as a cat, a bird, and a cupcake.

51 Wells, Rosemary ∗ *Yoko*
Illus. by the author ∗ Hyperion, 1998 ∗ 0-7868-0395-9
JAPANESE AMERICAN ∗ GRADES PRESCHOOL–2

Yoko, a kitten, is a Japanese American who is looking forward to her first day at school. Her mother has made her a beautiful lunch of sushi. The kids at school make fun of her lunch and Yoko is embarrassed. Yoko's teacher organizes an International Food Day, which allows the children to share their cultural traditions. Although only Timothy will try her sushi, Yoko is pleased to have one intrepid friend. There are more stories about Yoko and the kids from Hilltop School.

52 Wong, Janet S. ∗ *Alex and the Wednesday Chess Club*
Illus. by Stacey Schuett ∗ Simon & Schuster, 2004 ∗ 0-689-85890-6
ASIAN AMERICAN ∗ GRADES 2–4

Alex loves to play chess. He learned to play when he was four and his family helps him make chess fun. For example, his mother made a chessboard out of squares of bread so Alex could use food for the chess pieces—like a piece of banana for the king. Alex's enjoyment of chess is jeopardized when he plays with his neighbor, an older man called Uncle Hooya. Alex loses his games with Uncle Hooya and, eventually, he loses his enthusiasm for chess. For several years, Alex avoids playing chess. Finally, in the third grade, he joins the Wednesday chess club and his love for chess is rekindled. In the club, Alex learns that he is not the best. He wins some and loses some. At the City Tournament, Alex does have the satisfaction of beating Uncle Hooya's Little Cousin Hooya. A list of "Alex's Top Ten Chess Tips" follows the story.

THE IMPORTANCE OF BOOKS AND READING

READING AND BOOKS ARE VALUED IN MANY CULTURES and eras. Literacy provides opportunities to grow and improve. Reading opens doors to better jobs and a better self-image. *Goin' Someplace Special* could be the focus book in a program about the importance of reading. Children listening to this story will want to talk about what reading and libraries mean to them. Patricia Polacco's *Thank You, Mr. Falker* features a character who struggles to learn to read. By comparing the characters of 'Tricia Ann in *Goin' Someplace Special* and Trisha in *Thank You, Mr. Falker*, children can examine the obstacles each girl faced. 'Tricia Ann had to walk through the signs and sounds of segregation while Trisha had to endure the cruelty of her classmates. *Virgie Goes to School with Us Boys* can also be added to the comparison activity.

A survey of favorite books or authors would be a good related activity. Children can use different types of graphs (bar, pie, etc.) to chart the results. They can interview family and friends to find out what reading and libraries mean to them. Kay Winters's *Abe Lincoln: The Boy Who Loved Books* would be a good choice to connect with this activity, as would *Mr. George Baker*.

53 Hest, Amy ✴ *Mr. George Baker*
Illus. by Jon J Muth ✴ Candlewick, 2004 ✴ 0-7636-1233-2
African American ✴ Grades 1–3

Harry, who is white, runs across the yard to sit with Mr. George Baker, who is African American, on his front porch. Harry says, "He's a *hundred* years old, no kidding." Mrs. Baker comes out to the porch and gives Mr. Baker a paper bag with his lunch. Harry and George wait together, both with their red book bags. Then, it's time. The school bus arrives and they both get on. Harry goes to his class full of kids and Mr. George Baker sits with a small group of adults. Both groups are learning to read. This intergenerational story celebrates the importance of reading for all ages.

54 Howard, Elizabeth Fitzgerald ✳ *Virgie Goes to School with Us Boys*
Illus. by E. B. Lewis ✳ Simon & Schuster, 2000 ✳ 0-689-80076-2
AFRICAN AMERICAN ✳ GRADES 2–6

After the Civil War, black children were no longer prevented from learning to read and going to school. Virgie's brothers all go to school but Virgie, who is the youngest and a girl, is not encouraged to get an education. Her determination and spirit help her succeed. *Virgie Goes to School with Us Boys* won a Coretta Scott King Illustrator Honor Award.

55 McKissack, Patricia C. ✳ *Goin' Someplace Special*
Illus. by Jerry Pinkney ✳ Atheneum, 2001 ✳ 0-689-81885-8
AFRICAN AMERICAN ✳ GRADES 2–6

'Tricia Ann is hurt and frustrated by the signs of segregation as she travels through the city on her own. She sits in the "Colored Section" of the bus and is excluded from the fancy hotel and music hall. Each encounter undermines her confidence until she reaches her destination—the public library where "all are welcome." *Goin' Someplace Special* won a Coretta Scott King Illustrator Award.

56 Polacco, Patricia ✳ *Thank You, Mr. Falker*
Illus. by the author ✳ Philomel, 1998 ✳ 0-399-23166-8
EUROPEAN AMERICAN ✳ GRADES 2–6

Trisha loves books but learning to read is a struggle. At her new school in California, Trisha is bullied and called a "dummy." She is in fifth grade and still cannot read. Her teacher, Mr. Falker, praises her artistic talent but the kids still taunt her. Mr. Falker discovers her disability and he, along with a special reading teacher, help Trisha find success as a reader. A Note after the story explains that the book is autobiographical. The events in *The Bee Tree* (Philomel, 1993) are also mentioned in this book.

57 Winters, Kay ✳ *Abe Lincoln: The Boy Who Loved Books*
Illus. by Nancy Carpenter ✳ Simon & Schuster, 2003 ✳ 0-689-
82554-4
EUROPEAN AMERICAN ✳ GRADES 1–4

Abe Lincoln's love of learning is the focus of this biography. At
school, Abe absorbed letters, numbers, and words. At home, he listened to stories, often Bible stories told by his mother. After struggling with the hardships of frontier life, Abe's mother died. When his
father remarried, his new wife brought books to the Lincoln home.
Whenever he could, Abe read. And as he grew older, he studied on
his own and became a lawyer. His perseverance and dedication to
learning were qualities that helped him become the sixteenth president of the United States.

THE RIGHT TO READ

ANOTHER PERSPECTIVE ON THE IMPORTANCE OF LITERACY and how it impacts self-image can be found in *Ruby's Wish*. This book describes the restrictions put on females in China, where girls were not encouraged to go to school. Ruby's desire for an education earns her the admiration of her grandfather, who arranges for her to attend a university.

After a group of second-grade students heard *Ruby's Wish*, several children said: "That's not fair. Girls have the same rights as boys." This led to a discussion of other inequities, such as segregation. *Ruby's Wish* was followed by Marie Bradby's *More Than Anything Else*, and the children talked about the opportunities that they have now and how things were different in the past. Both books are based on actual events. *Running the Road to ABC*, which is set in Haiti, brings in another perspective on the importance of education.

By the end of second grade, students should be able to see the connection between the past and the present. They should be able to analyze the contributions of individuals and recognize the impact on how we live today. After reading *Running the Road to ABC*, children could make a chart showing what they do to get to school—what time they leave home, the length of their trip, the kind of transportation. After reviewing this chart, share *Read and Rise* and think about the impact of reading.

58 Bradby, Marie * *More Than Anything Else*
Illus. by Chris K. Soentpiet * Orchard Books, 1995 * 0-531-09464-2
AFRICAN AMERICAN * GRADES 2–6

> While living in West Virginia and working in the salt mines, young Booker T. Washington dreams of being able to read. This is a fictionalized account of an event from Washington's childhood.

59 Bridges, Shirin Yim ✷ *Ruby's Wish*
Illus. by Sophie Blackwell ✷ Chronicle, 2002 ✷ 0-8118-3490-5
ASIAN—CHINA ✷ GRADES 2–4

Ruby's grandfather allowed all of his grandchildren to take lessons, even the girls. Ruby loves to learn, but she knows how unusual it is for a girl to be educated in China. Ruby tells her dream of attending a university to her grandfather, who arranges for her to go. She becomes one of the first female university students in China. This book is a fictionalized account of the childhood experiences of the author's grandmother.

60 Lauture, Denizé ✷ *Running the Road to ABC*
Illus. by Reynold Ruffins ✷ Simon & Schuster, 1996 ✷ 0-689-80507-1
CARIBBEAN—HAITI ✷ GRADES 1–3

In Haiti, six children—three boys and three girls—wake while it is still dark. They eat breakfast. As dawn breaks, they are running—along narrow trails, past fields, and down hills—to the main road. They follow the road through the town and back into the country-side until they reach their destination—the schoolhouse.

61 Pinkney, Sandra L. ✷ *Read and Rise*
Photographs by Myles C. Pinkney ✷ Scholastic, 2006 ✷ 0-439-30929-8
AFRICAN AMERICAN ✷ GRADES PRESCHOOL–2

Reading takes you to other places, both real and imaginary. You dream and wonder, plan and learn. Numerous glowing, full-color photographs depict African Americans—young and old—enjoying the impact of reading. This book is part of the National Urban League initiative to promote reading within the African American community and to inspire African American children to believe in their dreams. Scholastic is a partner in the Read and Rise literacy campaign.

THE IMPORTANCE OF LANGUAGE

THERE ARE NUMEROUS OPPORTUNITIES THROUGHOUT the year to celebrate books, reading, language, and information. *Sequoyah* would be a great book to share during National Library Week in April or Children's Book Week in November or at a Right to Read celebration. Native American studies would also be enhanced by the use of *Sequoyah*. Some schools and libraries offer programs where the children research a famous person and then appear in a costume to present the report. *Sequoyah* would be a great book for this activity.

The legend of King Sejong of Korea and the creation of the Korean alphabet is described in the story *The King's Secret*. Like *Sequoyah*, the focus is on the importance of literacy for ordinary people. In many countries, reading and writing is restricted to the elite, to the wealthy and powerful. In both *Sequoyah* and *The King's Secret*, writing is made available to a wider audience.

Exploring another language would be a natural extension from reading these two books. The American Sign Language alphabet, and signs for specific words, would help children understand the importance of communication.

62 Farley, Carol ✳ *The King's Secret: The Legend of King Sejong*
Illus. by Robert Jew ✳ HarperCollins, 2001 ✳ 0-688-12776-2
ASIAN—KOREA ✳ GRADES 3–6

> In 15th-century Korea, only the nobility could read or write, and the language they used was Chinese. According to this legend, King Sejong designed a Korean alphabet to allow his people to communicate in their own language.

63 Heller, Lora ✳ *Sign Language for Kids: A Fun and Easy Guide to American Sign Language*
Illus. with photographs ✳ Sterling, 2004 ✳ 1-4027-0672-3
MULTICULTURAL ✳ GRADES 2–6

> Learn the American Sign Language alphabet, numbers, and more. Chapters feature signs for topics including School, Favorite Foods, Sports and Hobbies, Musical Instruments, and Clothing. There is a

section of Practical Words and Question Words, along with suggestions for constructing sentences. Color photographs depict children demonstrating the signs.

64 Rumford, James ✳ *Sequoyah: The Cherokee Man Who Gave His People Writing*
Translated into Cherokee by Anna Sixkiller Huckaby ✳ Illus. by the author ✳ Houghton Mifflin, 2004 ✳ 0-618-36947-3
NATIVE AMERICAN—CHEROKEE ✳ GRADES 3–6

Sequoyah did not seem destined for great achievements. He grew up in humble surroundings in the southern United States. In his fifties, he began to experiment with ways to capture the sounds of the Cherokee language, first designing a symbol for each word and then creating letters for specific sounds. His accomplishments allowed the Cherokee people to communicate in writing in their native language.

EXPLORING CHARACTER

COMPREHENSION STRATEGIES FOR READERS are enhanced by the use of graphic organizers. Children learn to gather information from texts and to organize it for improved understanding. One popular graphic organizer is the character map. For young children, a shape of a person is often used as the outline for information about the character—the head can be the character's name, one arm can be friends and the other family, the body can be a description of the character, and each leg can describe what the character does. Another organizer examines character traits. One column lists character traits while another asks for examples of that trait in the book.

Lowji Discovers America offers a strong central character, Lowji Sanjana, who could be featured in a character map. He is apprehensive, intrepid, hopeful, and open to new experiences. Readers could also chart the differences between his life in India and his life in America. Another character who could be the focus of a character map is Ray Halfmoon from *Indian Shoes*. Ray is a lively character who has some humorous adventures. Some of the chapters in *Indian Shoes* offer opportunities for prediction, too. For example, how will Ray and Grandpa solve the problem of Ray's missing pants?

Two books by Lisa Yee feature strong main characters: *Millicent Min: Girl Genius* and *Stanford Wong Flunks Big-Time*. Because the two books are connected, readers get insights into each character from different points of view.

Here is a sample of a chart for examining character traits.

Character Trait	Example from the Book
Lowji is **hopeful** about being in America.	He looks for "silver linings." For example, in America, he might get a pet—a dog, a cat, or perhaps a horse.
Lowji is **intrepid** and **curious**.	He follows footprints and handprints hoping to find a friend.
Lowji is **resourceful**.	He finds a way to get his landlady, Mrs. Crisp, to allow him to have pets—including goats!

65 Fleming, Candace ✳ *Lowji Discovers America*
Atheneum, 2005 ✳ 0-689-86299-7
INDIAN AMERICAN ✳ GRADES 3–6

Lowji Sanjana and his family have left their home in Bombay and settled in Hamlet, Illinois, where Lowji's mother will work at Ace Computers. Lowji's father, who was a gourmet chef in India, does not expect to find work right away. Lowji misses his large family; he especially misses his friend Jamshed. It is summer vacation, so how will he make friends in this new town?

Lowji and Jamshed had discussed the possible "silver linings" that might come from this move. Perhaps Lowji will finally be allowed to have a pet. Wrong! The landlady, Mrs. Crisp, is very clear that there will be no pets. Maybe Lowji will ride horses and round up cattle? Wrong again! The old movies of the American West are nothing like the small town of Hamlet. Slowly Lowji begins to adjust to his new environment. He meets some people, including Virgil and his pet pig Blossom, and he notices that a mysterious neighborhood girl is interested in him. Even Mrs. Crisp begins to heed his suggestions about getting a cat to chase the mice, a dog to protect the building from robbers, and two goats to eat the grass. It is almost like having pets!

As the summer passes, Lowji finds he is adjusting to life in America. He meets some boys at the bowling alley who burp in his face. When he burps right back at them, it is the start of a friendship. Lowji even solves the mystery of the footprints and handprints on the path in the woods. They belong to Tamika, the neighborhood girl whom he has seen riding her bike. Lowji and his family are not only adjusting to being in America, they are thriving.

66 Smith, Cynthia Leitich ✳ *Indian Shoes*
Illus. by Jim Madsen ✳ HarperCollins, 2002 ✳ 0-06-029531-7
NATIVE AMERICAN—CHEROKEE, SEMINOLE ✳ GRADES 3–6

Ray Halfmoon and his grandfather live in Chicago and enjoy many activities in the city, including going to Wrigley Field to watch the Chicago Cubs play baseball and going downtown to buy a hot dog. Their heritage is Cherokee and Seminole and occasionally they visit their family in Oklahoma and celebrate native traditions as well as enjoying everyday activities such as fishing.

Each of the six chapters in this book is a story that could stand alone as a read-aloud or for a discussion group. In the first story, Ray trades his orange hightop sneakers for a pair of moccasins for Grampa. In another chapter, Ray is supposed to wear a tuxedo to carry the ring in a friend's wedding but there are no pants. Ray and Grampa come up with a creative and humorous solution. During one Christmas, the weather is too treacherous to make the trip to Oklahoma so Ray and Grampa stay in Chicago and watch all the pets in their neighborhood. The final story is about a trip to Oklahoma, where a nighttime fishing expedition makes a special connection for Ray because Grampa used to fish like this with Ray's father.

67 Yee, Lisa ✳ *Millicent Min: Girl Genius*
Scholastic, 2003 ✳ 0-439-42519-0
CHINESE AMERICAN ✳ GRADES 4–6+

Millicent Min is 11 years old and has just finished her junior year of high school! It isn't easy being a genius. It's difficult to make friends—kids her own age seem immature while her high school classmates dislike being bested by a kid, especially a kid who carries a briefcase and plans to write her yearbook inscription in Latin. Her parents don't understand her and, besides, they have their own problems. Millie is closest to her grandmother, Maddie, but even that is going to change.

In this book, Millicent keeps a journal of the summer before her senior year. Her parents are letting her take a college course, but only if she also does something fun. Her mother decides that the "something fun" should be volleyball and she signs Millie up for the summer volleyball league. At college, Millie remains an outcast. Of course, it doesn't help that she loves her poetry class and practically begs to do extra work. Her one friend at college, Debbie, is really just taking advantage of Millie's brilliance by getting Millie to do her homework. Millie is crushed when she asks Debbie to go to the movies with her and Debbie says "you're just a child."

Just when Millie feels things cannot get any worse, her mother arranges for her to tutor Stanford Wong, her nemesis from elementary school. Stanford has to pass a summer school English class or he will have to repeat sixth grade. As Millie describes it—"I am to tutor my mortal enemy." Millie's days are filled with college, volleyball, and tutoring. One good thing does come out of the volleyball league, Millie makes a friend, Emily, and they enjoy trips to the mall and sleepovers.

Millie's first-person narration is filled with humor. Her tutoring sessions with Stanford are hysterical. There are some touching, realistic moments in the book, too, as when Emily realizes that Millie has not been honest with her about being a genius. Millie is a well-developed character who learns not only to accept herself but also to accept others.

68 Yee, Lisa ✷ *Stanford Wong Flunks Big-Time*
Scholastic, 2005 ✷ 0-439-62247-6
Chinese American ✷ Grades 4–6+

Stanford Wong needs to be tutored in English so he can enter seventh grade. Since Stanford is a top basketball player, passing English is even more important. This diary account describes a summer of basketball camp, summer school, and tutoring by none other than Millicent Min. Neither Stanford nor Millie are thrilled by the arrangement so they decide to keep it a secret. Their tutoring sessions are filled with humor as they call each other derogatory nicknames ("'Nerd,' she says. 'Geek,' I reply. Imbecile. Freak.") Millicent even turns a lesson on parts of speech into an opportunity to sneer at Stanford—"The *pea-brained* basketball player did not even attempt to study."

Besides dealing with Millicent, Stanford tries to keep conflicts with his parents, siblings, and relatives under control. His attraction to Emily, Millie's friend, and his grudging respect and friendship with Millie is described from his point of view, making this a great choice to read along with *Millicent Min, Girl Genius*. Stanford does become motivated and by the end of the summer he passes English and is named to the A-team. He even gets a library card. This is a great choice for discussion and a lot of fun as kids see themselves in the characters in these books.

CHAPTER TWO

Families, Friends, and Neighborhoods

ALL AROUND THE WORLD, CHILDREN ARE LISTENING to bedtime stories. They are playing with their friends and visiting the library. The books in this chapter explore some of the everyday experiences of children, their families, and their friends. There are books about children who are adopted, like *Jin Woo* and *Allison*. And there are books about taking trips and going on picnics. There are books about different neighborhoods—an African village (*It Takes a Village*), an urban street (*No Bad News*), and a rural town (*Down the Road*). There are connections among books of fiction, poetry, and biography. Sharing these books will promote discussion and encourage children to compare their experiences with those of the characters in these books.

IT TAKES A VILLAGE

THE WELL-KNOWN AFRICAN PROVERB "It takes a village to raise a child" is the focus for the books presented here. In fact, Jane Cowen-Fletcher uses that proverb for the title of her book about an older sister who is watching out for her younger brother only to discover that the whole village has been watching out for them both. In *For You Are a Kenyan Child*, another child in an African village receives the support and love of those around him.

Whoever You Are and *All the Colors of the Earth* could be the featured books in a program about the world's people. These books describe diversity while celebrating common humanity. Ann Morris's books present a world view on specific topics; for example, in *Houses and Homes*, the focus is dwellings. Children could create a mural that depicts their own homes. Or they could pick another topic, such as clothing, and find out about children's apparel around the world. *Children Just Like Me* would provide excellent information for this project.

69 Cowen-Fletcher, Jane ∗ *It Takes a Village*
Illus. by the author ∗ Scholastic, 1994 ∗ 0-590-46573-2
AFRICAN—BENIN ∗ GRADES PRESCHOOL–2

> While Mama is busy at the market, Yemi is responsible for her little brother, Kokou. The market is filled with people selling food and other wares. Yemi quickly becomes distracted by a vendor with peanuts and she loses track of Kokou. As Yemi searches for him, Kokou visits several vendors, who watch out for him. When Yemi finds him, she realizes that many people have cared for him and she thanks each one. When she tells Mama of the adventure, Mama repeats an African proverb—"It takes a village to raise a child." A Note following the story describes a rural open-air market.

70 Cunnane, Kelly ∗ *For You Are a Kenyan Child*
Illus. by Ana Juan ∗ Atheneum, 2006 ∗ 0-689-86194-X
AFRICAN—KENYA—KALENJIN ∗ GRADES 1–3

> Follow the daily activities of a young boy in a village in Kenya. He eats maize porridge for breakfast in his Mama's hut and then takes

Grandfather's cows to pasture. However, the activity in the village distracts him and he visits the tea shop, chases a black monkey, greets the village chief, and more. Finally, he remembers the cows. His grandfather has herded them together and together, they return home. Swahili phrases add to the poetic narrative, which is illustrated in bright, colorful paintings.

71 Fox, Mem * *Whoever You Are*
Illus. by Leslie Staub * Harcourt, 1997 * 0-15-200787-3
MULTICULTURAL * GRADES K–2

Beginning with the words "Little one, whoever you are, wherever you are, there are little ones just like you all over the world," this book celebrates diversity. The poetic text describes common activities—playing and going to school, for example—and common emotions such as sadness and joy. The colorful paintings by Leslie Staub extend the lyrical text. The message "inside, their hearts are just like yours" encourages readers to focus on the similarities among people, not the differences.

72 Hamanaka, Sheila * *All the Colors of the Earth*
Illus. by the author * Morrow, 1994 * 0-688-11132-7
MULTICULTURAL * GRADES PRESCHOOL–2

With a rhythmic text and lush illustrations, this book celebrates the many colors in the world and its people. A brown child roars in front of an image of a roaring brown bear. A russet-toned girl turns cartwheels in falling red leaves. The beauty of diversity shines forth in this celebration.

73 Kindersley, Anabel, and Barnabas Kindersley * *Children Just Like Me*
Illus. with photographs * DK, 1995 * 0-789-40201-7
MULTICULTURAL * GRADES 1–4

Inviting color photographs introduce readers to the diverse experiences of children around the world. There is Mohammad from Egypt and Bakang from Botswana as well as children from more than 140 other countries. As with other DK books, the information is presented on double-page spreads with numerous captioned photographs. Food, school, family, and friends are among the topics featured for each child. This is a great way to focus on similarities and differences.

74 Morris, Ann ✴ *Houses and Homes*
Photographs by Ken Heyman ✴ HarperCollins, 1992 ✴ 0-688-10168-2
Multicultural ✴ Grades Preschool–1

Color photographs show a variety of homes around the world, including tents, mud huts, and cabins. A map is included to show the locations of the homes. After sharing this book with children, make a map of the geographic locations. Other books from Ann Morris and Ken Heyman feature diverse experiences around the world.

ADOPTION

MANY BOOKS FOCUS ON THE EXPERIENCE OF ADOPTING a child from another country, particularly from China. Ed Young's *My Mei Mei* is a personal story that focuses on the experiences and feelings of his adopted daughter Antonia as the family adopts another daughter from China. At first, Antonia is excited about having a baby sister, then she is distressed by the extra attention that goes to the baby, and finally she accepts her new role as the big sister. Eve Bunting's *Jin Woo* tells a similar story. In this book, the first adopted child, David (who is depicted as Caucasian), is apprehensive about the arrival of the baby boy from Korea. Like Antonia, David adjusts to his changing family situation. In *Allison*, the focus of the story is on how Allison, an Asian child, adjusts to being adopted by parents from another culture.

How I Was Adopted: Samantha's Story and *We Wanted You* are reassuring books about loving families who have chosen to adopt.

75 Bunting, Eve ∗ *Jin Woo*
Illus. by Chris K. Soentpiet ∗ Clarion, 2001 ∗ 0-395-93872-4
KOREAN AMERICAN ∗ GRADES K–4

> David's parents have wonderful news. The baby they have been trying to adopt is arriving tomorrow. David, who is also adopted, has mixed feelings. Like any sibling, he is apprehensive about the impact the new baby will have on his relationship with his parents. When the baby, Jin Woo, arrives from Korea, David holds him. In the car, David makes Jin Woo laugh. At home, David's parents share a letter that they have written that reassures him. David gives Jin Woo the mobile of ducks and looks forward to being his big brother.

76 Cole, Joanna ∗ *How I Was Adopted: Samantha's Story*
Illus. by Maxie Chambliss ∗ Morrow, 1995 ∗ 0-688-11929-8
EUROPEAN AMERICAN ∗ GRADES PRESCHOOL–2

> Samantha tells about her home and her family. She discusses being adopted. Her parents explained how babies are born and about their decision to adopt a baby. They emphasize how happy they are to be a family and how much they love Samantha. In an introductory

note, the author describes some of the more difficult issues that children may ask. This book provides excellent information for families.

77 Rosenberg, Liz ✳ *We Wanted You*
Illus. by Peter Catalanotto ✳ Roaring Brook, 2002 ✳ 0-7613-1597-7
MULTICULTURAL ✳ GRADES PRESCHOOL–2

The title page depicts a young man holding his diploma and standing in front of a high school. From there, the text and illustrations describe the love the parents have shared with their adopted son, Enrique. This appears to be an interracial adoption as the illustrations show the parents as white and the child/young man as brown-skinned, perhaps Latino. With so many books featuring families adopting Chinese girls, this book provides another perspective on the experience.

78 Say, Allen ✳ *Allison*
Illus. by the author ✳ Houghton Mifflin, 1997 ✳ 0-395-85895-X
ASIAN AMERICAN ✳ GRADES K–3

Allison lives with her mother, father, and her doll named Mei Mei. One day, Allison puts on her kimono and realizes that she does not resemble her parents. Instead, with her dark straight hair, she looks more like her doll. Allison's parents describe how they brought her home from a country that is far, far away. Allison becomes withdrawn as she tries to understand her past. She acts out, destroying some of her parents' favorite items. When she sees a stray cat, she reaches out to care for it. As she and her family bring the cat into their home, Allison begins to understand and accept her family situation. She knows she belongs.

79 Young, Ed ✳ *My Mei Mei*
Illus. by the author ✳ Philomel, 2006 ✳ 0-399-24339-9
CHINESE AMERICAN ✳ GRADES K–3

Ed Young presents a personal story of adoption from the perspective of his older adoptive daughter, Antonia. Antonia describes flying home to America from China with her parents, Mommy and Baba (father). She pretends to be an older sister. Her dream comes true when she returns to China with her parents to adopt another baby who is named Rachel. The reality is not what Antonia expected. Her "Mei Mei" (little sister) is a baby who demands the time and attention of her parents. But as time passes, Antonia's dream of being a big sister becomes more real as she shares special moments with Rachel. Now both girls want another "Mei Mei."

EVERYDAY EXPERIENCES

LIBRARIANS AND TEACHERS KNOW THE IMPORTANCE of relating books to everyday experiences. Children need opportunities to use literature and language and to connect these to what they know. Simple experiences such as losing a tooth or flying kites or getting ready for bed help children "see themselves" in books. They can share personal experiences and find out about each other. Every child can relate to the experiences in these books. After sharing them, have the children discuss their own "loose tooth" moments or enjoy a pajama party in the library. A great springtime program could be building and flying kites.

Losing a Tooth

80 Beeler, Selby ★ *Throw Your Tooth on the Roof: Tooth Traditions from Around the World*
Illus. by G. Brian Karas ★ Houghton Mifflin, 2001 ★ 0-618-15238-5
MULTICULTURAL ★ GRADES K–3

> Learn about how children around the world deal with their lost teeth. In Korea, the tooth is thrown on the roof! Some teeth are left out to be taken by mice while others are swallowed by the dog. There is a world map showing the location of the tooth traditions along with basic facts about teeth.

81 Diakité, Penda ★ *I Lost My Tooth in Africa*
Illus. by Baba Wagué Diakité ★ Scholastic, 2006 ★ 0-439-66226-5
AFRICAN—MALI; AFRICAN AMERICAN ★ GRADES 1–3

> Amina lives in Portland, Oregon. She and her family travel to Bamako, Mali, to visit her father's family. Her tooth is loose and her father has told her that if you leave your tooth under a gourd, the African Tooth Fairy will leave you a chicken. Amina's tooth finally falls out and she gets *two* chickens. She cares for them and becomes caught up in the routine of the African village. Her hen lays eggs and Amina waits for them to hatch. As her family is leaving to return home, Amina runs to the chicken coop and sees some of the chicks hatching. This story is based on a family experience. It is written by

Penda Diakité, who is Amina's older sister. In an Author's Note, there is a picture of Amina (missing one tooth) holding her chicken.

82 Ruelle, Karen Gray ✶ *Dear Tooth Fairy*
Illus. by the author ✶ Holiday House, 2006 ✶ 0-8234-1929-0
UNIVERSAL ✶ GRADES K–2

Emily the cat cannot wait to lose her first tooth. She has written several letters to the Tooth Fairy suggesting possible gifts that she could receive for her tooth. Unfortunately, her tooth is stubborn and won't fall out. Her brother Harry suggests ways to remove it, but with no success. Finally, the tooth comes out. Emily places it under her pillow and receives a lovely bracelet. This is part of the series of books about these young cats' adventures.

Flying Kites

83 Compestine, Ying Chang ✶ *The Story of Kites*
Illus. by YongSheng Xuan ✶ Holiday House, 2003 ✶ 0-8234-1715-8
ASIAN—CHINA ✶ GRADES K–2

Three brothers, Ting, Pan, and Kùai, try to find a way to keep the birds from eating all the rice in their fields. They are tired of making noises and waving their arms. If only they could fly. Once they think about flying, they decide to create something that could be flown. After several failed attempts, they create three kites. One even makes music (there is a bamboo flute attached to it). The kites are a success and the brothers and their family open a kite factory. An Author's Note explains the origin of kites. Directions are included for making and flying a kite and some tips for kite safety.

84 Ichikawa, Satomi ✶ *My Pig Amarillo*
Illus. by the author ✶ Philomel, 2002 ✶ 0-399-23768-2
CENTRAL AMERICAN—GUATEMALA ✶ GRADES 1–3

Grandpa gives Pablito a pig that he names Amarillo. Pablito not only cares for Amarillo, but treats him as a friend. One day, Pablito returns home and Amarillo is missing. Pablito is distraught. Grandpa suggests that Pablito send a message into the sky by flying a kite on

All Saints' Day. Pablito makes a beautiful kite designed as the face of a pig and on All Saints' Day, he goes to the cemetery and releases his kite into the sky. As he watches his kite fly away, a cloud seems to form the shape of a pig. Pablito feels he has found the spirit of his pig.

85 Lin, Grace ✶ *Kite Flying*
Illus. by the author ✶ Knopf, 2002 ✶ 0-375-81520-1
ASIAN—CHINA ✶ GRADES PRESCHOOL–2

The whole family helps make a dragon kite to fly on a windy day. Bright, colorful illustrations show the three girls and their parents working and playing together. After the brief story, there is information about kites. This family is also featured in Lin's *Dim Sum for Everyone* (see in Chapter 3 under "Food").

86 Torres, Leyla ✶ *The Kite Festival*
Illus. by the author ✶ Farrar, Straus and Giroux, 2004 ✶ 0-374-38054-6
SOUTH AMERICAN—COLOMBIA ✶ GRADES 1–3

Fernando and his family go for a Sunday drive to San Vicente. It is the day of the Second Annual San Vicente Kite Festival and the Flórez family creates a kite. They buy bamboo strips from a vendor and form a hexagon. They use the map from the car to cover the frame. They attach it to the frame with Band-Aids and use paper napkins from their picnic basket for the tail. When the kite gets caught in a tree, Papa retrieves it, but the tail is damaged. Mama contributes her fabric belt to make a new tail. After a beautiful day of family togetherness, the family wins a basket of oranges for the most original kite. Instructions for making a hexagonal kite follow the text.

Going to Bed

87 Carlstrom, Nancy White ✶ *Northern Lullaby*
Illus. by Leo Dillon and Diane Dillon ✶ Philomel, 1992 ✶ 0-399-21806-8
NATIVE AMERICAN ✶ GRADES PRESCHOOL–1

A young child says good night to things in the world, including Grandpa Mountain, Grandma River, and Brother Bear. The rhythmic text sets just the right mood for bedtime. The setting of the book and the illustrations connect it to native people. An Author's Note describes the influence of the people and images of Carlstrom's new home in Alaska. Molly Bang's *Ten, Nine, Eight* (Greenwillow, 1983) is another book that features a character saying good night to specific objects as is the classic *Goodnight, Moon* (HarperCollins, 1947) by Margaret Wise Brown, illustrated by Clement Hurd.

88 Delacre, Lulu, selector ✳ *Arrorró mi niño: Latino Lullabies and Gentle Games*
Illus. by the selector ✳ Lee & Low, 2004 ✳ 1-58430-159-7
Hispanic American ✳ Grades Preschool–1

This is a perfect choice for bedtime . . . or for a pajama story time in the library. There are finger plays and rhymes along with lullabies. The illustrations are soft and reassuring, and each entry is presented in Spanish and English. There are instructions for the games and musical notation for the songs. This book was a Pura Belpré Honor Book for the illustrations.

89 Ho, Minfong ✳ *Hush! A Thai Lullaby*
Illus. by Holly Meade ✳ Orchard Books, 1996 ✳ 0-531-09500-2
Asian—Thailand ✳ Grades Preschool–1

Baby is sleeping and the mother wants everything to be quiet. Hush, she tells the mosquito, the lizard, the black cat, the gray mouse, the green frog, the fat pig, the white duck, the monkey, the buffalo, and the elephant. Finally, it is perfectly quiet and the mother falls asleep. Of course, the baby is now wide awake! The cut-paper collage with ink illustrations show the mother's gentle efforts to keep her toddler asleep. This book was a Caldecott Honor Book.

90 MacDonald, Margaret Read ✳ *Tuck-Me-In Tales: Bedtime Stories from Around the World*
Illus. by Yvonne Davis ✳ August House, 1996 ✳ 0-87483-461-9
Multicultural ✳ Grades Preschool–1

Folktales from Japan, Siberia, Liberia, Chile, Argentina, and the British Isles serve as reminders of the importance of adults—parents, caregivers, and teachers—using their voices as calming agents. Some stories include a chant or simple song (music is provided in the appendix). Lovely, rich watercolors add to the calm.

91 McBratney, Sam ★ _In the Light of the Moon and Other Bedtime Stories_

Illus. by Kady MacDonald Denton ★ Kingfisher, 2001 ★ 0-7534-5224-3

UNIVERSAL ★ GRADES PRESCHOOL–2

This Brit's collection of eight original bedtime stories are full of fun, adventure, and life's lessons for little ones. Appropriate for reading any time of day, they will work especially well when reader and listener can relax and enjoy them. Fanciful watercolors capture the playful mood of the people and critters in the stories.

LOVING FAMILIES

THERE ARE SO MANY STORIES IN WHICH PARENTS demonstrate their unwavering love for their children. In some books, the child needs to be reassured that the love of their mother and father will survive any of the child's missteps. In other books, the child describes the depth of his or her love for the family. Classic books such as *The Runaway Bunny* (HarperCollins, 1942) written by Margaret Wise Brown and illustrated by Clement Hurd can be updated with stories including *Mama, Do You Love Me?* and *Papa, Do You Love Me?* The 2006 Caldecott Medal winner, *The Hello, Goodbye Window*, continues this theme.

A school or public library could plan a parent/child story program featuring books in which families work together to solve problems. In *Down the Road*, Hetty spoils the family's plan to have eggs for breakfast and her parents help find a creative alternative. *Thunder Cake* is another popular story that features a child with a problem (fear of thunder) who is helped by a loving family member, her grandmother. Lenore Look's *Love As Strong As Ginger* encourages children to think about the many people in their families who help and care for them.

92 Joosse, Barbara M. ★ *Mama, Do You Love Me?*
Illus. by Barbara Lavallee ★ Chronicle, 1991 ★ 0-87701-759-X
NATIVE AMERICAN—INUIT ★ GRADES PRESCHOOL–1

An Inuit mother reassures her daughter that she is loved. Each time her daughter asks "Do you love me?" Mama provides an example of the depth and breadth of her love. Cultural information about the Inuit follows the text. This book connects with the next book, *Papa, Do You Love Me?*

93 Joosse, Barbara M. ★ *Papa, Do You Love Me?*
Illus. by Barbara Lavallee ★ Chronicle, 2005 ★ 0-8118-4265-7
AFRICAN—MAASAI ★ GRADES PRESCHOOL–1

In this companion book to *Mama, Do You Love Me?* a father in Africa declares his unwavering love for his son. The son poses questions that test the limits of his father's love. The father's love is constant. He is there to teach, protect, care for, and love his son . . .

always. The illustrations use designs from the Maasai and a glossary is included that explores elements of the Maasai culture.

94 Juster, Norton ✶ *The Hello, Goodbye Window*
Illus. by Chris Raschka ✶ Hyperion, 2005 ✶ 0-7868-0914-0
Multicultural ✶ Grades Preschool–1

A little girl loves to visit her grandparents, Nanna and Poppy, who have a big house with a back porch. But it is the kitchen window that makes the house special. It is the "Hello, Goodbye Window." You see people coming and going. You can check the weather or look out and count the stars. Visiting Nanna and Poppy is a special time and the "Hello, Goodbye Window" is the start and end of every visit. The childlike illustrations are full of color and movement. They are a perfect inspiration for children to make drawings of their own special places. This book received the 2006 Caldecott Medal.

95 Look, Lenore ✶ *Love As Strong As Ginger*
Illus. by Stephen T. Johnson ✶ Atheneum, 1999 ✶ 0-689-81248-5
Chinese American ✶ Grades 2–4

GninGnin (grandmother) works in a factory cracking crabs and removing the meat. Her granddaughter wants to visit the factory and help GninGnin work. On the day of the visit, the granddaughter experiences the hard, monotonous work and she realizes that her grandmother is making sacrifices to provide for a better future for the family. This book is based on the experiences of the author's grandmother, a Chinese American immigrant who worked in a cannery in Seattle in the 1960s and 1970s. Children in middle elementary grades (ages 7 to 9) will empathize with the grandmother's situation, as they think about the many people in their lives who help them. Interviewing an older relative or friend would be an extension activity for this book.

96 Polacco, Patricia ∗ *Thunder Cake*
Illus. by the author ∗ Philomel, 1990 ∗ 0-399-22231-6
EUROPEAN AMERICAN ∗ GRADES K–2

Patricia Polacco reflected on events from her childhood for this story. As a young girl, she was afraid of thunderstorms. While visiting her grandmother, a storm threatened. Instead of concentrating on the storm, her grandmother asked her to help make a special "thunder cake." Gathering the ingredients and making the cake provided a distraction. Then, when the storm arrived, the cake was done. A recipe for the cake is included.

97 Schertle, Alice ∗ *Down the Road*
Illus. by E. B. Lewis ∗ Harcourt, 1995 ∗ 0-15-276622-7
AFRICAN AMERICAN ∗ GRADES K–2

Hetty lives in the country. Today for the first time she is going down the road to the store to buy fresh eggs for tomorrow's breakfast. She feels special to be on her own. Coming home with the eggs, Hetty decides to pick some apples. Her basket of eggs tips and all are broken. When her parents find her hiding in an apple tree, they climb into the tree too and enjoy the view and the sweet apples. The next morning they have apple pie for breakfast. The parents in this story show their love for Hetty by taking a problem (broken eggs) and finding a creative solution (picking apples for an apple pie breakfast).

SIBLINGS AND FRIENDSHIP

SERIES BOOKS ARE AN IMPORTANT PART of developing fluency. Children find a book that is "just right" for them—a book they can read with ease and smoothness. These books allow readers to practice their skills and gain confidence in their ability. It's great to find series books that feature characters from diverse backgrounds, such as the friendship stories from Ann Cameron and the family books by Laurence Yep and Lensey Namioka. These books introduce children in grades 2 through 6 to characters and situations that are familiar and enjoyable.

Ann Cameron's stories about Julian, Huey, and Gloria are a perfect choice for middle-grade readers. They feature African American characters growing up, going to school, and enjoying their friends and family. *Gloria Rising* is one book in this series. Gloria's encounter with an astronaut, who later visits her class, helps her feel good about herself and improves a difficult situation with her fourth-grade teacher. Children who read *Gloria Rising* may want to read the other book about her, *Gloria's Way*, or one of the books that feature Julian and Huey. They could also research the space program, focusing on African Americans and on women. They could compare information in a biography of Mae Jemison with the information about Dr. Grace Street in *Gloria Rising*.

Laurence Yep's books about Teddy and his little brother Bobby feature two brothers growing up in San Francisco's Chinatown. As in the books by Ann Cameron, these are contemporary stories with lots of action and humor. And, as in the books about Gloria, readers could follow up with some research. In *Skunk Scout* the boys go on a camping trip with their Uncle Curtis. Learning about the woodland habitat would be a natural connection. *The Woods Scientist* (set in Vermont rather than the California of *Skunk Scout*) could encourage readers to observe in the habitats around their homes.

The books about the Yang family by Lensey Namioka are also books that feature cultural diversity and could be used to improve fluency and discuss family relationships.

98 Cameron, Ann ✳ *Gloria Rising*
Illus. by Lis Toft ✳ Farrar, Straus and Giroux, 2002 ✳ 0-374-32675-4
AFRICAN AMERICAN ✳ GRADES 2–4

Right before the start of fourth grade, Gloria Jones meets Dr. Grace Street in the grocery store. Dr. Street is an African American astronaut and she encourages Gloria to do her best and work to achieve her goals. At school, Gloria's fourth-grade teacher, Mrs. Yardley, who is nicknamed "the Dragon of Doom," misinterprets classroom situations and makes negative judgments about Gloria and her friends (including Julian and Latisha, from other books). A visit to the class from Dr. Street clears up the confusion and as a result, Mrs. Yardley becomes more tolerant of the students in her classroom. An Author's Note provides Internet sites about space and astronauts.

99   Naden, Corinne J., and Rose Blue ✳ *Mae Jemison: Out of this World*
Illus. with photographs ✳ Millbrook Press, 2003 ✳ 0-7613-2570-0
AFRICAN AMERICAN ✳ GRADES 2–5

On September 12, 1992, Mae Jemison became the first African American woman in space. From her birth in Alabama to her childhood in Chicago she studied and dreamed of being an astronaut. After graduating from Stanford, she earned a medical degree from Cornell. She worked as a physician, spending several years with the Peace Corps. Finally, in 1985, she applied to NASA. She waited two years before she was accepted and began to train to be an astronaut. This biography describes her training, mission in space, and subsequent activities. A timeline follows the text.

100 Cameron, Ann ✳ *Gloria's Way*
Illus. by Lis Toft ✳ Farrar, Straus and Giroux, 2000 ✳ 0-374-32670-3
AFRICAN AMERICAN ✳ GRADES 2–4

In this book, Gloria gives her mother a special valentine, she learns about keeping a promise, her father helps her understand fractions, and she helps train Julian's dog, Spunky. Each of the six chapters in this book is an independent story. Friends Gloria, Julian, Huey, and Latisha come from loving homes and receive support and advice from adults.

101 Namioka, Lensey ✳ *Yang the Eldest and His Odd Jobs*
Illus. by Kees de Kedfte ✳ Little, Brown, 2000 ✳ 0-316-59011-8
CHINESE AMERICAN ✳ GRADES 4–6

Eldest Brother, Yingwu Yang, is considered the most talented of the four Yang children. He is devoted to his music and dedicates all of his extra time to practicing the violin. When his violin needs a costly repair, Yingwu realizes that he must find a way to earn money. He finds some part-time jobs and begins to neglect his music. His hand is injured at his construction job and his future is in jeopardy. His siblings, particularly Third Sister, try to help him through this difficult time. With the love and support of his family, Eldest Brother works to rehabilitate his hand and finds renewed confidence in his musical ability. Related books in this series include: *Yang the Youngest and His Terrible Ear* (Little, Brown, 1992), *Yang the Third and Her Impossible Family* (Little, Brown, 1995), and *Yang the Second and Her Secret Admirer* (Little, Brown, 1998).

102 Yep, Laurence ✳ *Skunk Scout*
Hyperion, 2003 ✳ 0-7868-0670-2
CHINESE AMERICAN ✳ GRADES 3–6

This is the third book about Teddy and Bobby. Uncle Curtis is taking Teddy on a camping trip to celebrate his 10th birthday. Of course, younger brother Bobby gets to come, too. Teddy does not like to leave his home in Chinatown, while Bobby loves nature and the outdoors. The trip is a disaster. They get lost, their tent collapses (trapping Bobby and Uncle Curtis), it rains, and a skunk gets into their tent. The trip is also a great learning experience and Bobby realizes that there are many things about nature that he enjoys. In the Afterword, Yep explains how this book is based on experiences from his youth. *Cockroach Cooties* (Hyperion, 2000) and *Later, Gator* (Hyperion, 1995) also feature these two brothers.

103 Swinburne, Stephen R. * *The Woods Scientist*
Photographs by Susan C. Morse * Houghton Mifflin, 2002 *
  0-618-04602-X
EUROPEAN AMERICAN * GRADES 3–6

> After reading *Skunk Scout*, readers will find a lot of information in this nonfiction book. Susan Morse is a wildlife expert, conservationist, and photographer. The author features her experiences hiking in the woods in Vermont. There are details about the woodland habitat as well as information about scientific inquiry and observation. This is part of the excellent Scientists in the Field series.

BULLIES AND BULLYING

MANY SCHOOLS AND COMMUNITIES MUST DEAL with the issue of bullies and bullying. Christopher Myers's book *Wings* is a great choice to initiate a discussion on this topic. The main character, Ikarus Jackson, is different—he can fly—and thus attracts the taunts of bullies. Another character who has endured the attention of bullies is the one who speaks up to silence them. After reading this book, children can brainstorm strategies for dealing with bullies. They can also prepare a brochure about what to do and list the resources that are available for assistance.

In *Riding the Tiger* by Eve Bunting, the tiger represents gangs and bullies. The tiger tries to lure a new boy, Danny, into his trap. Danny's loneliness and his desire to belong make him the perfect target for the tiger.

In *Wings* and in *Riding the Tiger*, the illustrations add to the impact of the text. Myers's collages convey the dejection Ikarus feels when he is ostracized. At the beginning of *Riding the Tiger*, David Frampton's woodcuts depict the tiger as almost friendly, then sly, and finally threatening. The size of the tiger grows as the danger from him increases. Children can explore how each illustrator enhances the intensity of the story.

Christopher Myers's choice of the name Ikarus for the character who can fly is a clear connection to Icarus from ancient Greek mythology. Children may want to read *Wings* by Jane Yolen to discuss the link between the two stories.

104 Bunting, Eve * *Riding the Tiger*
Illus. by David Frampton * Clarion, 2001 * 0-395-79731-4
EUROPEAN AMERICAN * GRADES 4–6

Danny is new in town. He feels bored and alone until the tiger comes to him. The tiger knows his name and offers to give him a ride. Once on the tiger's back, Danny feels strong and proud. He watches as the people who pass shy away from them. The police warn him to get off, but Danny chooses to stay on, feeling the thrill of the tiger's power. When a girl comes up to them, the tiger asks her "Do you think the way I think?" and "Do you want what I want?" Danny begins to grow uneasy as the tiger sneers at a young man at the playground. The young man works with kids and offers them options. The tiger wants to control kids and is disdainful of the young man from the playground. Now Danny wants off, but the tiger seems to be larger and more powerful and he says "Don't even think about it." Finally, Danny realizes that he does have a choice, an option. He jumps off, falling roughly to the ground. Then Danny turns to help an old man knocked down by the tiger. Danny chooses not to belong to the tiger.

105 Myers, Christopher ✳ *Wings*
Illus. by the author ✳ Scholastic, 2000 ✳ 0-590-03377-8
AFRICAN AMERICAN ✳ GRADES 4–6

Ikarus Jackson can fly. He is different so others whisper and point at him. They laugh at him and taunt him. At school, the students and teacher belittle him, while a silent girl looks on. The girl has suffered herself as the focus of ridicule; now she watches, as Ikarus is the object of their derision. Finally, tired of the taunts, Ikarus falls to the ground amid shouts and laughter. The girl who has tried to be a shadow and avoid the cruel attention of the group—the silent girl—speaks. She yells "Stop!" She speaks words of affirmation and praise to Ikarus. Finding her own strength, she silences the bullies.

106 Yolen, Jane ✳ *Wings*
Illus. by Dennis Nolan ✳ Harcourt, 1991 ✳ 0-15-297850-X
GREEK, ANCIENT ✳ GRADES 2–6

This retelling of the myth from ancient Greece tells the story of Daedalus and his son Icarus. Daedalus was an artist and a prince. He was also proud of his abilities and accomplishments. He was so proud that he caused the death of his nephew, Talos, and was exiled from Athens. On the island of Crete, Daedalus built a labyrinth for King Minos, who kept the monstrous Minotaur there. Daedalus married and had a son whom he named Icarus, but, despite his settled life on Crete, Daedalus's heart was in Athens. Daedalus betrayed King Minos by revealing the secret of the labyrinth to Theseus, a young man from Athens, and King Minos imprisoned Daedalus and Icarus in a tower. Watching the birds from the window, Daedalus was inspired to create wings for their escape. As Daedalus and Icarus flew away from the tower, Icarus celebrated his freedom and neglected the warnings from his father. The pride of Icarus, son of the proud Daedalus, brought him too close to the sun. His wings disintegrated and Icarus was lost in the sea.

MULTICULTURAL FAMILIES

UNDERSTANDING FAMILIES—HOW THEY ARE UNIQUE and how they are similar—is a key element of learning for children. By examining cultural practices and family traditions, children develop an appreciation for diversity. Families are often the focus of school and library programs. Children draw the members of their family, labeling each person. They describe family foods, songs, and celebrations. Librarians and teachers use many books to show diverse family situations. The books described here feature children whose families represent more than one culture. Using these books, children can observe the contributions of different cultures.

107 Ada, Alma Flor * *I Love Saturdays y domingos*
Illus. by Elivia Savadier * Atheneum, 2002 * 0-689-31819-7
MULTICULTURAL * GRADES PRESCHOOL–2

> The young girl in this story visits both sets of grandparents each weekend. On Saturdays, she visits her English-speaking grandparents—her father's parents. On *los domingos*, she visits her mother's parents—*Abuelito y Abuelita*. Each double-page spread shows the activities she shares with her grandparents. Breakfast is scrambled eggs one day and *huevos rancheros* the next. There is Taffy the cat and *Canelo* the dog. The little girl counts in English and in Spanish and she listens to stories. Grandfather describes how he came to America from Europe; Abuelito describes the *rancho* in Mexico where he spent his childhood. There is even more diversity in her family since her Abuelita's family is Native American. Finally, it is the little girl's birthday and everyone is there for the multicultural celebration.

108 Friedman, Ina R. * *How My Parents Learned to Eat*
Illus. by Allen Say * Houghton Mifflin, 1984 * 0-395-35379-3
JAPANESE AMERICAN * GRADES 1–3

> A young girl whose mother is Japanese and whose father is American tells about her family. When her father was a sailor in Japan, he met a young Japanese woman. Each wanted to demonstrate an

appreciation for the other's culture so they learned about the food and traditions. As they shared their knowledge, their relationship developed. Now the young girl enjoys the heritage of each of her parents.

109 Hamanaka, Sheila ✴ *Grandparents Song*
Illus. by the author ✴ HarperCollins, 2003 ✴ 0-688-17852-9
MULTICULTURAL ✴ GRADES K–3

A young girl celebrates her diverse ancestry in this picture book. One grandmother was a Native American who married a green-eyed man who came "'cross the cold northern sea" (perhaps, Ireland). Her other grandmother came "across the Rio Grande" and married an African American whose ancestors were slaves. The text is rhythmic and framed in folk-art inspired illustrations in which images of a "family tree" are repeated. This book would be a great selection to share with children who have diverse family experiences.

110 Hausherr, Rosmarie ✴ *Celebrating Families*
Illus. with photographs ✴ Scholastic, 1997 ✴ 0-590-48937-2
MULTICULTURAL ✴ ALL AGES

Fourteen children invite the reader into their lives to meet their families, some traditional, some unique. Each double-page spread shares a family "portrait" and a summary of the child and family's background and favorite activities. Youngsters will appreciate their own families and gain an understanding of the family structure of many of their friends and peers.

YOUR NEIGHBORHOOD

AS CHILDREN GROW UP, THEY BEGIN TO NOTICE more about the world around them. They move from an egocentric view to one that encompasses a wider vision. The books described here present situations where children adjust to difficulties in their neighborhoods and their lives.

In *No Bad News*, Marcus is shown how to look for the good that is around him. Cooper (in *Cooper's Lesson*) finds a way to appreciate the present and the past. With *Creativity*, Charlie helps Hector adjust to his new home. *Superhero* is a fantasy story that will resonate with many children who wish they had special powers to make the world better. And even after Janna's grandfather passes away, his friends are there to look out for her and make her feel special in *Janna and the Kings*.

A cause-and-effect chart could be created for any of these books. Each character has a problem and finds a solution. For Marcus in *No Bad News*, the problem is his perception of his neighborhood. The men at the barbershop help him develop a positive approach to his world. Readers could talk about issues that they deal with and propose solutions.

111 Cole, Kenneth * *No Bad News*
Photographs by John Ruebartsch * Albert Whitman, 2001 * 0-8075-4743-3
AFRICAN AMERICAN * GRADES 1–4

Whenever Marcus needs a haircut, he and his mother always go to the barbershop together. Today, his mom is busy and Marcus walks there by himself. His journey takes him past signs of urban decay and he worries about the bad things that happen in his neighborhood. There are boarded-up buildings, young men drinking out of bottles in paper bags, police sirens, and people yelling. At the barbershop, Marcus is quiet and withdrawn. Mr. Jackson and some of the other men in the shop ask him what is wrong and Marcus describes his trip to the shop. Mr. Jackson starts to talk about the good news in the neighborhood and other customers join in. There are hard-working families, yards with beautiful gardens, neighbors helping each other, music, and more. An elderly man, Mr. Kelley, encourages Marcus to both *see* and *be* part of the good news. On his way home, Mar-

A Cause-Effect Chart for *No Bad News* might look like this:

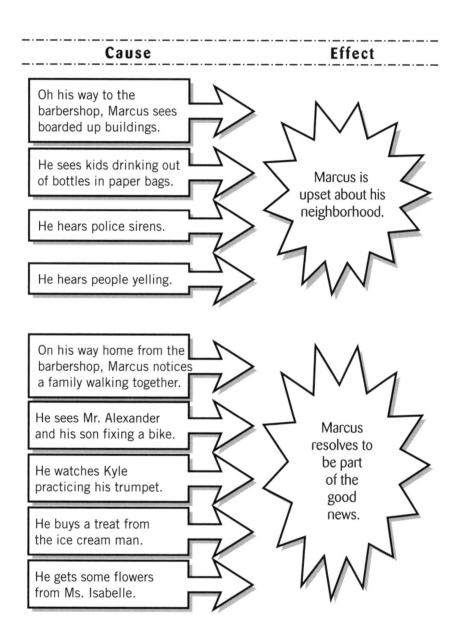

Cause | **Effect**

Oh his way to the barbershop, Marcus sees boarded up buildings.

He sees kids drinking out of bottles in paper bags.

He hears police sirens.

He hears people yelling.

Marcus is upset about his neighborhood.

On his way home from the barbershop, Marcus notices a family walking together.

He sees Mr. Alexander and his son fixing a bike.

He watches Kyle practicing his trumpet.

He buys a treat from the ice cream man.

He gets some flowers from Ms. Isabelle.

Marcus resolves to be part of the good news.

cus looks to see the good news and he reaches home promising to help make more good news. The black-and-white photographs are perfect for this realistic picture book. Once Marcus is looking for the good news, touches of color are added to the photographs to highlight the good things he sees, such as Mr. Alexander fixing a boy's bike, Kyle practicing his trumpet, and Ms. Isabelle and her flowers.

112 Shin, Sun Yung * *Cooper's Lesson*
Illus. by Kim Cogan * Children's Book Press, 2004 * 0-89239-193-6
KOREAN AMERICAN * GRADES 2–4

In his American neighborhood, Cooper feels like an outsider. With an American father and a Korean mother, he feels he does not belong. At the Korean grocery store, Mr. Lee, the owner, makes Cooper feel even more alienated. Mr. Lee talks to him in Korean, which Cooper can only partly understand. Frustrated and hurt, Cooper tries to take a hairbrush without paying for it. Mr. Lee catches him and decides that Cooper must work in the store to pay for the brush. As they spend time together, they develop a friendship. Mr. Lee shares some of his feelings about being an outsider—a foreigner in a new land. Cooper's mother comes to the store and Cooper begins to tell her what has happened—speaking in Korean! The text of this book is written in English and Korean.

113 Smith, Patricia * *Janna and the Kings*
Illus. by Aaron Boyd * Lee & Low, 2003 * 1-58430-088-4
AFRICAN AMERICAN * GRADES 1–3

Janna's best friend is her grandfather. On Saturdays, Janna and Granddaddy walk through the neighborhood talking to friends and relaxing at the corner store. Granddaddy always asks, "So, Princess Sugarlump, what should we do today?" Her answer is always the same, "I think you need a haircut, Granddaddy." All of Granddaddy's friends are at the barbershop sitting like kings in the high barbershop chairs. They fuss over Janna, making her feel like a real princess. After Granddaddy dies, Janna feels lost and alone. When she finally decides to walk around the neighborhood, it seems empty. She reaches the barbershop and the "kings" are there. They welcome Janna and ease the pain of her loss.

114 Steptoe, John ✳ *Creativity*
Illus. by E. B. Lewis ✳ Clarion, 1997 ✳ 0-395-68706-3
PUERTO RICAN AMERICAN; AFRICAN AMERICAN ✳ GRADES 3–6

Hector, the new kid in Charlie's school, is from Puerto Rico. Charlie is interested in Hector because they are similar but different: they both have brown skin and black hair, but Hector speaks Spanish. Charlie befriends Hector, helping him find his way around. Charlie asks his teacher about Hector's background and he talks to his parents, too, who discuss with him the creativity that can be found in the diversity of the world. At school, Charlie learns more about Puerto Rico and reflects on the influences of different cultures. After a group of boys in gym class make fun of Hector's appearance, especially his new but unpopular sneakers, Charlie tries to explain why the boys acted as they did. But Hector is still hurt. He knows his family cannot buy him another pair of shoes. Charlie goes home and finds a pair of new sneakers in his closet and gives them to Hector, who gives Charlie a shirt with a palm tree on it that was a gift from his grandmother in Puerto Rico. Charlie appreciates the creativity of sharing in his friend's heritage.

115 Tauss, Marc ✳ *Superhero*
Photographs by the author ✳ Scholastic, 2005 ✳ 0-439-62734-6
AFRICAN AMERICAN ✳ GRADES 1–4

Maleek loves comic books, especially those with superheroes. In fact, Maleek is a superhero. He has his own superhero costume and journeys around his city solving problems. He even has created a robot assistant named Marvyn. When the city parks disappear, Maleek and Marvyn time travel 500 years into the past to collect plants and flowers to help restore the parks. In his laboratory, Maleek creates "Gigundo Juice" and he pours it on the desolate areas of his city. Immediately, plant life appears, the parks are revitalized, and Maleek's superhero work is done for now. Vivid black-and-white photographs with unusual lighting and perspectives present Maleek's fantastic adventure.

LIBRARIES

Tomás and the Library Lady

116 Mora, Pat ∗ *Tomás and the Library Lady*
Illus. by Raul Colón ∗ Knopf, 1997 ∗ 0-679-80401-3
MEXICAN AMERICAN ∗ GRADES 1–3

Every summer Tomás and his family leave their home in Texas
and travel to Iowa. They are farm workers and their jobs
change with the seasons. In Iowa, Tomás is old enough to visit
the library on his own. The librarian welcomes him and helps
him find books on his favorite subjects. She even allows him
to borrow two books that have been checked out in her name.
Tomás loves sharing his books with his family—especially with
Papá Grande, his grandfather. All summer Tomás visits the
library and the library lady is there for him. On his last day in
Iowa, he brings her a *pan dulce* (sweet bread) from his
mother. The library lady gives him a new book.

This book is based on the story of Tomás Rivera, a migrant
worker who became a national education leader. The Tomás
Rivera Mexican American Children's Book Award was created
in Rivera's honor; *Tomás and the Library Lady* won the award
in 1997.

★

At the 2006 Annual Conference of the American Library
Association in New Orleans, there was a dramatization of this
wonderful story celebrating Tomás Rivera. Two actors played all
the roles and the stage setting and props were simple—suitcases,

shawls and hats, a couple of bookcases, and a stack of books. The actors captivated the audience as they brought the story of Tomás and his migrant family to life.

Through vignettes, the audience was introduced to the plight of the migrant worker and to the prejudices and stereotypes facing this population. The Mexican American culture and the importance of close family ties were emphasized. The determination of Tomás and the inspiring encouragement of one librarian were celebrated in this tribute to the real man who became Chancellor of the University of California at Riverside.

A panel discussion following the presentation featured author Pat Mora; Tim Wadham, youth services coordinator at the Maricopa County (AZ) Library District, who conceived the idea of staging *Tomás* as a play; José Cruz González , resident playwright for Childsplay, who took the book and scripted it; and David Saar, Childsplay artistic director and founder. The panel suggested visiting the Childsplay Web site (www.childsplayaz.org) for future plans of the traveling troupe or rights to presentation. Made possible through a grant to the Maricopa County Library District by the Arizona State Library Archives and Public Records Agency under the Library Services and Technology Act, which is administered by the Institute of Museum and Library Services, this project demonstrated that you *can change your world at your library!*

TOMÁS AND THE LIBRARY LADY shows that libraries within a neighborhood play an important role as a resource for knowledge and learning, but in the neighborhood they are also gathering places—to borrow materials for reading, listening, or viewing pleasure; to have questions answered; to see neighbors; to attend programs; to hold meetings; to share talents; to discuss books; or to read a newspaper from another city.

Each of the books featured here describes the impact of the library on the lives of the characters. After reading any of these books have the children describe their own feelings about libraries. Make a book or bulletin board of their responses.

Then take children on a trip to the local library. Do they each have a library card? Have them collect information: What is the library's name? Is there a story behind that name? Is it just the street or neighborhood name or was it named for a well-known person in the community? Introduce your students to the librarian and explore the children's and teen areas together. See what computers are available to help find information for a report, or if there are any for simply playing games.

117 Heide, Florence Parry, and Judith Heide Gilliland ∗ *The House of Wisdom*

Illus. by Mary GrandPré ∗ DK, 1999 ∗ 0-789-42562-9
MUSLIM ∗ GRADES 3–6

Ishau is the son of the chief translator to the Caliph of ancient Baghdad. He marvels at the wisdom and knowledge passed down through the ages and how it's expanded and readied for future scholars as he is sent to gather manuscripts and books from the far reaches of the historic Middle East. Paintings pulsating in the background of the boxed text add to the excitement and energy of expanding the universe of information.

118 Miller, William ∗ *Richard Wright and the Library Card*

Illus. by R. Gregory Christie ∗ Lee & Low, 1997 ∗ 1-880000-57-1
AFRICAN AMERICAN ∗ GRADES 3–6

This fictionalized account tells how Richard Wright wanted to learn to read and be able to use the library, but since only whites were allowed, he feared he would never quench his hunger for books. At one of his first jobs, he gathered the courage to ask his white boss to lend him his library card. At the library, he pretended to be getting books for Mr. Falk. He devoured all that he could. He saw books and reading as his ticket to freedom.

119 Ruurs, Margriet * *My Librarian Is a Camel: How Books Are Brought to Children Around the World*
Boyds Mills, 2005 * 1-59078-093-0
MULTICULTURAL * GRADES 3–5

Stories of "mobile libraries" bring attention to the arrival of books for children by feet, on wheels, and even by boat in different settings around the world. Maps and photographs make a pleasing scrapbook of library services from Australia to Zimbabwe.

120 Spinelli, Jerry * *The Library Card*
Scholastic, 1997 * 0-590-46731-X
MULTICULTURAL * GRADES 4–6

Award-winning author Jerry Spinelli tells four stories of young people and the impact obtaining a library card can have on their lives. A favorite character is April Mendez who moves from New York City to a farm in Pennsylvania—a mushroom farm, with quite a distinct odor! She doesn't miss the city except for the library. She loves to read and had spent many hours at the city library. One day she packs a lunch and decides to go for a hike—to see the surrounding hills and trees and to try to get away from the smell. Suddenly a truck with B-O-O-K-S written on it comes over the hill. She learns what a bookmobile is and makes a friend besides. Use this book as a great way to stimulate conversation or writing about any individual's encounter with a library card.

121 Stewart, Sarah * *The Library*
Illus. by David Small * Farrar, Straus and Giroux, 1995 * 0-374-34388-8
EUROPEAN AMERICAN * GRADES K–4

This rhythmic tribute to Elizabeth Brown, a born bookworm, touches on the joy, the fun, the dangers, the sacrifices, and the gift of a devoted reader when she gave her houseful of books to the city to establish a library, which she could then visit and continue to read on and on.

Reflections

In 2003 I attended the IFLA (International Federation of Library Associations) Conference in Berlin, Germany. Arriving in late July—in a summer of extreme heat for that part of the world—we found our quaint Kronprintz hotel nestled in trees. Opening the windows (did I mention, no air-conditioning?) admitted enough of a breeze to keep us comfortable if we didn't move too quickly. The modern Convention Center, with air-conditioning, was a welcome refuge and, as usual, the conference program was filled with interesting sessions about library innovations, services, and needs around the world.

At one meeting, two children's librarians from Egypt shared slides of the Bibliotheca Alexandrina, a new public library (www.bibalex.org/English/index.aspx) erected near the site of the famous Library of Alexandria, which was destroyed probably around 30 A.D. This new $200 million structure was designed by an Oslo architecture and landscape firm to be not only a functional library, but also a monument to civilization. The slides showed a massive cylinder emerging from the ground near the sea, at an angle. The disc-shaped roof suggests the sun rising over the Mediterranean Sea and the aluminum and glass roof panels resemble microchips. The outer wall consists of nearly 6,500 granite panels bearing characters from all the known alphabets.

The library is designed to have seven levels and house up to 8 million volumes. It also houses a planetarium, a library school, a digitization laboratory and a conference center. The women told us the Children's Library was not part of the original plan and was added just four months before the formal inauguration. The Children's Library serves primary school-aged children (no children under 6 at this time) and has 3,000 titles in Arabic, English, and French. Students use computer labs, A-V materials, televisions, and the Web site to "Ask a Librarian." No parents are allowed in this section of the library in order to give the children the chance to freely choose their own materials.

—Kathy East

Activity

After reading the description of the library at Alexandria, try to draw or make a model of this unique building. Or design a unique library of your own! What are important elements to consider? The shape of the building—perhaps have it look like a book? The need for a theater? The reflection from CDs hanging in the entry hallway? Or consider designing a specific kind of library with a unique shape. A zoo library shaped like an ape? Or a transportation library shaped like a train? Design and give yourself an award for some outstanding innovation!

Enjoy books that connect with ancient Egypt, such as *How the Amazon Queen Fought the Prince of Egypt*, *The Winged Cat*, and others listed here.

122 Bower, Tamara ✳ *How the Amazon Queen Fought the Prince of Egypt*
Illus. by the author ✳ Atheneum, 2005 ✳ 0-689-84434-4
EGYPTIAN, ANCIENT ✳ GRADES 4–6+

Based on a story from an ancient Egyptian scroll, a tribe of Amazon women stand against an invading Egyptian army. When the queen and prince fight face-to-face to a draw, they see each other as equals and decide to form an alliance. The illustrations for this book are based on ancient Egyptian and Assyrian art. Portions of the text are rewritten in picture-writing for added interest and understanding.

123 Cushman, Doug ✳ *The Mystery of King Karfu*
HarperCollins, 1996 ✳ 0-06-024797-5
UNIVERSAL ✳ GRADES PRESCHOOL–2

This humorous picture book is set in 1938 and sends wombat detective Seymour Sleuth to Egypt to help Professor Slagbottom to find the stolen Stone Chicken of King Karfu. The yellow notebook paper format is kid-friendly, showing notes, pictures, and other clues, so the reader can play sleuth as well. A nice starting point for a writing exercise to develop other mysteries worthy of solving.

124 Lattimore, Deborah Nourse * *The Winged Cat: A Tale of Ancient Egypt*

Illus. by the author * HarperCollins, 1992 * 0-06-023636-1
EGYPTIAN, ANCIENT * GRADES 4–6+

Merit is a serving girl in the ancient temple of the Pharaoh. When the High Priest, Waha, drowns a sacred cat, Merit is a witness. To find the truth, the Pharaoh sends them both to the Netherworld, where Merit and Waha are tested. With help from the cat's spirit, Merit succeeds. The cat is given another life and the High Priest is destroyed. The illustrations replicate design elements from ancient Egypt using hieroglyphics and ancient symbols.

125 Love, D. Anne * *Of Numbers and Stars: The Story of Hypatia*

Illus. by Pam Paparone * Holiday House, 2006 * 0-8234-1621-6
EGYPTIAN, ANCIENT * GRADES 3–6

Hypatia was a brilliant woman of the 4th century in Alexandria, Egypt, in a time and place when most young girls did not learn to read or write. But Hypatia became so well educated that she was recognized as an authority in mathematics, astronomy and philosophy. Her father was a

mathematician and believed in his daughter. A sparse text
tells of her early training. Additional information is available in
an Author's Note that tells of the price she paid for her fame.
The artwork lends a "sense of ancient Egypt" to this
extraordinary tale.

126 Trumble, Kelly ✳ *The Library of Alexandria*
Illus. by Robina MacIntyre Marshall ✳ Clarion, 2003 ✳ 0-395-
75832-7
EGYPTIAN, ANCIENT ✳ GRADES 5–6+

This history of the most famous library in the ancient world
tells of its founding in the 3rd century when Ptolemy I began
collecting hundreds of thousands of valuable books, almost all
in Greek. Many were collected from other cultures and were
translated into Greek. The library is believed to have contained
more than half a million books. Alexandria was known as the
greatest center for learning. Many of the great works of the
geographer Eratosthenes, who measured the circumference of
the world, were housed in the library, along with works of
astrologists, physicians, and others. However, the library did
not survive. During the reign of Julius Caesar, a fire targeting
the Egyptian fleet in the harbor at Alexandria spread and the
library went up in flames. At the end of the text, a short Note
tells of the creation of the Bibliotheca Alexandrina,
inaugurated in 2002.

SPORTS AND TEAM SPIRIT

SPORTS STORIES ARE POPULAR WITH MANY READERS. Readers like books with characters that are "just like them." They appreciate stories that present everyday situations. Like the books about Julian, Gloria, and Huey mentioned under "Siblings and Friendship" earlier in this chapter, *The Real Lucky Charm* and *The Real Slam Dunk* fill an important need for readers looking for transitional chapter books. Marcus and Mia are modern African American kids who go to school, argue, and face realistic problems. The basketball connection adds to the appeal.

When the opening chapter of *The Real Slam Dunk* was read to a group of fourth-graders, they were eager to keep reading the book. They said "You should get more than one copy of that book for us" and "I liked the basketball action." One student commented that she was on a co-ed team, so she recognized some of the potential problems. *Hoop Girlz* and *Strong to the Hoop* are also basketball-themed books for this age group.

Basketball poetry would be great to share with these fiction books. *Hoop Kings* and *Hoop Queens* are action-packed rhymes about male and female players. *The Basket Counts* offers more verses about this sport.

Biographies about popular sports figures are also an excellent resource to encourage reading fluency. Many children understand the context of a sport. They know the vocabulary—goal, quarterback, touchdown, and score. With this familiarity, they feel confident about reading books with a sports context. The biographies listed below are recent and feature significant achievements such as the first Asian American to win an Olympic Gold medal (*Sixteen Years in Sixteen Seconds: The Sammy Lee Story*) and two brothers who have succeeded in professional football (*Game Day*). These would be excellent choices to promote a discussion about working against the odds to achieve your goals.

Fiction

127 Bledsoe, Lucy Jane ✴ *Hoop Girlz*
Holiday House, 2002 ✴ 0-8234-1691-7
MULTICULTURAL ✴ GRADES 5–6+

River Borowitz-Jacobs, grade 6, wants to play for the WNBA. She is disappointed when she does not make the A-Team in her town, Azalea, Oregon. Now she cannot play in the Oregon Coast Tournament. And her hopes of being the MVP and going to a free summer basketball camp are dashed. Coach Glover is very blunt about why she was not chosen, and River is determined to find a way to succeed. Along with other girls who have been assigned to the B-Team, River forms a team called Hoop Girlz.

There are obstacles to this team of second string players and Coach Glover encourages River to overcome them. Her parents and older brother Zack are supportive, too. Zack even agrees to help the team, eventually becoming their coach so they can enter the tournament. The team really comes together. Zack even helps design a play for Jennifer, who is in a wheelchair. But when River is finally offered a spot on the A-Team she must make a choice. She chooses the Hoop Girlz. They make it to the tournament and into the finals, where they lose to the A-Team. Emily Hargraves, a WNBA player from the town, awards the MVP trophy to Rochelle Glover of the A-Team and to the entire team of Hoop Girlz for their outstanding teamwork. The basketball action during the tournament is quick and exciting.

128 Coy, John ✴ *Strong to the Hoop*
Illus. by Leslie Jean-Bart ✴ Lee & Low, 1999 ✴ 1-880000-80-6
AFRICAN AMERICAN ✴ GRADES 2–6

James is 10—too young to play on the main court with his older brother Nate. When Nate's teammate Luke is injured, James is allowed to join the game. He must guard Marcus, one of the biggest and best players. Marcus talks trash, like "You can't guard me" and "Get out of here or I'll push you out," but James is determined to stay in the game. With the teams tied at 14, Marcus leaves James to double-team another player. James gets the ball and shoots the game-winning shot. Another team comes to play the winners and James is allowed to continue to play. The mixed-media illustrations in this book are a combination of photographs cut and layered onto scratchboard drawings and will attract many readers.

129 Richardson, Charisse K. ✴ *The Real Lucky Charm*
Illus. by Eric Velasquez ✴ Dial, 2005 ✴ 0-8037-3105-1
AFRICAN AMERICAN ✴ GRADES 3–5

Mia and Marcus are 10-year-old African American twins. In this, the second book about them, Mia and her friend Gabbie sign up for a girl's basketball team. There is not enough interest in that team, so the girls' and boys' teams are merged, becoming co-ed. The new team includes Mia's brother, Marcus. Mia enjoys the new arrangement and plays with confidence. When she receives a basketball charm as a gift, she decides that the charm brings her good luck so she relaxes her efforts at practice and at school. Losing the charm helps her learn a lesson about responsibility and hard work. Themes of friendship, responsibility, sports, and competition add to the appeal of this book.

130 Richardson, Charisse K. ✴ *The Real Slam Dunk*
Illus. by Kadir Nelson ✴ Dial, 2005 ✴ 0-8057-3050-0
AFRICAN AMERICAN ✴ GRADES 3–5

Marcus Robinson loves basketball and Jason Carter is his favorite player. His class is going on a field trip to the Giants Basketball Practice Day and Marcus will be the official class greeter and meet his hero. Marcus got this honor by winning the class math contest. Usually, Marcus is ambivalent about school but he has shown that he could apply himself and win when the prize is right. At the Practice Day, Jason Carter greets each student and talks about his accomplishments and work ethic. He also discusses the importance of school and his desire to be a chemist when his playing days are over. Mia, Marcus's twin, tells Jason of her plans to be a news reporter and Marcus's plans to be a basketball player. Jason encourages Marcus and all his classmates to "always dream more than one dream."

Poetry

131 Adoff, Arnold ∗ *The Basket Counts*
Illus. by Michael Weaver ∗ Simon & Schuster, 2000 ∗ 0-689-80108-4
MULTICULTURAL ∗ GRADES 3–6

Arnold Adoff focuses on basketball in these free-verse poems. The illustrations depict diverse participants—males, females, blacks, and whites. One poem features a player in a wheelchair who can "pop the sharpest wheelchair wheeeelies." The design of the poems is very creative. Read these along with *Hoop Kings* and *Hoop Queens* and encourage kids to try writing their own poetic reflections.

132 Smith, Charles R., Jr. ∗ *Hoop Kings*
Illus. with photographs ∗ Candlewick Press, 2004 ∗ 0-7636-1423-8
MULTICULTURAL ∗ GRADES 3–6

Twelve prominent NBA players are featured in these poems, including Allen Iverson, Vince Carter, Kobe Bryant, Jason Kidd, and Tracy McGrady. The poems combine word play and a knowledge of basketball. For example, Tim Duncan is featured in "Money in the Bank," which celebrates his ability to finesse, shooting bank shots that require lots of practice and rely on understanding geometric angles. The poem about Shaquille O'Neal is an acrostic poem for the letters "SHAQ" and appears on a fold-out page that shows a lifesize picture of the bottom of one of O'Neal's enormous shoes. The illustrations are photographs of the players placed on a lively background of lines and bright colors.

133 Smith, Charles R., Jr. ∗ *Hoop Queens*
Illus. with photographs ∗ Candlewick Press, 2004 ∗ 0-7636-1423-8
MULTICULTURAL ∗ GRADES 3–6

Like *Hoop Kings* this book features 12 players, but they are from the WNBA. Included are Sheryl Swoopes, Chamique Holdsclaw, Lisa Leslie, Nykesha Sales, and Teresa Weatherspoon. There is lots of action in the words and in the design of the book. For Chamique Holdsclaw, the poem "Fire Starter" describes her "Racing reversing leaping and snaking, jumping twirling taking and making." The picture shows her leaping to make a shot. Bright orange flames frame the action. The typography is designed for dramatic impact and typesize is changed to add to the energy. Readers could try formatting their own writing using these poems as models.

Biographies

134 Adler, David A. ✳ *America's Champion Swimmer: Gertrude Ederle*
Illus. by Terry Widener ✳ Harcourt, 2000 ✳ 0-15-201969-3
EUROPEAN AMERICAN ✳ GRADES 2–5

Gertrude Ederle was born in 1906 at a time when women had limited opportunities. Like those who overcame barriers because of their ethnicity, Ederle faced similar inequities. She learned to swim on a family trip to Germany. Back at home, she became a member of the New York Women's Swimming Association. Not only did she compete and win races, she also broke down gender barriers. In August 1926, she swam across the English Channel, becoming the first woman to do so while also beating the men's record. Her achievement was celebrated with a parade in New York City. An Author's Note provides information about Ederle's life following her swim across the Channel.

135 Adler, David A. ✳ *Joe Louis: America's Fighter*
Illus. by Terry Widener ✳ Harcourt, 2005 ✳ 0-15-216480-4
AFRICAN AMERICAN ✳ GRADES 2–6

During the Great Depression, many Americans looked for heroes to sustain them. Joe Louis became such a figure, particularly to the African American community. This biography describes Louis's rise as a boxer and the difficulties he faced, especially when dealing with the prejudiced attitudes of this era. As he competed against white fighters, many white fans cheered his opponents. In 1936, however, he faced a German fighter, Max Schmeling, and many white fans in America began to support Joe Louis. When Louis lost his first fight with Schmeling, many Germans hailed it as a victory for the Nazi agenda. Two years later, the men fought again, an event broadcast around the world. This time, Joe Louis won. When World War II began, Louis served in the army. After the war, he continued to box, retiring in 1949. He attempted a comeback, but it was unsuccessful. When he died in 1981, Louis was hailed as the greatest heavyweight fighter ever.

136 Barber, Tiki, and Ronde Barber, with Robert Burleigh ✷ *Game Day*
Illus. by Barry Root ✷ Simon & Schuster, 2005 ✷ 1-4169-0093-4
African American ✷ Grades 2–5

Ronde and Tiki Barber both play in the National Football League. They are twins who grew up playing football and supporting each other. This book explores their childhood experiences playing on the same team, Tiki as a running back and Ronde as a blocker. Tiki scores the points and gets the glory and Ronde begins to feel left out. His mother and his coach try to help him see the importance of his role, but Ronde still feels unappreciated. In the big game against the Knights, the coach runs a surprise play in which Tiki laterals the ball to Ronde, who scores. Both brothers realize that they succeed by working as a team. *By My Brother's Side* (Simon & Schuster, 2004) and *Teammates* (Simon & Schuster, 2006) are two more books by the Barber twins.

137 Bolden, Tonya ✷ *The Champ: The Story of Muhammad Ali*
Illus. by R. Gregory Christie ✷ Knopf, 2004 ✷ 0-375-82401-4
African American ✷ Grades 2–5

Born Cassius Marcellus Clay, Jr. in 1942, Ali grew up in Louisville, Kentucky, during segregation. When he was 12, he began learning to box. After more than ten years of training and practice, he had his first fight, which he won. Cassius Clay went on to win the gold medal at the Olympic Games in Rome, Italy, in 1960. He continued to fight, but he also became more politically active. He joined the Nation of Islam, changed his name to Muhammad Ali, and, eventually, refused to be drafted into military service. Crowds of people berated him; he was banned from boxing; he faced imprisonment. As he appealed his case, Ali chose to speak about his beliefs. People began to support his decision. When Ali was allowed to box again, he was more popular than ever. His fights were worldwide events; he was, once again, the champ. After his retirement it became evident that years of boxing had impacted his health. Even so, he has maintained a public image, supporting causes of freedom and peace. The dramatic illustrations use bright colors, striking angles, and creative print design to support the action of the biography.

138 Bruchac, Joseph ✶ *Jim Thorpe's Bright Path*
Illus. by S. D. Nelson ✶ Lee & Low, 2004 ✶ 1-58430-166-X
Native American ✶ Grades 2–4

This picture book focuses on Jim Thorpe's early life. Beginning with the birth of Jim and his twin brother Charlie in Indian Territory in Oklahoma, the author describes their childhood and the influence of their parents, especially their father. Hiram Thorpe was one of the few Native Americans in the region who could read and write English. He valued education as a way to improve the life of Indians. Both boys were sent to an Indian boarding school where Charlie became ill and died. Jim's father continued to demand that Jim become educated. Eventually, Jim attended the Carlisle Indian School in Pennsylvania. There he attracted the attention of coach Pop Warner. Jim became involved in track and football. His athletic skill would bring him recognition in many sports and he would become an activist for equal rights for Native Americans.

139 Krull, Kathleen ✶ *Wilma Unlimited*
Illus. by David Diaz ✶ Harcourt, 1996 ✶ 0-15-201267-2
African American ✶ Grades 2–4

Wilma Rudolph was born in Clarksville, Tennessee, in 1940. She was a sickly child with 19 older brothers and sisters. When she was almost 5 years old, she contracted both scarlet fever and polio. She was not expected to walk again, but she persevered, doing exercises and wearing a brace that allowed her to walk and attend school. Still, she wanted more. She continued her exercises until one day at church she removed her brace and began to walk. Her strength grew and she began to participate in sports, eventually winning a full athletic scholarship to Tennessee State. There, she continued to train and in 1960 she participated in the Olympic Games in Rome, Italy, where she won three Olympic gold medals. Wilma Rudolph's achievements have served as an example of the importance of determination and courage.

140 McDonough, Yona Zeldis ✴ *Hammerin' Hank: The Life of Hank Greenberg*
Illus. by Malcah Zeldis ✴ Walker Books, 2006 ✴ 0-8027-8997-8
JEWISH AMERICAN ✴ GRADES 2–6

Hank Greenberg played baseball in the 1930s and was one of the first professional Jewish players in the game. Like Jackie Robinson, he faced discrimination and hostility. Both fans and players made anti-Semitic jeers. His family did not support his decision to play baseball and his religious commitments sometimes conflicted with his baseball schedule. Still, Greenberg continued to achieve in the sport. After his retirement, he became the first Jewish player elected to baseball's Hall of Fame.

141 Robinson, Sharon ✴ *Promises to Keep: How Jackie Robinson Changed America*
Illus. with photographs ✴ Scholastic, 2004 ✴ 0-439-42592-1
AFRICAN AMERICAN ✴ GRADES 4–6+

The author, Sharon Robinson, is Jackie Robinson's daughter. She provides personal insights into the life and experiences of her father. Chapters focus on the years before Jackie Robinson became the first black player in major league baseball, the discrimination and bigotry that he endured, and his years after baseball as a civil rights activist. Numerous archival photographs and documents add to the presentation. This book is a personal tribute to a man who was not only a baseball hero but also a pioneer for equal rights and opportunities.

142 Yoo, Paula ✳ *Sixteen Years in Sixteen Seconds: The Sammy Lee Story*
Illus. by Dom Lee ✳ Lee & Low, 2005 ✳ 1-58430-247-X
KOREAN AMERICAN ✳ GRADES 2–4

Sammy Lee, a Korean American, grew up in California during the 1930s. At that time, public swimming pools were open only one day each week for people of color. Sammy watched the divers and, on the day the pool was open for him, Sammy practiced diving. With determination and the help of a demanding coach, Sammy's diving continued to improve. He also maintained his academic excellence— he was the first nonwhite to be the student body president of his school and he received a full scholarship to Occidental College in Los Angeles. Still, his dream was to compete in the Olympics, although his father wanted him to become a doctor. The cancellation of the 1940 Olympics delayed his dream and the death of his father in 1943 made him focus on a medical career. In 1948, Dr. Sammy Lee participated in the Olympics in London, England, and became the first Asian American to win a gold medal. An Author's Note provides additional information. This book received an honorable mention for illustrations in the 2006 Asian/Pacific American Awards for Literature.

TRAVEL AND ADVENTURE

SEVERAL BOOKS FOCUS ON TRAVELING AND LEARNING about historical sites. In *Sienna's Scrapbook*, Sienna chronicles her family's trip from their home in Connecticut to a family reunion in North Carolina. In *The Jones Family Express*, Steven tries to find something special to give his Aunt Carolyn at the annual block party. Aunt Carolyn has been traveling and sends postcards to Steven, making him feel special.

Both of these books have illustrations that could be models for extension projects. The collages in *The Jones Family Express* include simulated postcards from Aunt Carolyn, stamps from around the world, and colorful mixed-media pictures of Steven, his family, and his neighborhood. What a great opportunity to make your own family collage! The illustrations in *Sienna's Scrapbook* are designed to simulate a scrapbook. There are photographs, drawings, and captions. Many pages look like lined paper that would be used for a child's report. *Tripper's Travels* and *Around the World* also use a "scrapbook" format that could serve as a model for projects.

After sharing these books with children, suggest they make their own travel or history scrapbooks. These could feature important sites in their state or neighborhood. Children could also plan an imaginary trip, use a map to plot the route, and research places to visit along the way. Postcards could be simulated to highlight areas of interest. *P Is for Passport* could also be used as a model for a class ABC project on locations that celebrate diversity.

143 Chapman, Nancy Kapp ✶ *Tripper's Travels: An International Scrapbook*
Illus. by Lee Chapman ✶ Marshall Cavendish, 2005 ✶ 0-7614-5240-0
UNIVERSAL ✶ GRADES 3–6

Tripper is a dog who travels the world and chronicles his trip in this humorous scrapbook. Many illustrations are drawings of Tripper in exotic locales; others are photographs of famous places with cartoon images of Tripper glued into the picture. The captions provide details about locations including Paris, Rome, Cairo, Nairobi, Moscow, Delhi, Tokyo, Canberra, Mexico City, and Washington, D.C. A list of foreign words in eight languages completes the text. Children will enjoy finding pictures of famous places and gluing in pictures of themselves.

144 George, Lindsay Barrett * *Around the World: Who's Been Here?*
Illus. by the author * Greenwillow, 1999 * 0-688-15269-4
UNIVERSAL * GRADES 3– 6

This picture book is the account of a teacher's year traveling around the world and reporting back to her class about the wildlife she sees. The illustrations depict animals and terrain of her global trip. Her letters to the class share important facts, reflect her startling discoveries, and answer many of the questions the reader has wondered about too. This is a great book to start a world tour of any social studies or science topic. The paintings are wonderfully realistic and add to the knowledge gained by this fictional trip.

145 Hull, Maureen * *Rainy Days with Bear*
Illus. by Leanne Franson * Lobster Press, 2004 * 1-894222-85-7
UNIVERSAL * GRADES PRESCHOOL–2

Bear lives with an author who is always busy writing a book. Weeks of rain have inspired Bear to take a trip. The author's advice is to "Go in your imagination." With delightful, childlike enthusiasm, Bear goes to Trinidad to learn to play steel drums (the kitchen to bang on pots and pans), to Switzerland to play his alpine horn (the living room to blow on a long tube made from paper towel rolls taped together), and to Russia to dance (bouncing on his bed after watching a video about Russia). The pictures are colorful, and feature traditional costumes. In the end, Bear and the author take a real trip—to Costa Rica, to the rain forest!

146 Parker, Toni Trent * *Sienna's Scrapbook: Our African American Heritage Trip*
Illus. by Janell Genovese * Chronicle Books, 2005 * 0-8118-4300-9
AFRICAN AMERICAN * GRADES 3–6

On the way to a family reunion in North Carolina, Sienna, her parents, and her little brother Davey visit sites that are significant in African American history. After leaving their home in Hartford, Connecticut, they stop in New Haven to tour a replica of the *Amistad*. They visit Harlem in New York City and learn about the Harlem Renaissance. They go to Louis Armstrong's home in Queens and Amateur Night at the Apollo. They stop in Philadelphia, Baltimore, Washington, D.C., and Virginia before reaching North Carolina, where they visit a civil rights museum, a plantation, and, finally, the family reunion.

147 Scillian, Devin ✷ *P Is for Passport: A World Alphabet*
Illus. ✷ Sleeping Bear Press, 2003 ✷ 1-58536-157-7
MULTICULTURAL ✷ GRADES 2–6

Each letter of the alphabet provides a word to explore the diversity of the world. A rhyme introduces the locations and items being explored and then a few paragraphs expand the presentation. For example, "A" describes Africa and some animals there—ape, antelope, aardvarks, and more. A also highlights the Amazon and America, the Andes, Australia, and Asia. While "I" features Ireland, Iceland, and Islands and "P" celebrates the diversity of People in the world. A variety of artists illustrate these letters. A natural extension would be to have children create their own alphabet book.

148 Steptoe, Javaka ✷ *The Jones Family Express*
Illus. by the author ✷ Lee & Low, 2003 ✷ 1-58430-047-7
AFRICAN AMERICAN ✷ GRADES 2–4

Steven's Aunt Carolyn goes traveling every summer. He loves getting postcards from her and he looks forward to the day when he can go on a trip with her. It's time for the annual block party and Aunt Carolyn will be there. Because she has made him feel special, Steven wants to give her something that lets her know he thinks she is special, too. He looks in the stores on Nostrand Avenue but nothing seems quite right. His Uncle Charles lets Steven rummage through the stuff at his house and Steven is able to create an original gift for his aunt. It's a big toy train with pictures of the family in each window. Aunt Carolyn loves the gift and has a surprise for Steven, a postcard with the message "Good for one trip with Aunt Carolyn."

FAMILY GATHERINGS

WHAT DO YOU DO AT A FAMILY GATHERING? Do the kids play games and the grown-ups sit around and talk? Are there special foods? Do you listen to stories and dance to your favorite songs? These are some of the questions that could emerge from reading these family stories.

We Had a Picnic This Sunday Past and *Knoxville, Tennessee* describe the activities at gatherings of two African American families. *Halmoni and the Picnic* describes the relationship between a Korean girl, Yunmi, and her grandmother as they prepare for a picnic with Yunmi's American classmates. Patricia Polacco tells a personal story that connects her childhood experiences with the present day. After reading these stories, have students interview family members about their experiences at family gatherings. Have them write a story from those interviews.

149 Choi, Nyul Sook ✳ *Halmoni and the Picnic*
Illus. by Karen M. Dugan ✳ Houghton Mifflin, 1993 ✳ 0-395-60626-3
KOREAN AMERICAN ✳ GRADES 2–4

> Yunmi loves her grandmother, Halmoni, and she wishes that she could find a way to help her feel more comfortable about being in America. Yunmi's friends, Anna Marie and Helen, want to help. When their third-grade teacher announces that they need a chaperone for the annual picnic in Central Park, the girls volunteer Halmoni. Halmoni is delighted and begins to prepare special Korean treats for the picnic. Yunmi is worried that her classmates will not relate to her grandmother, but her worries are groundless. Halmoni is the hit of the picnic.

150 Giovanni, Nikki ✳ *Knoxville, Tennessee*
Illus. by Larry Johnson ✳ Scholastic, 1994 ✳ 0-590-47074-4
AFRICAN AMERICAN ✳ GRADES PRESCHOOL–2

> A young girl celebrates her love of summer in the country. She enjoys going with her family to the church picnic, where there is okra, greens, cabbage, barbecue, buttermilk, homemade ice cream, and more. She goes barefoot and eats fresh corn from "daddy's gar-

den." The poetic text is accompanied by brilliantly colored paintings that show the lush green of summer and the love of family and friends.

151 Polacco, Patricia ✳ *When Lightning Comes in a Jar*
Illus. by the author ✳ Philomel, 2002 ✳ 0-399-23164-1
EUROPEAN AMERICAN ✳ GRADES 2–4

> Trisha is so excited about the family reunion. She checks with Gramma that all the special foods and games and family will be there. Gramma reassures her and adds "we might catch lightning in a jar." As the picnic begins, the tables are loaded with food, including favorite Jell-O salads. After eating, there is the annual baseball game, followed by croquet, races, and seed-spitting. The family looks at photo albums and finally, there are stories. After the stories, the kids are gathered and given canning jars. They catch lightning bugs and then let them go. At the end of the book, a new family reunion is beginning. Now Trisha is the hostess (and the author, Patricia Polacco), but the traditions are the same. Trisha in this story is also in *Thank You, Mr. Falker* (see Chapter 1, under "The Importance of Books and Reading").

152 Woodson, Jacqueline ✳ *We Had a Picnic This Sunday Past*
Illus. by Diane Greenseid ✳ Hyperion, 1997 ✳ 0-7868-0242-1
AFRICAN AMERICAN ✳ GRADES 1–3

> At this picnic, there is so much food. Grandma brings biscuits and chicken. There are ears of corn, cinnamon bread, cranberry muffins, and cookies shaped like angels. There are aunts and uncles and cousins; there are old folks and babies. After greeting each other, playing games, and catching up on what has been happening, everyone sits down at the long picnic table. Everyone wonders where Cousin Martha is. She always bakes a dreaded dried-out apple pie. When she arrives, very late and very rushed, she has been too busy to cook. She brings store-bought cake! What a wonderful picnic.

CHAPTER THREE

Traditions—Food, Art, Poetry, Music, and Celebrations

TRADITIONS ARE A GREAT WAY TO LEARN ABOUT THE WORLD.
Children can relate to the way families celebrate birthdays, weddings, and holidays. They can explore different foods and learn about music and art. In this chapter there are books that feature customs from around the world. Children can examine the tradition of making baskets and the importance of that tradition to three cultures—African American (*Circle Unbroken*), Native American (*Weaving a California Tradition*), and Nepalese (*I, Doko*). They can read about (and listen to) jazz. They can see how poetry reflects the emotions of people from many cultures. By exploring the traditions of different people, children develop an understanding for and appreciation of diversity.

FOOD

TO UNDERSTAND OUR GLOBAL SOCIETY, children are expected to learn about the practices of diverse social, ethnic, and cultural groups. Restaurants and food offer an ideal way to promote comparisons among peoples. Sharing the books listed here can lead to a discussion of favorite foods that reflect the heritages of a group of children. A visit to a neighborhood restaurant can connect with a study of the roles of community helpers. Of course, tasting foods is a natural activity.

There is a menu on the end papers of *Big Jimmy's Kum Kau Chinese Take Out*. Children could use this menu to order food and compute the total cost. They could pretend to pay for their food and make change. Or the menu could be used as a model to create menus for other ethnic restaurants. *Dim Sum for Everyone!* shows another Chinese dining experience. Children might enjoy using chopsticks after reading *The Story of Chopsticks*.

Bee-bim Bop! includes a recipe, as does *Saturday Sancocho*. Children could bring in favorite recipes that represent their family traditions and a cookbook could be prepared. An international celebration could evolve from reading these books.

153 Compestine, Ying Chang * *The Story of Chopsticks*
Illus. by YongSheng Xuan * Holiday House, 2001 * 0-8234-1526-0
ASIAN—CHINA * GRADES K–2

Did you ever wonder about the origin of chopsticks? Here is an entertaining story of how they might have been created. Long ago, Kùai, the youngest child, was always hungry. Everyone ate with their fingers, so the food had to be cool. Kùai always got pushed aside by the older members of his family, especially his brothers. One day, Kùai used sticks from the kindling pile to spear his food while it was still hot. His family applauded his ingenuity and began to eat with sticks which they called "Kuan zi," which means "quick one." Soon all the people in the village was using the sticks and even the emperor used them. There is an Author's Note about chopsticks, a description of how to use them, and a recipe for "Sweet Eight Treasures Rice Pudding."

154 Lewin, Ted ∗ *Big Jimmy's Kum Kau Chinese Take Out*
Illus. by the author ∗ HarperCollins, 2002 ∗ 0-688-16026-3
Chinese American ∗ Grades 1–3

A young boy helps out at his father's Chinese restaurant. Food is delivered, the kitchen is cleaned, and the foods are prepared for cooking—chopping, dicing, slicing, and shredding. Menus are folded and the restaurant is opened. People order food and it is packed for take out. As the day draws to a close, the young narrator has his favorite food—pizza!

155 Lin, Grace ∗ *Dim Sum for Everyone!*
Illus. by the author ∗ Knopf, 2001 ∗ 0-375-81082-X
Chinese American ∗ Grades K–2

At a restaurant in Chinatown, Ba-Ba (the father), Ma-Ma (the mother), and their three daughters enjoy dim sum, a meal of a variety of foods in small dishes. A Note explains dim sum.

156 Park, Linda Sue ∗ *Bee-bim Bop!*
Illus. by Ho Baek Lee ∗ Clarion, 2005 ∗ 0-618-26511-2
Korean American ∗ Grades 1–3

A young girl helps her mother prepare a traditional Korean dish, Bee-bim Bop. The rhyming text makes this a fun choice for reading aloud. A recipe is included. An Author's Note is accompanied by a picture of the author and her nephew and niece working in the kitchen.

157 Torres, Leyla ∗ *Saturday Sancocho*
Illus. by the author ∗ Farrar, Straus and Giroux, 1995 ∗ 0-374-36418-4
South American ∗ Grades 1–3

When Maria Lili visits her grandparents on Saturdays, they make chicken sancocho, a thick stew. This week there is no food and no money, but Mama Ana has a plan. She trades eggs with the vendors in the market and she accumulates the necessary ingredients for the stew. The setting is a rural village in South America and a recipe is included. This book can also lead to a discussion of bartering.

PROVERBS AND SAYINGS

FINISH THIS PHRASE—"EARLY TO BED, EARLY TO RISE . . ." Or this one—"An apple a day . . ." Many cultures have familiar sayings and proverbs; often they reflect the beliefs and traditions of the group. Sharing collections of phrases and sayings from around the world allows children to analyze the traditions of diverse cultures.

After reading *Fortune Cookie Fortunes*, children could create their own predictions. Ashley Bryan's *The Night Has Ears: African Proverbs* can be used to show that many cultures have sayings that are used to guide behaviors. *Off to the Sweet Shores of Africa* introduces nursery and nonsense rhymes from Africa. *Skip Across the Ocean* features nursery rhymes from around the world. As some children may not know some traditional proverbs, be sure to introduce a general collection of them, such as *A Word to the Wise*.

158 Benjamin, Floella, collector ✳ *Skip Across the Ocean: Nursery Rhymes from Around the World*
Illus. by Sheila Moxley ✳ Orchard Books, 1995 ✳ 0-531-09455-3
MULTICULTURAL ✳ GRADES PRESCHOOL–2

Chapters divide the rhymes by "Lullabies," "Action Rhymes," "Nature," and "Grab Bag." There are rhymes from Peru, Nigeria, Norway, Australia, China, and more. Some of the rhymes are presented in both their original language and an English translation. Some have suggestions for finger plays or activities. This is an entertaining collection that introduces rhymes from many peoples.

159 Bryan, Ashley ✳ *The Night Has Ears: African Proverbs*
Illus. by the author ✳ Atheneum, 1999 ✳ 0-689-82427-0
AFRICAN ✳ GRADES 1–3

Ashley Bryan has organized this collection of African sayings with a tribal connection for each one (although many of the sayings occur in more than one tribe). Some of the proverbs are meant to instruct; others provide insights into human nature. Brilliantly colored illustrations provide vivid support for each proverb. Some samples: "Do not try to fight a lion if you are not one yourself. Swahili." and "As a crab walks, so walk its children. Kpelle." Encourage children to connect these proverbs to sayings that are familiar to them, such as "the apple does not fall far from the tree." If you are sharing these with older children, see if they can write some proverbs that guide behaviors.

160 Hurwitz, Johanna, selector * *A Word to the Wise and Other Proverbs*
Illus. by Robert Rayevsky * HarperCollins, 1994 * 0-688-12065-2
MULTICULTURAL * GRADES 1–3

"Too many cooks spoil the broth" and "Birds of a feather flock together" are two of the maxims in this brief collection of sayings. Each statement is illustrated with a full-page picture that literally depicts the circumstances. After reading these, librarians and teachers will want to explore the deeper meaning of the sayings, asking "Why does one good turn deserve another?" or "How does the early bird get the worm?" This collection will stimulate thought and discussion.

161 Lin, Grace * *Fortune Cookie Fortunes*
Illus. by the author * Knopf, 2004 * 0-375-81521-X
CHINESE AMERICAN * GRADES PRESCHOOL–2

A young Chinese American girl and her family share their fortune cookie fortunes. As the girl observes her family, the fortunes seem to come true. A Note about the origin of fortune cookies is appended.

162 Unobagha, Uzo * *Off to the Sweet Shores of Africa, and Other Talking Drum Rhymes*
Illus. by Julia Cairns * Chronicle Books, 2000 * 0-8118-2378-4
AFRICAN * GRADES PRESCHOOL–2

The Author's Note at the beginning of this book explains that these rhymes connect with Unobagha's West African heritage but have been expanded to include images from all around Africa. They also connect with Mother Goose rhymes in their simple language and enchanting rhymes. Some of the verses are nonsensical, like a hare climbing a baobab tree and a clay pot dancing with a broom. Others are rhythmic with creative language—"Bomboy blew his bamboo flute . . . Hootie-tootie-bom-bamboo!"—that children will enjoy reciting. A glossary follows the collection of rhymes. Select some of the rhymes to put on poetry charts for young children to see and say.

CELEBRATIONS

CELEBRATIONS ARE A PART OF EVERY CULTURE. There are holidays and birthdays, weddings and fiestas. The books included here feature diverse groups enjoying their families and their heritage. After reading any of these books, children could discuss their own traditions. Are there special foods for a birthday party, as in *Henry's First-Moon Birthday*? Do they wear special clothes for an ethnic celebration, as Amelia does in *Amelia's Show-and-Tell Fiesta*? Have they ever been in a wedding? Or celebrated Chinese New Year?

Plan a party that reflects the cultural traditions of your group. Invite family members—parents, grandparents, aunts, uncles, and more. Maybe someone will come dressed in a traditional costume or play a song from their heritage or bring a special treat to share. Celebrations offer a great opportunity to learn about diverse experiences of the young people in your classroom or library.

Birthdays

163 Kleven, Elisa ★ *Hooray, a Piñata!*
Illus. by the author ★ Dutton, 1996 ★ 0-525-45605-8
HISPANIC AMERICAN ★ GRADES PRESCHOOL–1

Clara is eagerly awaiting her birthday party. Her friend, Samson (who is African American) goes with her to pick out the piñata for the party. He thinks she should get a huge, scary, thundercloud monster but she picks out a little dog. Clara plays with her piñata dog, naming him Lucky and pretending he is real. She even dreams about him. As Clara becomes more attached to Lucky, she does not want to break him at the party. Samson understands this. On the day of her party he arrives early, bringing her another piñata to break. Lucky is saved and Clara has a terrific birthday celebration.

164 Look, Lenore ★ *Henry's First-Moon Birthday*
Illus. by Yumi Heo ★ Atheneum, 2001 ★ 0-689-82294-4
CHINESE AMERICAN ★ GRADES 1–3

JenJen likes to think she is in charge of her baby brother's first moon celebration marking Henry's one-month birthday. With Grandmother there to cook, to write Loong (the baby's Chinese name), to help clean up messes, to make red eggs, and to get JenJen dressed for the party, it is the best family celebration. The bright, child-like art adds many details to this energetic story.

165 Lopez, Loretta ✶ *The Birthday Swap*
Illus. by the author ✶ Lee & Low, 1997 ✶ 1-880000-47-4
Mexican American ✶ Grades Preschool–2

Lori searches for the perfect gift for Cookie, her teenage sister. There will be a family reunion in Mexico and celebrating Cookie's birthday will be part of the festivities. However, Cookie has a surprise for Lori. Since Lori's birthday is in the winter, Cookie has "swapped" birthdays with her so that Lori can be the focus of the big outdoor family celebration. The games, the piñata, and the mariachi band are wonderful, but the best surprise for Lori is her new puppy.

166 Madrigal, Antonio Hernandez ✶ *Erandi's Braids*
Illus. by Tomie dePaola ✶ Putnam, 1999 ✶ 0-399-23212-5
Mexican ✶ Grades Preschool–2

Erandi is excited about her seventh birthday and the new dress she expects as a gift which she can wear to the village fiesta. While helping her mother with fishing, she realizes any money in their poor household will need to be spent on a new net. Walking with her mother to the barbershop, she sees her mother offer to sell her hair. When told her hair is not long enough, Erandi offers to sell her beautiful braids. Now there is enough money to buy a net, a dress, and a doll for Erandi, who knows her hair will soon grow back, just as long and just as beautiful. This book is set in the Tarascan Indian village of Patzcuaro in the hills of Mexico in the 1950s.

167 Soto, Gary ✶ *Chato and the Party Animals*
Illus. by Susan Guevara ✶ Putnam, 2000 ✶ 0-399-23159-5
Mexican American ✶ Grades K–3

Chato, a proud Spanish-speaking cat decides to surprise his friend Novio Boy with a birthday party complete with cake, a disc jockey, a piñata and games. The dumpster-diving cat almost misses his own party! Acrylic paint on scratch board depicts cultural signs, symbols, and designs. Soto and Guevara have collaborated on two other Chato books: *Chato's Kitchen* (Putnam, 1995) and *Chato Goes Cruisin'* (Putnam, 2005).

Holidays—Chinese New Year

168 Berkeley, Jon ✶ *Chopsticks*
Illus. by the author ✶ Random House, 2005 ✶ 0-375-83309-9
ASIAN—CHINA ✶ GRADES PRESCHOOL–2

A small mouse named Chopsticks lives in a floating restaurant in the Hong Kong harbor. Enormous wooden dragons guard the entrance to the restaurant. During a Chinese New Year celebration one of the dragons speaks to the little mouse of his desire to be free and to fly over all the world. The mouse agrees to seek out the old woodcarver who created the dragon. The woodcarver teaches the mouse a magical tune to play on an old wooden whistle when the moon is full. The magic works and every full moon the mouse and dragon go soaring.

169 Compestine, Ying Chang ✶ *D Is for Dragon Dance*
Illus. by YongSheng Xuan ✶ Holiday House, 2006 ✶ 0-8234-1887-1
ASIAN—CHINA ✶ GRADES PRESCHOOL–2

Celebrate Chinese New Year with this colorful alphabet book. Acrobats balance on Balls. Firecrackers and Dragon Dancers keep the Evil Spirits away. There are Noodles, Oranges, and Steamed Dumplings for the celebration. Z for Zodiac concludes the alphabet. Additional information, including a recipe for New Year's Dumpling Delight, follows the text.

170 Compestine, Ying Chang ✶ *The Runaway Rice Cake*
Illus. by Tungwai Chau ✶ Simon & Schuster, 2001 ✶ 0-689-82972-8
ASIAN—CHINA ✶ GRADES 2–4

This original story has elements of the gingerbread man folktale. The Chang family has only enough rice flour to make one *nián-gāo*, the New Year's rice cake. When Mama opens the steamer, the rice cake runs away. It runs past chicks, pigs, and villagers but it cannot be caught. Finally it bumps into an old woman and Mama Chang catches the cake. Even though they are very hungry, the Changs decide to share the cake with the old woman. The nián-gäo is so delicious that the old woman eats it all and runs away in embarrassment. The family returns home with nothing. Their neighbors have heard of their kindness and come to share their food, but there is still not enough for everyone. The two older brothers decide to let their younger brother eat first and when he uncovers the food, more food magically appears. There is a celebration for everyone, ending with the parade, dragons, and firecrackers for Chinese New Year.

171 Kudler, David * *The Seven Gods of Luck*
Illus. by Linda Finch * Houghton Mifflin, 1997 * 0-395-78830-7
ASIAN—CHINA * GRADES K–3

As the traditional celebration for the New Year approaches, Sachiko and Kenji learn that there is not enough money for the rice, beans, potatoes, and radishes. The children try to earn money by selling the hairpins and chopsticks they have decorated. However, in the snowy village, no one wants to buy these. Instead, the children trade them for hats. On the way home, they pass the shrine of the Seven Gods of Luck and decide to give a hat to each of the gods as protection from the fast falling snow. The gods come to life and reward the children for their thoughtfulness with soup, rice cakes, walnuts, and fish. Their mother is surprised and the children are delighted at their good luck!

**172 Simonds, Nina, Leslie Swartz, and the Children's Museum,
Boston * *Moonbeams, Dumplings and Dragon Boats: A Treasury
of Chinese Holiday Tales, Activities and Recipes***
Illus. by Meilo So * Harcourt, 2002 * 0-15-201983-9
ASIAN—CHINA * ALL AGES

Information about Chinese festivals is presented here including Chinese New Year and the Lantern Festival, Qing Ming and the Cold Foods Festival, the Dragon Boat Festival, and the Mid-Autumn Moon Festival. Games, foods, stories, projects, riddles, and more are given for each festival. There are directions for making a kite, information about the Chinese Zodiac, and a recipe for Moon Cakes and Moon Cookies. There are resource lists for adults and young readers as well as Internet sources. This is a super resource for celebrations.

173 Wong, Janet S. ✶ *This Next New Year*
Illus. by Yangsook Choi ✶ Farrar, Straus and Giroux, 2000 ✶ 0-374-35503-7
MULTICULTURAL ✶ GRADES PRESCHOOL–2

In this neighborhood, everyone celebrates Chinese New Year. The narrator, a boy who is half Korean, celebrates with *duk gook*, a Korean soup made by his mother. His friend, who is French and German, celebrates by eating take-out Thai food. The boy's whole family cleans out the dust from the past year, which is symbolic of sweeping out the bad luck. The boy takes a bath and puts on clean clothes. He attends the parade where there are dragons and firecrackers. He is filled with hopes and dreams for a bright new year. An Author's Note briefly describes some of the lunar new year traditions.

Holidays–Christmas

174 dePaola, Tomie ✶ *The Night of Las Posadas*
Illus. by the author ✶ Putnam, 1999 ✶ 0-399-23400-4
HISPANIC AMERICAN ✶ GRADES 1–3

In the introduction, dePaola explains that this celebration originated in Spain and continues in Mexico and the American Southwest. It celebrates the sheltering of Mary and Joseph in the stable on Christmas Eve. Today communities reenact the search for shelter. They knock on doors and are turned away (often by devils) until they come to a place where they are accepted. In this book, which takes place in the mountains above Santa Fe, Sister Angie's niece, Lupe, and Lupe's new husband, Roberto, will portray Maria and José (Mary and Joseph) in the celebration. This is a special day for Sister Angie, celebrating her 50 years as a nun. A carving has been made for the church. As Christmas Eve approaches, Sister Angie falls ill and then Lupe and Roberto become stuck in the snow. As the townspeople wait for them to arrive, another couple appears, dressed in the appropriate costumes. They say they are friends of Sister Angie. After the celebration, the new couple disappears. When Sister Angie goes into the church, she sees that the carvings of Maria and José are covered in fresh snow, indicating that the statues were the couple who miraculously came to the ceremony. A Note following the story explains some of the variations of the celebration of Las Posadas.

Tomie dePaola has many other books about Christmas, including *The Legend of the Poinsettia* (Putnam, 1994), *An Early American Christmas* (Holiday House, 1987), *The Legend of Old Befana* (Harcourt, 1980), and *The Story of the Three Wise Kings* (Putnam, 1991).

175 Feliciano, José ✳ *Feliz Navidad: Two Stories Celebrating Christmas*
Illus. by David Diaz ✳ Scholastic, 2003 ✳ 0-439-51717-6
Hispanic American ✳ Grades Preschool–3

Dazzling color paintings accompany the lyrics to the popular holiday song by José Feliciano. The second "story" evolves from the introduction describing the Puerto Rican Christmas celebration of *parranda* with carolers, musicians, dancing, and food. The festivities continue from house to house culminating in a cookout for families, friends, and neighbors. Diaz's illustrations of the Spanish words of the song depict the parranda while the English words show images of the Santa, Christmas tree, and gifts of an American Christmas. After reading this book, a sing-along would naturally follow.

176 Horn, Sandra Ann ✳ *Babushka*
Illus. by Sophie Fatus ✳ Barefoot, 2002 ✳ 1-84148-353-2
European—Russia ✳ Grades Preschool–2

This holiday story from Russian folklore retells the story of Babushka, an old woman who is so busy cleaning that she nearly misses the chance to be part of a special event. Babushka has a dream about a baby in a stable. The baby is poor; he does not even have a decent blanket. Babushka gathers gifts for him and sets out to find the baby. Along the way, she meets others who desperately need her gifts and she gives them away. When she arrives at the stable, she is sad because she has nothing but her basket. But she realizes that her

##ʻ

kindness to others has been appreciated and that her best gift for the baby is her love. Instead of stopping to tidy the stable, Babushka lets the work wait. She holds the baby, sharing her love. The acrylic paintings are whimsical and touching. Compare this story with Tomie dePaola's *The Legend of Old Befana* (Harcourt, 1980).

177 Hoyt-Goldsmith, Diane ✷ *Three Kings Day: A Celebration at Christmastime*
Photographs by Lawrence Migdale ✷ Holiday House, 2004 ✷ 0-8234-1839-1
HISPANIC AMERICAN ✷ GRADES 3–5

Focusing on a girl, Veronica, whose family lives in a Puerto Rican community in New York City, the author describes the traditional celebration of Three Kings Day. This holiday is part of twelve days of festivities beginning with Christmas Eve. Three Kings Day is celebrated on the final day. The nonfiction text includes background information about Puerto Rico and the native Taíno people. Excellent color photographs complement the text. For example, when discussing folk art carvings, there are photographs of carvings from Puerto Rico as well as a picture of Veronica watching a *santero* carve wood for a Three Kings display. The celebration includes music, gifts, and special foods; there is even a parade. A glossary is included.

178 Johnston, Tony ✷ *A Kenya Christmas*
Illus. by Leonard Jenkins ✷ Holiday House, 2003 ✷ 0-8234-1623-2
AFRICAN—KENYA ✷ GRADES K–2

Fantasy elements bring a magical touch to this Christmas story. Long ago, when the narrator, Juma, was 10, he and his rich aunt Aida planned a special Christmas for the village. Aunt Aida has come to visit and brings a red suit for Father Christmas. Juma arranges for Ole Tunai to wear the suit and Tembo the elephant is borrowed for Father Christmas to ride. Chicken feathers have been gathered to simulate snow. All of the villagers gather on Christmas Eve and Father Christmas arrives riding Tembo and distributing gifts until they are gone. Later, back in the hut, Juma and Aunt Aida celebrate their surprise until Ole Tunai appears. He is upset that Tembo would not let him ride. So, who delivered the gifts? They look outside to see Father Christmas riding on an elephant through the starry sky and shouting "Happy Christmas." As the book concludes, Juma is an old man telling this story to his grandchildren.

Holidays—St. Francis of Assisi's Day

179 Madrigal, Antonio Hernandez ✶ *Blanco's Feather*
Illus. by Gerardo Suzan ✶ Rising Moon, 2000 ✶ 0-87358-743-X
MEXICAN ✶ GRADES PRESCHOOL–2

In the tradition of her Mexican family, Rosalia is anxious to take her pet chicken, Blanco, to the special blessing for all animals, the celebration of Saint Francis of Assisi's Day. When she searches for the pet, however, she cannot find her. Not wanting to be late at church, Rosalia takes one of the hen's feathers to be blessed. Some laugh at her, but the priest sprinkles the feather with holy water and instructs Rosalia to rub the feather on Blanco's head. Much to Rosalia's surprise, when she finds Blanco, she also finds newborn chicks. Using the feather, all receive Saint Francis's blessing of protection. Brightly colored whimsical paintings help tell the story.

180 Weller, Frances Ward ✶ *The Day the Animals Came: A Story of Saint Francis Day*
Illus. by Loren Long ✶ Philomel, 2003 ✶ 0-399-23630-9
HISPANIC AMERICAN ✶ GRADES 1–3

This story recalls the New York City tradition of blessing the animals on the Feast of Saint Francis. Ria and her family have recently arrived in New York City from an island in the Caribbean. Ria loves animals and is pleased that Mrs. Blum, her baby-sitter, is taking her to the cathedral for the blessing of the animals. Ria realizes she is the only one without an animal to be blessed. She rounds up an errant duck and the duck's owner allows Ria to carry him to the blessing. The beautiful fold-out pages show the menagerie of animals marching down the massive cathedral's main aisle.

Fiesta

181 Chapra, Mimi ✳ *Amelia's Show-and-Tell Fiesta / Amelia y la fiesta de "muestra y cuenta"*
Illus. by Martha Avilés ✳ HarperCollins, 2004 ✳ 0-06-050255-X
CUBAN AMERICAN ✳ GRADES PRESCHOOL–1

Amelia is starting school in America. She is eager to learn and wants to participate. When the teacher asks for special items to share for show-and-tell, Amelia knows just what to do. She will wear her fiesta dress from her home in Cuba. At home, she tries it on and she watches the three colorful layers of the skirt fan out when she twirls. But, at school the next day, Amelia is chagrined. No one else is in a special outfit and she is embarrassed. Her teacher understands her dilemma and helps Amelia recover her confidence and speak about her dress. While Amelia describes the fiesta in her former home, she begins to feel more at home in America.

The text is presented in English and Spanish and there are Spanish words sprinkled through the English text.

182 Elya, Susan Middleton ✳ *F Is for Fiesta*
Illus. by G. Brian Karas ✳ Putnam, 2006 ✳ 0-399-24225-2
HISPANIC ✳ GRADES PRESCHOOL–3

This book opens with a glossary of the Spanish words with pronunciation and the meaning of the word in English. For example: *Abuela* (ah Bweh lah) Grandma. There is an Author's Note that explains the Spanish alphabet. Then, the alphabet book begins. Letters are presented in a rhyming text accompanied by bright, colorful illustrations. The theme for the book is celebrating a fiesta, so words like *globos* (balloons), *salsa* (sauce, music, a dance), and *velas* (candles) get you ready for a party.

183 Orozco, José-Luis, selector, arranger, and translator ✳ *Fiestas: A Year of Latin American Songs of Celebration*
Illus. by Elisa Kleven ✳ Dutton, 2002 ✳ 0-525-45937-5
HISPANIC AMERICAN ✳ GRADES PRESCHOOL–3

Orozco has selected more than 20 rhymes and songs that connect to Latin American holidays and celebrations. In the preface he writes

"Latino culture is very family-oriented and welcomes any occasion to get people together." The month-by-month arrangement makes it easy to include these songs throughout the year. Each song has an introduction, musical notation, and the lyrics in Spanish and English.

Weddings

184 Look, Lenore ∗ *Uncle Peter's Amazing Chinese Wedding*
Illus. by Yumi Heo ∗ Atheneum, 2006 ∗ 0-689-84458-1
CHINESE AMERICAN ∗ GRADES 1–3

Uncle Peter calls Jenny his "special girl." She has always enjoyed the extra attention he has given her. Now he is getting married and Jenny is anxious and sad. As the whole family prepares for the wedding, Jenny feels left out. Uncle Peter's bride, Stella, is in the spotlight. But Stella finds a perfect way to involve Jenny in the celebration and Jenny whispers to her "Welcome to the family." Traditions of a Chinese wedding are incorporated into the text and could connect with wedding experiences of the readers. Sharing information about other ceremonies is another possibility.

185 Onyefulu, Ifeoma ∗ *Here Comes Our Bride! An African Wedding Story*
Illus. with photographs ∗ Frances Lincoln Children's Books, 2004 ∗ 1-84507-047-X
AFRICAN—NIGERIA ∗ GRADES 1–3

Strikingly beautiful photographs tell the story of marriage in Benin City, in Nigeria. A young boy is anxious to attend a wedding. He has even picked out the couple! He soon finds out that a wedding is not just about joining two persons, it is about joining two families. There is the proper request of the woman's hand to her grandfather. And the bride's family produces a list of things the groom's family must gather together. There is even some teasing as part of the acceptance of this union. There are also several celebrations complete with gifts and cake! That young boy can't wait for the next wedding! A small map helps readers understand where Nigeria is in Africa. Boxed text includes explanations of foods and traditions.

186 Soto, Gary ✳ *Snapshots from the Wedding*
Illus. by Stephanie Garcia ✳ Putnam, 1997 ✳ 0-399-22808-X
MEXICAN AMERICAN ✳ GRADES 1–3

Maya is the flower girl in Isabel's wedding. Maya describes the other participants, including Danny, the ring bearer, and Father Jaime. There is Tía Marta crying and throwing rice after the ceremony. Then, the reception begins. The mariachis arrive to play music and there is *pollo con mole* and *arroz y frijoles*. Everyone dances until the cake is cut and Isabel throws her bouquet. The celebration is over and Maya falls asleep in the car on the way home. The illustrations for this book are photographs of three-dimensional artwork. Figures have been molded from clay, decorated with paint and fabrics, and posed in vignettes. This book received the Pura Belpré Illustration Award.

ARTISTIC TRADITIONS

FEATURE THE BOOK *Julio's Magic* at a program or library class visit. It is an inspiring book about creativity and compassion. Julio sacrifices his own opportunity to win a contest. Instead, he helps an aging artist, Iluminado, to finish his work and send it to the judges. Many children will connect with the themes in this book and understand the importance of helping others. Maya Ajmera and John D. Ivanko's *To Be an Artist* depicts children around the world enjoying many artistic activities.

Connect these books to biographies about artists, such as *Action Jackson* and *Diego*. Or, read these books before going to a museum or gallery. Follow up with an art activity, such as looking for wood or stones to decorate with paint. Maybe you will find a dragon-shaped stick or a gnarled stone that inspires a painting of a bear. Children will enjoy the opportunity to imagine and create.

187 **Ajmera, Maya, and John D. Ivanko** ✶ ***To Be an Artist***
Illus. with photographs ✶ Charlesbridge, 2004 ✶ 1-57091-503-2
MULTICULTURAL ✶ GRADES PRESCHOOL–4

> The wonder of art and its universal language are featured in numerous photographs of children around the world dancing, singing, drawing, drumming, painting, playing instruments, writing, and otherwise showing off their talents. All photographs are labeled with the countries of origin of the featured children.

188 **Dorros, Arthur** ✶ ***Julio's Magic***
Illus. by Ann Grifalconi ✶ HarperCollins, 2005 ✶ 0-06-029004-8
MEXICAN ✶ GRADES 1–3

> Iluminado is a master wood carver and he is teaching Julio his craft. Julio wants to win the woodcarving contest that is held in a distant city, but Iluminado chooses not to enter the contest. As Julio walks to Iluminado's home, he passes the houses of other carvers and see their work. When he is with Iluminado, Julio notices how carefully Iluminado caresses the wood with his fingers but how he strains to see his work. The two journey to the mountainside and search for pieces of wood to use for their carvings. The pieces of wood seem to

"speak" to them, encouraging them to release the shapes within. They return to their homes and begin carving. Julio takes time out to help the aging artist. As the contest approaches, Julio prepares his entry. He visits Iluminado and helps him finish his carvings by painting them with beautiful colors and designs. Then they agree to send the carvings they did together to the contest, but Julio does not put his name on them. When the winner is announced, it is Iluminado. The final page of the story shows Julio looking at the carvings that he has kept under his bed—carvings he did not send to the contest. Julio says, "Next year." Beautiful collage illustrations capture the artistry of the Mexican carvings and the strength of the friendship that crosses generations.

Origami

189 Falwell, Cathryn ✳ *Butterflies for Kiri*
Illus. by the author ✳ Lee & Low, 2003 ✳ 1-58430-100-7
JAPANESE AMERICAN ✳ GRADES 1–3

For her birthday, Kiri has received a book about origami and a package of colorful paper. Kiri carefully follows the directions for making a butterfly. Her first effort tears after only a few steps and Kiri gives up, for now. When she tries again, she uses notebook paper so she does not wreck the special origami paper. This time, she follows more steps before the paper tears. Kiri continues to practice her origami and to enjoy other artistic activities like using chalk, paint, and clay. On Saturday, Kiri creates a collage to celebrate the beautiful spring day. She succeeds in folding a yellow piece of paper into an origami butterfly, which she adds to her collage. Directions for making an origami butterfly follow the story.

190 Wells, Rosemary * _Yoko's Paper Cranes_
Illus. by the author * Hyperion, 2001 * 0-7868-2602-9
JAPANESE AMERICAN * GRADES PRESCHOOL–2

Little Yoko moves with her family to California, leaving her
grandparents behind in Japan. In January, when it is time for
Obaasan's birthday, Yoko has no money for a gift. She decides
to send her grandmother paper cranes she has made from
beautiful papers, to remind her grandmother of the cranes
that visit her pond in warmer weather. Yoko's message, written
in Japanese says, "I will come back to Japan, just like the
cranes." In simple text and beautifully designed pictures
using traditional colors and patterns of origami paper, the
power of love of family, no matter how near or far, is gently
celebrated. Although Wells has depicted Yoko as a cat, this
story has a universal appeal.

$$*$$

Demonstrating or showing the paper folded cranes would be a
perfect complement to reading these books. Young children could
follow up with a folding paper activity—maybe something as
simple as a little paper cup folded from waxed paper, so the child
can experience at least one drink to celebrate the project.

191 Greenberg, Jan, and Sandra Jordan * _Action Jackson_
Illus. by Robert Andrew Parker * Roaring Brook Press, 2002 *
0-7613-1382-5
EUROPEAN AMERICAN * GRADES 3–6

This book focuses on May and June 1950 and the creation of Jackson Pollock's painting _Lavender Mist_. In an old weathered barn, Pol-
lack spreads a canvas sheet on the floor. Using house paint, he
drizzles, spatters, flings, swirls, and sprays. He layers colors, whirling

around the canvas with an inspired vision. He paints for hours and then leaves the barn for almost a week. Then he returns and "dances" on the canvas spreading more colors and designs. A reproduction of the painting, *Number One, 1950 (Lavender Mist)* is included as are two pages of biographical information on Jackson Pollock. Notes and sources are appended.

192 Winter, Jonah ✳ *Diego*
Translated from English by Amy Prince ✳ Illus. by Jeanette Winter ✳
  Knopf, 1991 ✳ 0-679-81987-8
Mexican ✳ Grades 2–6

The artist Diego Rivera is featured in this bilingual (Spanish and English) biography. He struggled in school but he loved colors and shapes and drawing. He attended art school but he chafed at the restrictions and began to paint what he saw around him. Celebrations, fighting, and everyday people were among his subjects. He studied in Paris and Italy and returned to Mexico where he began to paint murals. After the text, additional information about Diego Rivera is included.

BASKETS AND BASKET WEAVING

Reflections

In the late 1990s, I visited Charleston, South Carolina, to attend a workshop. In the off-hours, I found this charming city a wonderful corner of the world to explore. In the town square were tents displaying baskets, and at every stall men and women were weaving with the long reeds of the sweetgrass plant. The traditional patterns and shapes of the baskets and other objects have remained the same through generations of the Gullah culture. I was taken by the unusual shapes of the baskets. To find *Circle Unbroken*, a book celebrating this artform, has been a pleasure. —Kathy East

BASKETWEAVING CAN BE A SIMPLE CRAFT to share with youngsters. Supplies are readily available at craft or fabric stores at very reasonable prices. The secret is to have well-soaked reeds so they will be pliable. Many books show the basic cross beginning for the bottom of the basket and then follow the simple "in and out" and "over and under" weave. To finish the rim may be a bit tricky, but the dedicated basketmaker, even a beginner, will catch on and produce a lovely finished product, even on the first try! What a nice surprise to receive even a small basket as a gift for the holidays, Mother's Day, or any occasion when a gift is appropriate. Classrooms, art classes, and library programs are all perfect places to make this "surprise."

As part of a weaving program, share *Circle Unbroken* or *I, Doko* and discuss the importance of baskets to the people in these stories. Introduce children to Carly Tex in the photo essay *Weaving a California Tradition*.

193 Raven, Margot Theis ★ *Circle Unbroken: The Story of a Basket and Its People*
Illus. by E. B. Lewis ★ Farrar, Straus and Giroux, 2004 ★ 0-374-31289-3
African American ★ Grades 3–6

A grandmother recounts the history of her people and their skill at making baskets as she teaches her granddaughter the sweetgrass pattern of circle on circle, coil on coil. Going back generations, to when her ancestors were in Africa, Grandma tells how a young boy learned to make ropes, nets, drums, and baskets. That boy was captured, taken across the ocean, and sold into slavery, but he continued to sew baskets and began to teach others. The tightly sewn circles of the basket serve as a metaphor for the circle of family that carries on the tradition of the technique and design. A Note tells "More About Sweetgrass Baskets," which are also called "coil" or "Gullah" baskets.

194 Yamane, Linda ★ *Weaving a California Tradition: A Native American Basketmaker*
Illus. by Dugan Aguilar ★ Lerner, 1997 ★ 0-8225-2660-3
Native American ★ Grades 4–6

Eleven-year old Carly Tex is proudly learning the art of Western Mono basketweavers. In this photoessay, the reader sees how this California Indian family lives as most Americans do, but how their native culture brings an additional dimension to their lives. Baskets have so many uses. Today many of those traditional uses have been replaced by modern items, but the skill and pride in the colors and designs is preserved. Since making a 6-inch replica of a cradleboard, Carly has wanted to learn about the kinds of plants needed for weaving. With her family she gathers the materials and demonstrates the twining and coil methods of making baskets. Carly uses her weaving skills to design a gathering basket for the Basketweavers Showcase at Tuolumne Rancheria. This little girl becomes a friend to every reader through her beautiful smile and gentle pride in her heritage.

195 Young, Ed ✶ *I, Doko: The Tale of a Basket*
Illus. by the author ✶ Philomel, 2004 ✶ 0-399-23625-2
ASIAN—NEPAL ✶ GRADES 2–6

In this tale from Nepal, a family's history is told by the basket, called Doko. The basket is owned by Yeh-yeh, whose wife, Nei-nei, uses it to carry her baby boy while she works in the field. Later, they use it to gather wood and, sadly, Doko carries Nei-nei to her grave after an epidemic. The baby boy grows up, marries, and has a son named Wangal; the aging Yeh-yeh lives with the young couple. When the father becomes a burden, Doko is used to carry him to the temple steps to be abandoned. Young Wangal asks a question that saves his grandfather. The story concludes with a lesson on how to treat elders. The paint and collage illustrations bordered in gold add a delicacy to the pages.

JAZZ

BOOKS WITH MUSICAL ELEMENTS PROVIDE OPPORTUNITIES to encourage children to be active learners. They often have rhyme and rhythm and are wonderful for reading aloud. These books encourage participation as children snap their fingers, clap their hands, and move their arms. Playing music is a natural extension that makes for lively programs.

Chris Raschka has created several books that feature African American jazz musicians. *Charlie Parker Played Be Bop, Mysterious Thelonious,* and *John Coltrane's Giant Steps* would be excellent choices for a program about jazz. They could be paired with Walter Dean Myers's poetic celebrations in *Jazz.* Andrea Davis Pinkney's biographies of jazz artists such as Duke Ellington could also be included. *Once Upon a Time in Chicago* introduces another well-known jazz musician and his music. Visit the Jazz Resource Library at the Web site for the Thelonious Monk Institute of Jazz (www.monkinstitute.com/index11. html). Select Jazz Resource Library for access to a timeline, famous firsts, biographies, and audio snippets from well-known jazz pieces.

For one class of second graders, *John Coltrane's Giant Steps* was the featured book. The librarian shared the book and then played a CD of the music. The music teacher followed up on this by reading other jazz books, playing music, and discussing the roots of jazz. Another library visit featured *Shake, Rattle and Roll* and everyone grooved to the sounds of Elvis Presley and Buddy Holly.

Another activity could be to look at how Chris Raschka uses color to depict music and compare this with Brian Pinkney's illustrations in *Duke Ellington.*

196 George-Warren, Holly ✳ *Shake, Rattle and Roll: The Founders of Rock and Roll*
Illus. by Laura Levine ✳ Houghton Mifflin, 2001 ✳ 0-618-05540-1
MULTICULTURAL ✳ GRADES 5–6+

Just as jazz shook up the world in the 1920s and 1930s, rock and roll exploded in the 1950s. Fifteen musical pioneers are featured in this book, each with a one-page essay opposite a colorful full-page illustration. Bill Haley, Little Richard, Chuck Berry, Wanda Jackson, Elvis Presley, Buddy Holly, and Richie Valens are among those included.

Walter Dean Myers and Christopher Myers

In *Jazz*, Walter Dean Myers and Christopher Myers provide a dazzling tribute to jazz music and musicians. The father-and-son team previously worked together on another musical book, *Blues Journey* (Holiday House, 2003). Both books use poetic language and striking illustrations to explore the mood, emotion, and energy of music. Walter Dean Myers is well known as an author of books for young adults. His book *Monster* received the first Michael L. Printz Award for young adult literature and he was the recipient of the 1994 Margaret A. Edwards Award (both from the American Library Association). Several of his books have been Newbery Honor books and he has been recognized by the Coretta Scott King Award Committee on numerous occasions. The first book that Christopher Myers illustrated, *Shadow of the Red Moon*, was written by his father. They collaborated on *Harlem*, which received an Honor Award from both the Caldecott Committee and the Coretta Scott King Award Committee. Christopher Myers has also written books, including *Wings*, which is featured in Chapter 2.

The "Three Voices" poem in *Jazz* would be a great poem to read along with Chris Raschka's *John Coltrane's Giant Steps*. Both books convey music through words and rhythm along with inventive images. "Three Voices" shows the role of three instruments—bass, piano, and horn—in a jazz song, while *John Coltrane's Giant Steps* describes the interaction of four elements in the creation of jazz.

197 Myers, Walter Dean ✳ *Jazz*

Illus. by Christopher Myers ✳ Holiday House, 2006 ✳ 0-8234-1545-8

AFRICAN AMERICAN ✳ GRADES 4–6+

From the opening poem describing the rhythm of jazz—the love and the heart and the soul of the music—this book celebrates a truly American art form. There is a tribute to Louis Armstrong, a poem about bebop, and one about a jazz vocalist. Poems describe the creation of jazz in "Session I" and "Session II." The book's introduction provides an overview of the development of jazz, and the book concludes with a glossary of jazz terms and a jazz timeline. Christopher Myers's paintings are fantastic. Bright colors are presented against dark, contrasting backgrounds, resulting in vivid images filled with energy. *Jazz* received a Coretta Scott King Honor Award for the illustrations.

198 Pinkney, Andrea D. ✳ *Duke Ellington: The Piano Prince and His Orchestra*

Illus. by Brian Pinkney ✳ Hyperion, 1998 ✳ 0-7868-0178-6

AFRICAN AMERICAN ✳ GRADES 2–6

As a child, Duke Ellington wanted to play baseball, not the piano. But when he heard ragtime music as a young man, he changed his mind. He taught himself to play the piano. Later he formed a band and headed to New York City and started playing small clubs. Finally Ellington and his band made it to the best club in Harlem—the Cotton Club. Duke Ellington and his Orchestra played favorites as well as original music. They experimented, painting colors with music and creating jazz. An essay after the biography describes more about jazz and Ellington's career until his death in 1974. This book received a Caldecott Honor Award and a Coretta Scott King Illustrator Honor Award.

199 Raschka, Chris ✱ *Charlie Parker Played Be Bop*
Illus. by the author ✱ Orchard, 1992 ✱ 0-531-08599-6
African American ✱ Grades 1–3

In a rhyming text, the music of jazz great Charlie Parker is described. Repetition and nonsense words (such as "Be bob," "Fisk, fisk," "Boomba, boomba," and "Zznnzznn") create a beat that slides, snaps, and pops. The staccato rhythm encourages participation through clapping, snapping fingers, and movement.

200 Raschka, Chris ✱ *John Coltrane's Giant Steps*
Illus. by the author ✱ Atheneum, 2002 ✱ 0-689-84598-7
African American ✱ Grades 2–6

Chris Raschka's creative presentation explores jazz music by showing the interactions between four elements—a box, a snowflake, some raindrops, and a kitten. First comes the tempo from the raindrop. The box joins in and lays down the foundation of the song. The snowflake brings in harmony and the cat provides the melody. For a while, the music flows, but when the tempo becomes too fast and the foundation is too heavy and the harmony and melody are discordant, the music stops and begins again. It finally achieves the smooth colorful sound of *Giant Steps*.

201 Raschka, Chris ✱ *Mysterious Thelonious*
Illus. by the author ✱ Orchard, 1997 ✱ 0-531-30057-9
African American ✱ Grades 2–6

Thelonious Monk was a creative and innovative jazz pianist and composer. Chris Raschka is a creative and innovative author and illustrator. In this book, Raschka uses squares of color placed throughout each page to convey the concept of the 12 musical tones of the chromatic scale. The text of the book appears in words or parts of words on each color square, making for a vibrant presentation that jumps across each page, showing the energy and imagination of Thelonious Monk. Monk's composition "Misterioso" is the inspiration for this book and could be played while doing a choral reading. Each reader could hold colorful cards with the words and word fragments on them and deliver their parts in a format like the one in the book.

202 Winter, Jonah ✳ *Once Upon a Time in Chicago: The Story of Benny Goodman*

Illus. by Jeanette Winter ✳ Hyperion, 2000 ✳ 0-786-80462-9
JEWISH AMERICAN ✳ GRADES 1–3

From his beginnings in a large family of Jewish immigrants, Goodman became a popular and successful jazz musician. This biography describes his childhood in a Chicago neighborhood filled with musicians. His parents worked hard but with 12 children there was never enough money. At the local synagogue, Benny and two of his brothers received musical instruments. As a child, Benny was shy but he loved to play the clarinet and he communicated through music. He became so good that his father found money for special lessons. Benny soon appeared on stage; he began to earn money and attract attention. After the tragic death of his beloved father, Benny Goodman continued to achieve knowing that his success would have made his father proud.

MUSIC AND DANCE

THERE ARE MANY STORIES ABOUT MUSIC AND DANCE—for example, *Salsa*, which features a Puerto Rican American family, and *Rap a Tap Tap*, which highlights a famous African American tap dancer, Bill "Bojangles" Robinson. *Jose! Born to Dance* introduces readers to an acclaimed Mexican American dancer and choreographer. And there are stories about rhythm and beat, like *My Family Plays Music* and *Violet's Music*. One special book, *Moses Goes to a Concert*, describes the experiences of a deaf child at a concert.

All of these books could be extended by playing music, learning dances, and moving and shaking. In a school setting, these stories could be coordinated with activities in music or physical education. In a public library, there might be community resources to support a program on salsa, tap dancing, or other music/dance activities.

203 Colón-Vilá, Lillian * *Salsa*
Illus. by Robert Collier-Morales * Piñata Books, 1998 * 1-55885-220-4
PUERTO RICAN AMERICAN * GRADES 1–3

Rita describes the rhythm and joy of salsa. Her Puerto Rican American family and friends play and dance to the lively music. Uncle Jorge plays the *timbales*. Cuban Canary plays the trumpet. Her brother Alberto, who still lives in Puerto Rico, describes how to spin and twirl. Play salsa music and move to the beat. This book is written in English and Spanish.

204 Cox, Judy * *My Family Plays Music*
Illus. by Elbrite Brown * Holiday House, 2003 * 0-8234-1591-0
AFRICAN AMERICAN * GRADES 1–3

A young girl describes the musical activities of her large extended family. Her mom plays the fiddle in a country-and-western band. Her dad plays cello in a string quartet. There's sister Emily and her clarinet, brother Paul on guitar, Aunt Saffron playing vibes, Uncle Woody on saxophone, and more. The young girl plays along with each of them. Tambourine, cymbals, cowbell, maracas, and rhythm sticks are among her musical accompaniments. A glossary describes types of music (big band, bluegrass, jazz, etc.) and musical terms (percussion, strings, etc.) Children will have fun trying to play some of the percussion instruments that the young girl enjoys.

205 Dillon, Leo, and Diane Dillon ✴ *Rap a Tap Tap: Here's Bojangles—Think of That!*
Illus. by the authors ✴ Scholastic, 2002 ✴ 0-590-47883-4
AFRICAN AMERICAN ✴ GRADES PRESCHOOL–1

The rhythmic text and repetition of "Rap a tap tap—think of that!" make this a great book to share with young children. They join in on the refrain and they move and groove to the lively beat. The book describes the dancing of Bill "Bojangles" Robinson, an incredible tap dancer. An Afterword gives additional information about his life, including the fact that he was "the highest paid black entertainer" during the Great Depression. *Rap a Tap Tap* received a Coretta Scott King Illustration Honor Award.

206 Johnson, Angela ✴ *Violet's Music*
Illus. by Laura Huliska-Beith ✴ Dial, 2004 ✴ 0-8037-2740-2
AFRICAN AMERICAN ✴ GRADES PRESCHOOL–1

Even when she was a baby, Violet made music, shaking her rattle and hoping that others would join in. No one did. When she was 2, she played her horn and looked for other players, but still she played alone. In kindergarten, there were lots of kids but none of them loved music the way she did. Violet kept looking. Several years passed until one day at the park she found three musicians—Angel, Randy, and Juan. Now they are a band, playing together and sharing their love of music.

207 Millman, Isaac ✴ *Moses Goes to a Concert*
Illus. by the author ✴ Farrar, Straus and Giroux, 1998 ✴ 0-374-35067-1
EUROPEAN AMERICAN ✴ GRADES 1–3

What is like to go to a concert when you cannot hear? Moses and his classmates are deaf. They go on a field trip to a concert and enjoy the experience, especially meeting the percussionist, who is also deaf. She follows the music through the vibrations she feels through her feet. The children get to experiment with the percussion instruments and then return to school. Along with the written text of the book, there are drawings of some of the action being told in American Sign Language. Children could try to learn some of the signs and retell the story. An illustration of the hand alphabet follows the text.

208 Reich, Susanna * *José! Born to Dance: The Story of José Limón*
Illus. by Raúl Colón * Simon & Schuster, 2005 * 0-689-86576-7
MEXICAN AMERICAN * GRADES 2–4

Born in Mexico in 1908, José Limón became a successful dancer and choreographer. This picture-book biography describes his childhood in Mexico and the impact of his early life on the modern dance movements he created. Limón's family came to America to escape the civil war in Mexico. As an adult, Limón moved to New York City to study art and, later, dance. This book was the 2005 Winner of the Tomás Rivera Mexican American Children's Book Award.

Reflections

The Wood County District Public Library building was recently renovated. The newly created atrium includes a cozy fireplace for casual reading, a "New Books" browsing area, magazines and newspapers, and several computers. It also has marvelous acoustics that gave birth to an idea—to buy a piano and schedule concerts and recitals.

Buying and reconditioning the piano was accomplished through extensive fundraising, a benefit concert, and a generous gift from a corporate business. Of course, once we had the piano, we needed a celebration! A group of sixth-graders from Toledo worked with their art teacher to make a special banner. The children stepped into different colors of watercolor paint and then danced—to jazz music—across the length of a sheet of bright orange paper. The footprints became the background for a long set of black-and-white piano keys. That paper was attached to another long sheet—glued down in 3-D waves—and kids' handprints, cut from various colors of paper, were glued to the piano keys. Debbi Chocolate's *The Piano Man*, illustrated by Eric Velasquez, was displayed under the banner.   —Kathy East

Making Music

Many books feature musical experiences. In *The Piano Man*, a girl celebrates the musical talents of her grandfather, a man who played the piano for silent movies, vaudeville, and for musical revues. *A Pianist's Debut* is a nonfiction book exploring the development of a young concert pianist. There is even a book about Polly, a dog that loves listening to the piano.

Children can create their own artistic interpretations of music or musical instruments. How would violin music and all those strings be attached to notes on a mural? Perhaps sets of drumsticks could make a sun shape on the front of a circle of cloth replicating a drum face? Think of other musical instruments and styles of music and plan a bold way to "celebrate" the shape and sound of each instrument.

209 Beirne, Barbara * *A Pianist's Debut: Preparing for the Concert Stage*

Illus. with photographs * Carolrhoda Books, 1990 * 0-87614-432-6

KOREAN AMERICAN * GRADES 4–6

This book describes Leah Yoon's love of piano and music. She started playing when she was 2 years old and had "ear training" from the grandmother who raised her. At age 5 she began taking lessons. Her dream was to attend Juilliard School for Performing Arts in New York City. This photoessay documents Leah's first piano, first competition, first prize, and even her visit to the White House before performing at the Kennedy Center. Youngsters learn how intense a program and routine must be followed to balance school, lessons, practicing, performing, and having a life with family and friends. Although this title is a bit dated, the rigors of performance are realistically documented and the importance of family support and the unselfish dedication needed to reach a dream are emphasized.

210 Chocolate, Debbi * *The Piano Man*

Illus. by Eric Velasquez * Walker, 1998 * 0-802-78646-4
AFRICAN AMERICAN * GRADES 1–3

With great pride, a young girl recalls her grandfather's many musical jobs, demonstrating the numerous ways piano music has entertained audiences through the years. Grandfather played for silent movies, on Broadway, with any number of famous singers and dancers, and even married a dancer—the girl's grandmother. The impact of the "talking pictures" sent Grandfather to tuning pianos for a living. The reader understands Grandfather's love for music and how he passed that love on to one little girl.

211 Miller, William * *The Piano*

Illus. by Susan Keeter * Lee & Low, 2000 * 1-880000-98-9
AFRICAN AMERICAN * GRADES 1–3

Tia, an African American girl, takes a job as a maid in the home of an elderly white woman, Miss Hartwell. Tia was drawn to the home by the sound of music. While Tia works, she listens to the music Miss Hartwell plays on the record player. Tia notices the beautiful piano in the parlor and she presses the keys. She is delighted with their sound. As Tia experiments on the piano, her desire to learn to play grows. She asks Miss Hartwell to teach her. Demonstrating scales and chords makes Miss Hartwell's hands ache and Tia helps ease her pain. They share their love of music. The characters in this story come from diverse ethnic and economic

backgrounds. They also come from different generations—
Miss Hartwell is elderly and Tia appears to be preadolescent—
which allows for extension activities in which young people
visit older citizens and perform or share gifts.

212 Montparker, Carol * *Polly and the Piano*

Illus. by the author * Amadeus Press, 2004 * 1-57467-093-X
EUROPEAN AMERICAN * GRADES 3–6

Polly is the adopted dog of a very talented piano player. Laurel
gives lessons to children, who love that a dog is always under
the piano enjoying the beautiful classical music. Polly proves
to be such fun and such an inspiration that when Laurel gets
the chance to play at Carnegie Hall, guess who accompanies
her on stage! This beautiful picture book, with lush watercolor
illustrations, is based on the author's real-life experiences. A
CD of classical piano music is included. Talk about the kind
of music your dog likes. What CD would you play to help
express your dog's appreciation of music?

POETRY

THE POEMS IN THESE COLLECTIONS CAPTURE THE MOODS and emotions of different cultures. Janet S. Wong shares personal insights into her diverse heritage. Shonto Begay explores the traditions of his Navajo people. *Words With Wings* presents images of the experiences of African Americans. Ed Young creates a beautiful poem about China that is presented in a creative format with stunning paper-collage illustrations. Children reading these poems will want to create images in words and pictures that connect to their own heritages. The poems in *Poems to Dream Together / Poemas para soñar juntos* are written in both English and Spanish and connect with the experiences of the author in Mexico and California. And James Berry provides an opportunity to go *Around the World in Eighty Poems.*

213 Alarcón, Francisco X. ✳ *Poems to Dream Together / Poemas para soñar juntos*
Illus. by Paula Barragán ✳ Lee & Low, 2005 ✳ 1-58430-233-X
MEXICAN AMERICAN ✳ GRADES 4–6+

What do you dream of? Maybe you see ancient buildings, like the adobes, and you wonder about the people who built them so long ago. Or perhaps you dream of your future. Presented in English and Spanish, the poems in this book celebrate families, the earth, and imagination. There are poems about "Questions," "Daydreaming," and "Nightmares." In the poem "Life Is a Dream," a family looks at an album of photographs and feels the love of their togetherness. Some of the poems explore the author's experiences growing up in California and Mexico.

214 Begay, Shonto ✳ *Navajo: Visions and Voices Across the Mesa*
Illus. by the author ✳ Scholastic, 1995 ✳ 0-590-46153-2
NATIVE AMERICAN—NAVAJO ✳ GRADES 4–6+

Shonto Begay explores the mysticism, beauty, and symbolism of his Navajo heritage in these poems and paintings. "Creation" celebrates the four worlds that led to the present world. Another poem describes the tribal fair. Throughout the collection there is an appreciation for remembering and the past. Songs, prayers, chants, and stories honor the Navajo people and their customs. Beautiful paintings show the dignity, strength, and imagery of the Navajo.

215 Berry, James, selector ✴ *Around the World in Eighty Poems*
Illus. by Katherine Lucas ✴ Chronicle, 2001 ✴ 0-8118-3506-5
MULTICULTURAL ✴ GRADES 1–5

Poems from more than 50 countries demonstrate the wide and lively appeal of poetry and document the variety of experiences in everyday lives of children around the world. These poems remind us of our similarities.

216 Berry, James R. ✴ *Isn't My Name Magical? Sister and Brother Poems*
Illus. by Shelly Hehenberger ✴ Simon & Schuster, 1999 ✴ 0-689-80013-4
AFRICAN AMERICAN ✴ GRADES 1–4

The poems in this book are written from the point of view of a sister, Dreena, and her brother, Delroy. Their poems reflect their different personalities. Dreena loves imaginative play and magic and her poems are mostly written in free verse. Delroy craves action and adventure and there is more of a rhyming pattern to his poems. The bright, colorful illustrations add beautiful details to the word pictures and connect with the Jamaican American heritage of the children.

217 Rochelle, Belinda, selector ✴ *Words with Wings: A Treasury of African American Poetry and Art*
Illus. ✴ HarperCollins, 2001 ✴ 0-688-16415-3
AFRICAN AMERICAN ✴ GRADES 4–6+

The words of well-known poets such as Gwendolyn Brooks, Alice Walker, Paul Laurence Dunbar, Langston Hughes, Nikki Giovanni, and Maya Angelou are paired with strong images by artists including Jacob Lawrence, William H. Johnson, Romare Bearden, and Henry Ossawa Tanner. The combination is powerful, providing images in words and pictures of the struggles and triumphs in the African American experience. Alice Walker's "Women" honors the strength of the generation of women who worked long, difficult hours to provide a better future for their children. Maya Angelou celebrates the "Human Family." These poems connect to the history and heritage of many African American people.

218 Wong, Janet S. ✳ *A Suitcase of Seaweed and Other Poems*
Illus. by the author ✳ Simon & Schuster, 1996 ✳ 0-689-80788-0
Asian American ✳ Grades 5–6+

The poems in this book are divided into three parts: Korean Poems, Chinese Poems, and American Poems. This reflects the author's background and presents emotions and experiences from her life. For the Korean Poems, there is an introduction about Wong's Korean mother. The first poem describes her parents when they met and is called "Love at First Sight." Other poems in this section explore food, customs, and everyday experiences. The Chinese Poems section is introduced with background information about Wong's father, who came to America when he was 12. These poems celebrate her family, especially her grandfather, and explore customs like the "Tea Ceremony." Finally, the American Poems explore Wong's emotions about her heritage, customs, and experiences. The final poem, "Quilt," uses the quilt as a metaphor for the diversity of her family and the warmth of their love.

219 Young, Ed ✳ *Beyond the Great Mountains: A Visual Poem About China*
Illus. by the author ✳ Chronicle, 2005 ✳ 0-8118-4343-2
Asian—China ✳ Grades 4–6

Using paper collage on delicate rice paper, Ed Young has created a loving salute to his native land. The pages are cut so that each page is slightly larger than the one before and the book is designed to be opened with the spine at the top (like a calendar). The color of each page is different and the lines of the poem are written on the exposed edges of the pages. When the book is opened, the reader experiences beautiful colors and the poetic language of the author's celebration of China. The illustrations incorporate Chinese characters that often serve as the inspiration for the design of the collages. The brief text and beautiful pictures make this a unique opportunity to experience Young's sense of China.

CHAPTER FOUR

Traditions—Folktales

FOLKTALES OFFER MANY OPPORTUNITIES TO EXPLORE cultural traditions. They also allow readers to compare and contrast, to analyze plot sequence, to demonstrate comprehension, and to understand the characteristics of this genre. Since they are part of the oral tradition of literature, they are great for retelling, dramatization with props, and the development of presentation skills.

In this chapter there are traditional stories from around the world. Some are familiar, such as versions of Cinderella and the Gingerbread Man. Others are less well known—for example, *The Great Ball Game*, a pourquoi story from the Muskogee people, and *The Hungry Coat*, a noodlehead story from Turkey. There are fables, cumulative tales, stories of trickery, and stories of strength. Find a globe and begin a trip around the world with these wonderful stories.

CINDERELLA

THERE ARE HUNDREDS OF CINDERELLA STORIES from around the world and many have been made into picture books. A program or study unit could focus on these stories. Readers could examine each story for common elements and create a chart to answer "What Makes a Cinderella Story?" Possible categories are:

- What is the character's name?
- Where does the story take place?
- Does she live in the ashes or cinders and/or work as a servant?
- Does she have a stepmother and/or stepsisters?
- Is there a magical creature (like a fairy godmother)?
- Is there a ball or dance or party?
- Is there a time limit at the party?
- Is there a slipper or lost object?

Children can add other categories as they read more stories. Four recent Cinderella stories are listed below and additional versions and variants are included.

220 dePaola, Tomie ✳ *Adelita: A Mexican Cinderella Story*
Illus. by the author ✳ Putnam, 2002 ✳ 0-399-23866-2
MEXICAN ✳ GRADES 2–4

Adelita's mother dies after she is born and her father remarries. Shortly after the marriage, Adelita's father dies and Doña Micaela and her two daughters take over the house. Adelita becomes a servant, working in the kitchen with her nurse Esperanza. When Señor Gordillo plans a *fiesta* for his son Javier, Adelita is kept too busy to prepare herself to go. Esperanza helps her and she arrives at the party as the beautiful *Cenicienta*—Cinderella. Javier falls in love with her but she leaves the fiesta and returns home. Javier searches for her, finds her, and they are married. The text of this folktale includes many Spanish phrases that are explained in context as well as in a glossary following the story.

**221 McClintock, Barbara, reteller; from the Charles Perrault version
✳ *Cinderella***
Illus. by the reteller ✳ Scholastic, 2005 ✳ 0-439-56145-0
EUROPEAN—FRANCE ✳ GRADES 2–4

Charles Perrault retold many classic folktales for the French court in
the late 1600s. This European version is often the one children are
familiar with. There is the gentle daughter of a noble family whose
mother dies and whose father remarries. The stepmother relegates
her to the life of a servant. She dresses in rags and does the bidding
of her stepmother and two stepsisters. There are two grand balls and
a fairy godmother and a lost glass slipper, which, of course, fits the
servant girl, Cinderella.

222 San Souci, Robert D. ✳ *Cendrillon: A Caribbean Cinderella*
Illus. by Brian Pinkney ✳ Simon & Schuster, 1998 ✳ 0-689-80668-X
CARIBBEAN ✳ GRADES 2–4

When her father remarries a proud and vain woman (Madame
Prospèrine), young Cendrillon becomes a servant in her father's
home. Cendrillon's godmother uses her magic to send Cendrillon to
the birthday celebration for handsome Paul. There, Paul sees her and
falls in love but, like Cinderella, Cendrillon leaves the party, loses her
slipper, and is reunited with Paul who loves her even in her rags.

223 Sierra, Judy ✳ *The Gift of the Crocodile: A Cinderella Story*
Illus. by Reynold Ruffins ✳ Simon & Schuster, 2000 ✳ 0-689-82188-3
ASIAN—INDONESIA—SPICE ISLANDS ✳ GRADES 2–4

Set in the Spice Islands in Indonesia, this folktale has many elements
of a traditional Cinderella: a stepmother and stepsisters as well as a
girl who does all the work and sleeps in the ashes. Damura's kindness
toward an ancient crocodile ("Grandmother Crodocile") brings her
good fortune and the prince. In an unusual ending, Princess Damura
is eaten by a crocodile only to be spit out and brought back to life by
Grandmother Crocodile. A Folklore Note describes the origin of this
retelling.

Additional Cinderella versions and variants:

Climo, Shirley. *The Egyptian Cinderella*. Illustrated by Ruth Heller. Crowell, 1989. 0-690-04822-X

Climo, Shirley. *The Irish Cinderlad*. Illustrated by Loretta Krupinski. HarperCollins, 1996. 0-06-024396-1

Climo, Shirley. *The Korean Cinderella*. Illustrated by Ruth Heller. HarperCollins, 1993. 0-06-020432-X

Climo, Shirley. *The Persian Cinderella*. Illustrated by Robert Florczak. HarperCollins, 1999. 0-06-026763-1

Huck, Charlotte. *Princess Furball*. Illustrated by Anita Lobel. Greenwillow, 1989. 0-688-07837-0

Louie, Ai-Ling, reteller *Yeh-Shen: A Cinderella Story from China*. Illustrated by Ed Young. Philomel, 1982. 0-399-20900-X

Martin, Rafe. *The Rough-Face Girl*. Illustrated by David Shannon. Putnam, 1992. 0-399-21859-9

Pollock, Penny. *The Turkey Girl: A Zuni Cinderella Story*. Illustrated by Ed Young. Little, Brown, 1996. 0-316-71314-7

San Souci, Robert D., reteller. *The Talking Eggs: A Folktale from the American South*. Illustrated by Jerry Pinkney. Dial, 1989. 0-8037-0619-7

Steptoe. John. *Mufaro's Beautiful Daughter: An African Tale*. Illustrated by the author. Lothrop, Lee & Shepard, 1987. 0-688-04045-4

GINGERBREAD MAN

THE POPULAR GINGERBREAD MAN STORIES can be used in many creative ways. Young children can chart the sequences of various versions; they can also make puppets and scenery that enhance the retellings. These books can be used to highlight different cultural elements; they are also helpful in teaching different presentation skills. Children have the opportunity to speak and to perform. They learn the conventions of a "cumulative" folktale—stories that add on. Many children like to try to write their own cumulative stories, using the folktale as a model.

Using these books connects with several content areas, including writing, analyzing literary texts, sequencing, genres, and studying cultural traditions. Recent Gingerbread Man stories include *The Gingerbread Man* (Aylesworth) and *The Gingerbread Boy* (Egielski). Jan Brett's *The Gingerbread Baby* is a popular picture book story with an original ending, while *The Runaway Latkes*, *The Runaway Rice Cake*, and *The Runaway Tortilla* bring in elements from different cultures. Make a sequence chart of what the runaway item meets along the way, what the refrain is, and what happens at the end of the story. Make props and encourage retelling.

224 Aylesworth, Jim, reteller ✳ *The Gingerbread Man*
Illus. by Barbara McClintock ✳ Scholastic, 1998 ✳ 0-590-97219-7
EUROPEAN ✳ GRADES PRESCHOOL–2

The well-known cumulative story of the gingerbread man who runs away is presented with colorful illustrations. In this version, there are two main repeated phrases that could be compared with the phrases in other versions. This little man runs away from a husband, a wife, a butcher, a cow, and a sow until he is eaten by a fox. Children will enjoy the illustrations depicting humans and animals dressed in old-fashioned clothing.

225 Brett, Jan ✶ *The Gingerbread Baby*
Illus. by the author ✶ Putnam, 1999 ✶ 0-399-24166-3
EUROPEAN—SWITZERLAND ✶ GRADES PRESCHOOL–2

When Matti and his mother make a gingerbread man, Matti opens the oven before the cooking time is completed and a gingerbread baby jumps out. Matti's mother begins the chase and is joined by other characters. Matti stays in the house where he makes a gingerbread house for the baby. This book can be used as a model for how a folktale can be the springboard for a new original tale.

226 Compestine, Ying Chang ✶ *The Runaway Rice Cake*
Illus. by Tungwai Chau ✶ Simon & Schuster, 2001 ✶ 0-689-82972-8
ASIAN—CHINA ✶ GRADES 2–4

This original story has elements of the gingerbread man folktale. The Chang family has only enough rice flour to make one *nián-gäo*, the New Year's rice cake. When Mama opens the steamer, the rice cake runs away. It runs past chicks, pigs, and villagers but it cannot be caught. Finally it bumps into an old woman and Mama Chang catches the cake. Even though they are very hungry, the Changs decide to share the cake with the old woman. The nián-gäo is so delicious that the old woman eats it all and runs away in embarrassment. The Changs return home with nothing. Their neighbors have heard of their kindness and come to share their food, but there is still not enough for all. The two older brothers decide to let their younger brother eat first and when he uncovers the food, more food magically appears. There is a celebration for everyone, ending with the parade, dragons, and firecrackers for Chinese New Year. A Note describes "Celebrating Chinese New Year" and there are two recipes for nián-gäo. After reading this book it would be fun to celebrate with this sweet treat.

227 Egielski, Richard ✶ *The Gingerbread Boy*
Illus. by the author ✶ HarperCollins, 1997 ✶ 0-06-026030-0
EUROPEAN AMERICAN ✶ GRADES PRESCHOOL–2

The setting for this book is an urban apartment, so when the gingerbread boy runs away, he encounters appropriate characters. He runs away from a woman and a man, a rat, construction workers, musicians, and a policeman. In the park zoo, he encounters a fox and meets his fate. The unusual setting and characters make this version a great choice for comparison activities.

228 Kimmel, Eric A. * *The Runaway Tortilla*
Illus. by Randy Cecil * Winslow Press, 2000 * 1-890817-18-X
MEXICAN AMERICAN * GRADES PRESCHOOL–2

In Texas, Tía Lupe and Tío José make delicious tortillas that are so light that one tortilla rolls away. The characters chase after her, including familiar animals of the Southwest such as rattlesnakes, jackrabbits, and donkeys. In the end, Señor Coyote tricks her into being eaten.

229 Kimmelman, Leslie * *The Runaway Latkes*
Illus. by Paul Yalowitz * Albert Whitman, 2000 * 0-8075-7176-8
JEWISH AMERICAN * GRADES PRESCHOOL–2

On the first night of Hanukkah, Rebecca Bloom is at the synagogue making potato pancakes (latkes). Three of her latkes jump out of her pan and roll away saying a rhyming refrain. Many people, including the rabbi and the cantor, chase after them. The latkes jump into the river, which miraculously changes into applesauce. Rebecca and all who have been giving chase enjoy a bite of the delicious potato pancakes. After reading this book, children may want to explore the traditions of Hanukkah.

SYMBOLS OF STRENGTH

MANY CULTURES HAVE STORIES AND LEGENDS about individuals with special talents. From China, *The Sons of the Dragon King* features nine sons searching for their strengths. From Ghana in West Africa, there is the story of *Anansi the Spider*. Each of Anansi's six sons uses his skill to help rescue Anansi. Native American totem poles also provide symbolic images that connect to stories. In *Whale in the Sky*, Thunderbird saves the salmon from Whale. After hearing stories from different cultures, readers will enjoy creating their own symbols that highlight their strengths. If a reader enjoys reading, football, running, and music, the design might incorporate a book, a football, a sports shoe, and a musical note. Children can discuss using symbols to represent activities and emotions. In Ed Young's *Voices of the Heart*, Chinese characters provide the inspiration for images of emotions such as "shame," "respect," and "mercy." Learning about the Chinese Zodiac is another extension.

230 Demi ✳ *The Dragon's Tale: And Other Fables of the Chinese Zodiac*
Illus. by the author ✳ Henry Holt, 1996 ✳ 0-8050-3446-3
ASIAN—CHINA ✳ GRADES 2–4

> The 12 animals of the Chinese Zodiac are featured with a detailed illustration, a fable, and a phrase. "The Rat's Tale" describes the importance of appreciating what you are. "The Tiger's Tale" shows how a fox (or any small creature) must think quickly to survive. "The Rabbit's Tale" connects with Henny Penny and Chicken Little stories in which "the sky is falling." The phrases, like those from Aesop, teach a lesson. For example, after "The Rabbit's Tale" is the phrase "If someone tells a falsehood, one hundred will repeat it as true." A book of *Aesop's Fables* would be another connection. See the section on Fables later in this chapter.

231 Hoyt-Goldsmith, Diane ✳ *Totem Pole*
Photographs by Lawrence Migdale ✳ Holiday House, 1990 ✳ 0-8234-0809-4
NATIVE AMERICAN—TSIMSHIAN ✳ GRADES 2–4

> David's family belongs to the Eagle Clan of the Tsimshian people. In this nonfiction photoessay, David describes his father's work as a

woodcarver working on a totem pole. David and his father talk about the process of carving. There is a spirit in the wood, and the woodcarver must reveal the hidden spirit. Carving is an important part of the heritage of the Tsimshian people. David's father teaches David about other traditions—songs, dances, legends, and ceremonial clothing. Color photographs show the totem pole being carved while the text explains each element of the pole and why it has been selected. For example, Raven is included because he brought light to the Indian people. Finally, the pole is done and there is a ceremony for "Raising the Pole." There is a glossary and a folktale, "The Legend of the Eagle and the Young Chief," is included in the text.

232 McDermott, Gerald, adapter ✳ *Anansi the Spider: A Tale from the Ashanti*

Illus. by the adapter ✳ Henry Holt, 1972 ✳ 0-8050-0310-X
AFRICAN—GHANA ✳ GRADES 1–4

Anansi the spider leaves his six sons and falls into trouble. Each of his sons uses his special skill to rescue Anansi. See Trouble sees the trouble and alerts Road Builder, who builds a road. River Drinker drinks the river so that Game Skinner can cut open the fish that has swallowed Anansi. Once Anansi is released from the fish, Falcon snatches him up. Stone Thrower hits Falcon. Anansi falls out of the sky but lands on Cushion. On the way home from the rescue, Anansi and his sons find a beautiful globe of light that is taken into the sky to be the moon. This book received a Caldecott Honor Award.

233 Siberell, Anne ✳ *Whale in the Sky*

Illus. by the author ✳ Dutton, 1982 ✳ 0-525-44021-6
NATIVE AMERICAN—NORTHWEST COAST ✳ GRADES 1–3

This legend from the Northwest Coast Indians uses woodcuts to depict the story of Salmon's rescue. Long ago, Thunderbird watched over all the creatures. When Whale tried to swallow salmon and chase them out of the sea and into the river, Thunderbird grabbed Whale and lifted him into the sky. He dropped Whale on a mountain. Whale promised to stay out of the river, so Thunderbird allowed him to return to the sea. The story was carved into a totem pole with Thunderbird on the top. The woodcut illustrations are a perfect complement to this story of carving a totem pole.

234 Young, Ed ✳ *The Sons of the Dragon King: A Chinese Legend*
Illus. by the author ✳ Atheneum, 2004 ✳ 0-689-85184-7
ASIAN—CHINA ✳ GRADES 2–4

The Dragon King observes each of his nine sons to discover his special gift. Bei-She spends his days proving his strength, and the Dragon King gives him the job of supporting the roofs of buildings. The symbol for Bei-She can be found carved on the columns of China's greatest buildings. Chi Wen, the second son, seems to just stand on the roof and stare into the distance. The Dragon King realizes that Chi Wen would be an excellent sentinel and now his image is seen on the tops of buildings. Finally, the Dragon King finds a role for each son that matches his ability. The illustrations combine ink-and-brush paintings with intricate cut-paper designs.

235 Young, Ed ✳ *Voices of the Heart*
Illus. by the author ✳ Scholastic, 1997 ✳ 0-590-50199-2
ASIAN—CHINA ✳ GRADES 2–4

Focusing on 26 Chinese characters that use the symbol of the heart, Ed Young creates new images that represent emotions and virtues. Words such as *contentment, respect, panic, rudeness, mercy,* and *loyalty* are presented. The concepts may seem abstract to many children; however, the beauty of the illustrations and book design encourage readers to reflect and savor the thoughtful presentation. Calligraphy and cut paper provide a counterpoint to the brief descriptions of each word.

FOLKTALES FROM SIX CONTINENTS

SOCIAL STUDIES PROGRAMS FOCUS on cities, states, countries, and continents. Using folktales, librarians and teachers can explore continents and demonstrate how stories often reflect regional language, topography, and art.

Folktales are part of the oral tradition of a native people. They often teach a lesson or explain a natural phenomenon, and children will enjoy identifying the characteristics of these tales. Find a folktale from each inhabited continent. (Of course, there are no folktales from Antarctica because of its inhospitable climate. When you communicate this information to children, be sure to show informational books about Antarctica.) Then share these folktales, focusing on the elements that connect each story to its place of origin. In *Moon Rope* from Peru, for example, the story takes place in the mountains. Use a globe, preferably one with raised relief features, to show how the Andes Mountains dominate the topography of Peru. In *The Biggest Frog in Australia*, explain that the animals are native to Australia—koalas, kookaburras, wombats, and more.

Africa

236 Bryan, Ashley ∗ *Beautiful Blackbird*
Illus. by the author ∗ Atheneum, 2003 ∗ 0-689-84731-9
African—Zambia—Ila ∗ Grades 2–4

Long ago in Africa, all of the birds were very colorful but they had no markings on their feathers. Blackbird was considered the most beautiful. Ringdove asks Blackbird to mark his feathers with black, giving him a ring around his neck. Blackbird agrees and soon all of the birds want black markings, and he obliges them. Blackbird also stresses the importance of being proud of who you are and how you look. His message, "Color on the outside is not what's on the inside," is one that many children will relate to. This book received the Coretta Scott King Award for Illustration.

South America

237 Ehlert, Lois ＊ *Moon Rope: A Peruvian Folktale / Un lazo a la luna: Una leyenda peruana*
Illus. by the author ＊ Harcourt, 1992 ＊ 0-15-255343-6
SOUTH AMERICAN—PERU ＊ GRADES 2–4

Fox wants to go to the moon and he convinces Mole to go too. The birds take their grass rope up to the moon and the two start to climb. Mole loses his grip on the rope and falls. He is rescued by the birds, but he is mocked by the animals who have been watching. Now, Mole stays deep in his hole and only comes out when he will be alone. Fox continues up to the moon. When there is a full moon, you can see his face looking down. The big full moon on the last page of the story is printed in silver ink. When you tip the book, you can see a face in the moon. In a Note, Lois Ehlert explains that the color and design of Peruvian textiles, ceramics, etc., were an inspiration for the illustrations in this book. This is a "pourquoi" folktale that answers the "why" questions of why moles stay underground and why there is a face in the moon.

Europe

238 Lunge-Larsen, Lise ＊ *The Race of the Birkebeiners*
Illus. by Mary Azarian ＊ Houghton Mifflin, 2001 ＊ 0-618-10313-9
EUROPEAN—NORWAY ＊ GRADES 3–6

This vibrant, legendary account tells of the danger and difficulty in the safe delivery of Prince Hakon of Norway from his family's enemies. The infant prince and his mother are aided by the Birkebeiners, a group of men loyal to the former king. Their dangerous nighttime journey across the icy mountains is dramatically portrayed in the colored woodcuts by Caldecott-winning artist Mary Azarian. This folktale portrays the spirit of Norway's people and the challenge of survival.

North America

239 McDermott, Gerald, reteller ✷ *Raven: A Trickster Tale from the Pacific Northwest*
Illus. by the reteller ✷ Harcourt, 1993 ✷ 0-15-265661-8
NATIVE AMERICAN—PACIFIC NORTHWEST ✷ GRADES 2–4

Raven is sad that the people live in darkness so he steals a ball of light from the home of the Sky Chief. The light becomes the sun and the people are thankful. This book is part of a collection of trickster tales from Gerald McDermott, including *Zomo the Rabbit: A Trickster Tale from West Africa* (Harcourt, 1992), *Coyote: A Trickster Tale from the American Southwest* (Harcourt, 1994), and *Jabuti the Tortoise: A Trickster Tale from the Amazon* (Harcourt, 2001).

Australia

240 Roth, Susan L. ✷ *The Biggest Frog in Australia*
Illus. by the author ✷ Simon & Schuster, 1996 ✷ 0-689-80490-3
AUSTRALIAN ✷ GRADES 1–3

In Australia, the biggest frog drinks up all of the water. Other animals—Koala, Wombat, Echidna—try to get the water back. When the eels make Frog laugh, all of the water spills back out into the world. Illustrated with bold, colorful collages, this book includes a glossary describing some of the Australian terms, animals, and plants.

Asia

241 Young, Ed ✷ *The Lost Horse: A Chinese Folktale*
Illus. by the author ✷ Harcourt, 1998 ✷ 0-15-201016-5
ASIAN—CHINA ✷ GRADES 2–4

A wise man named Sai owns a fine horse. During a storm, the frightened horse runs away. Sai's neighbors are upset about his loss, but Sai is philosophical. When the horse returns, bringing a mare, the neighbors are pleased for Sai, but he is still philosophical. With each new development, Sai maintains his equanimity. A version of this folktale is also included in *Zen Shorts* (see under "Making Choices" below).

Reflections

Norway—a land just as beautiful and pristine as it looked on the cover of my fifth-grade social studies book! It is a country I have always thought I would like to visit, and on this trip as a precursor to the IFLA meeting in Oslo in the summer of 2005, I was not disappointed. The train ride from the city of Bergen on the west coast to the capital city of Oslo displayed the beauty of the mountains, the deep gorges, the glorious fjords, the charming villages, and the absence of traffic and neon lights.

All this beauty and tranquility is in sharp contrast to the traditional literature and stories filled with frightful tales of trolls—big trolls, clever trolls, hidden trolls, and ugly trolls. Of course in these stories the trolls are outsmarted by people, who are always more clever!

—Kathy East

Norway and Its Trolls

Here are books that focus on Norway and trolls. Hand out outline maps of the country of Norway. Allow youngsters to move that shape around until it becomes a part of a sleeping troll, or a part of the caves in which trolls live, or use the shape to make troll faces. The only requirement is that each troll have wild hair, a long nose, and an ugly face!

Look for other unusual creatures in folktales from around the world—the Hairy Man in *Wiley and the Hairy Man* or perhaps the giant in *Jack and the Beanstalk*. How many creatures can you find?

242 Batt, Tanya Robyn * *The Princess and the White Bear King*

Illus. by Nicoletta Ceccoli * Barefoot Books, 2004 * 1-84148-339-7

EUROPEAN—NORWAY * GRADES 2–5

In this folktale, a princess dreams of a beautiful golden crown and then finds it when she is carried off by the great white bear. She briefly returns to her family, and her mother gives her a knife and a candle. Back with the bear, the princess lights the candle in her bedchamber and discovers the bear is a handsome prince under the spell of the Troll Queen. Now that his secret is known, he must marry the Troll Queen. The princess follows him east of the sun and west of the moon to the great glass mountain. After three trials, she outsmarts the Troll Queen and the princess and prince are married and live happily ever after.

243 Lunge-Larsen, Lise * *The Troll with No Heart in His Body and Other Tales of Trolls, from Norway*

Illus. by Betsy Bowen * Houghton Mifflin, 1999 * 0-395-91371-3

EUROPEAN—NORWAY * GRADES 2–5

Each story in this collection is introduced by a storyteller—the Troll Lady. She says "Like fire, a good troll story is slightly dangerous, spellbinding, and warming." The trolls in these stories are quarrelsome, ugly, boastful, and tricky. This is an authentic collection made more dramatic by the woodcuts used to create landscapes, creatures with lots of sharp teeth, and visual images of those mean and frightening trolls.

POURQUOI STORIES

AFTER READING FOLKTALES FROM DIFFERENT CONTINENTS, a classroom or library program can focus on elements found in many traditional stories. For example, the number three is often seen in folktales—three bears or three billy goats. And folktales often have unusual creatures—trolls, mermaids, or hairy men.

Pourquoi stories explain why things happen in nature. *The Great Ball Game*, tells why birds fly south in winter. *Jabutí the Tortoise* explains why the tortoise has a cracked shell. And do you know why snakes cannot be trusted? *The Singing Snake* explains this, while another tale, *Coyote Steals the Blanket*, demonstrates the trickiness of the coyote. *The Hatseller and the Monkeys* is from West Africa and tells why nutrition is important to learning.

Moon Rope and *Raven* (featured in the section "Folktales from Six Continents" above) could fit in this program too.

Make a list of the "why" statements that are found in folktales and identify the origin of each story, too. Children will learn that the "why" convention is often used in folktales. They will enjoy trying to write their own "why" stories.

244 Bruchac, Joseph, reteller ★ *The Great Ball Game: A Muskogee Story*

Illus. by Susan L. Roth ★ Dial, 1994 ★ 0-8037-1539-0
NATIVE AMERICAN—MUSKOGEE ★ GRADES 2–4

When the Birds and the Animals had an argument, they decided to play a game to settle the issues. Bat could not decide which side was right for him. The Birds sent him away, so the Animals allowed him on their team. The game began and both teams played well. As the sun set, the Birds looked as if they would win until Bat swooped out, took the ball, and won the game. As a penalty, the Birds had to leave the area for half of each year. The collage illustrations use paper collected from around the world. And the ball game depicted is lacrosse, a game that originated among the Native Americans.

245 Czernecki, Stefan, and Timothy Rhodes ✱ *The Singing Snake*
Illus. by Stefan Czernecki ✱ Hyperion, 1993 ✱ 1-56282-399-X
AUSTRALIAN ✱ GRADES 2–4

Old Man organizes a contest to find the animal with the most beautiful singing voice. Snake wants to win but realizes his voice is only average. When he hears the beautiful song of Lark, he swallows her and, holding her in the back of his throat, he allows her song to come from his mouth. He wins the contest, but, because he cheated, the animals refuse to speak to him again. His voice becomes a "hiss" that answers the pourquoi—why do snakes make a hissing sound. Also, all cheaters are now known as "snakes in the grass." Australian animals including Dingo, Kookaburra, and Wallaby are among the participants in the contest. The colorful art is reminiscent of the patterns of aboriginal paintings.

246 Diakité, Baba Wagué, reteller ✱ *The Hatseller and the Monkeys: A West African Folktale*
Illus. by the reteller ✱ Scholastic, 1999 ✱ 0-590-96069-5
AFRICAN—WEST AFRICA ✱ GRADES 1–3

From the continent of Africa comes this story with a familiar plot. BaMusa joyfully sells hats, walking from town to town and carrying the hats on his head. One day, he hurries off without eating and becomes so tired he must stop and rest under a mango tree. The monkeys in the tree steal his hats. BaMusa awakes and must outwit the monkeys, but he is so tired he cannot think straight. He eats some mangoes and, with a full stomach and a clear head, he tricks the monkeys into throwing him his hats. He reaches his destination and sells all the hats. The lesson in this story is "it is with a full stomach that one thinks best." An Author's Note explains that this story has been retold around the world, including *Caps for Sale* by Esphyr Slobodkina.

247 McDermott, Gerald, reteller ＊ *Jabutí the Tortoise: A Trickster Tale from the Amazon*

Illus. by the reteller ＊ Harcourt, 2001 ＊ 0-15-200496-3
SOUTH AMERICAN ＊ GRADES 2–4

Jabutí, the tortoise, plays songs that are enjoyed by most of the animals in the rain forest. Animals that Jabutí has tricked, however, are not amused. The birds love Jabutí's music—except for Vulture. Vulture is jealous of Jabutí and wants to harm him. When the birds fly to a festival with the King of Heaven, Vulture agrees to take Jabutí there too. On the journey, Vulture drops Jabutí, who falls to the earth and cracks his smooth shell. Three birds help find the pieces and put them together. Now tortoises have cracked-looking shells and those three birds, Toucan, Macaw, and Hummingbird, have bright, colorful feathers. A Note from the reteller provides some background on the "Jabutí" stories, linking them to the stories of Brer Terrapin seen in African American stories as well as in stories from Aesop.

248 Stevens, Janet, reteller ＊ *Coyote Steals the Blanket: A Ute Tale*

Illus. by the reteller ＊ Holiday House, 1993 ＊ 0-8234-0996-1
NATIVE AMERICAN—UTE ＊ GRADES 2–4

Coyote is always causing trouble. One day, he sees some blankets spread out on rocks in the desert. They are so beautiful he must have one. He grabs one only to be chased by the rock. No matter what he does, Coyote cannot escape the rolling rock. Mule Deer, Big Horn Sheep, and Hummingbird try to help but nothing works until Coyote returns the blanket. Then, Hummingbird whirs her wings and cracks the rock into pieces. Coyote still does not learn his lesson. He steals more blankets and the chase begins again. This is why coyotes cannot be trusted.

NOODLEHEADS

MANY FOLKTALES FEATURE "NOODLEHEADS." These characters are usually sweet and simple-minded. They often follow every instruction literally. Readers laugh at their mistakes; they enjoy the silly situations. *Goha the Wise Fool* includes several stories about Goha's foolishness, and many of the stories in *Kibbitzers and Fools* could be classified as "noodlehead" stories. Another popular story of silliness features *Epossumondas*. These stories are great for creative dramatics. Children enjoy acting out the preposterous circumstances. In several of the stories, as in *Epossumondas* and *The Six Fools*, the plot is episodic with lots of opportunities for visual humor.

How many silly people (or animals) are there in the world? Just read these books and begin making a list.

249 Demi * *The Hungry Coat: A Tale from Turkey*
Illus. by the author * Simon & Schuster, 2004 * 0-689-84680-0
EURASIAN—TURKEY * GRADES 2–6

> Here is a tale from the Turkish folk philosopher Nasrettin Hoca. In this story, Nasrettin is invited to a banquet. Along the way there are a series of misfortunes and when he arrives he is dirty and smells like a goat. The guests shun him and Nasrettin leaves. He hurries home, bathes, and dresses in a beautiful silk coat with golden threads. Returning to the party, he is given food and beverages. To the amazement of the other guests, Nasrettin puts everything into his coat. He explains that the guests shunned him when he arrived in shabby clothes, but they welcome him in this coat, so it must be that the coat is really the honored guest. His friends understand his lesson and celebrate his wisdom. An Afterword explores the roots of this story.

**250 Hurston, Zora Neale, collector; adapted by Joyce Carol Thomas
  * *The Six Fools***
Illus. by Ann Tanksley * HarperCollins, 2006 * 0-06-000646-3
AFRICAN AMERICAN * GRADES 2–6

> A young man realizes that his fiancee and her parents are fools. In frustration, he says he will search the world for three equal fools. If

he succeeds, the wedding will go ahead. It is no surprise to the reader that there are plenty of fools for him to find. He finds a man trying to jump into his trousers, a farmer trying to lift his cow to eat the grass growing on the barn roof, and a woman trying to catch sunshine with a wheelbarrow. An Adapter's Note looks at the tradition of laughing at the foolishness of others.

251 Johnson-Davies, Denys ✴ *Goha the Wise Fool*
Illus. by Hag Hamady and Hany ✴ Philomel, 2005 ✴ 0-399-24222-8
EURASIAN—TURKEY; MIDDLE EASTERN ✴ GRADES 3–6

Stories about Goha are prolific throughout the Middle East. In many stories, he is a fool; in others, he displays great wisdom. These 15 stories show the strengths and weaknesses of this humorous character. In "Goha Counts His Donkeys" and "Goha Buys a New Donkey," he is a classic "noodlehead"—a character whose behavior is absurd. In "Goha Outthinks the Three Wise Men," Goha shows his mettle by answering three impossible questions. The illustrations are striking. They are colorful fabric designs appliqued on a textured beige background cloth. A Note following the stories describes their origin and shows the illustrators at work. They are tentmakers who work in a small store in the Old Islamic Quarter in Cairo. Information about the history of tentmaking and about the Goha stories is also included.

252 Montes, Marisa ✴ *Juan Bobo Goes to Work: A Puerto Rican Folktale*
Illus. by Joe Cepeda ✴ HarperCollins, 2000 ✴ 0-688-16234-7
CARIBBEAN—PUERTO RICO ✴ GRADES 2–5

Juan Bobo tries to do things right, but when his mother sends him out to earn money, he proves to be a hard worker who can't get his day's earnings safely home to his Mama. She tells him to hold the coins in his hands, but he puts the coins in his pockets, full of holes! And he puts milk the farmer gives him as pay in a burlap bag and, of course, it all drips out by the time he gets home. One day a sick girl who is the daughter of a rich man sees Juan Bobo dragging a ham on the ground behind him. All the cats and dogs are nibbling on the meat. The girl laughs and laughs—just what she needs to do to recover. It turns out that Bobo's foolishness proves rewarding for him and his mama. The brightly painted illustrations capture this boy's antics and add to the humor of each of the situations. This book was selected as an Honor Book for Illustration for the Pura Belpré Award.

253 Salley, Colleen ✳ *Epossumondas*
Illus. by Janet Stevens ✳ Harcourt, 2002 ✳ 0-15-216748-X
AMERICAN ✳ GRADES K–3

Epossumondas is a sweet little possum whose mama and auntie (both human females) dote on him. When Epossumondas visits his auntie, she gives him something to take home. But by the time he gets there, the item is almost unrecognizable. His mama tries to give him instructions about what to do, but he is always one step behind. Children love hearing what Epossumondas will do next. The sequential events in this story make it great for retelling or acting out. *Epossumondas* is a retelling of a classic story from the American South. Companion volumes with this character are *Why Epossumondas Has No Hair on His Tail* (Harcourt, 2004) and *Epossumondas Saves the Day* (Harcourt, 2006).

254 Stewart, Dianne ✳ *Gift of the Sun: A Tale from South Africa*
Illus. by Jude Daly ✳ Farrar, Straus and Giroux, 1996 ✳ 0-374-32425-5
AFRICAN—SOUTH AFRICA ✳ GRADES 2–4

Thulani looks for the easy way out. Milking his cow is too much work so he sells the cow and gets a goat. The goat eats his dried corn so he gets a sheep. After shearing the sheep, he decides that three geese will be easier, but his wife, Dora, makes him sell the geese and buy seeds for planting. Thulani buys seeds but they are sunflower seeds. Dora thinks they are worthless. As the sunflowers grow, they produce many seeds and Thulani collects the seeds and feeds the chickens, who lay extra eggs. With the eggs, he buys another sheep and then another cow. Lazy, foolish Thulani is now successful!

255 Taback, Simms * *Kibitzers and Fools: Tales My Zayda Told Me*
Illus. by the author * Viking, 2005 * 0-670-05955-2
JEWISH—EUROPEAN—EASTERN EUROPE * GRADES 3–6

The 13 stories in this collection are from traditional stories from the Jewish people in Eastern Europe. Many Yiddish words are included in the text and the pictures and several of the stories are accompanied by sayings that capture the essence of the tale. For example, in "The Umbrella," two friends go for a walk when it begins to rain. One has an umbrella that is full of holes. His friend asks why he brought such a useless item only to be told that the umbrella's owner did not think it would rain. The saying "Be with a fool and you will suffer the consequences" is a perfect end to this silly story. In another "noodlehead" story, Hershel sees a man he believes he recognizes but he is wrong. Instead of acknowledging his mistake, he comments that the man has changed—even his name! There is a lot of fun in this collection. *Kibitzers and Fools* received a Sydney Taylor Book Honor Award for Younger Readers in 2005.

MAKING CHOICES

THE STORIES IN THIS SECTION TEACH PHILOSOPHICAL lessons about choices and values. Some are folktales while others are retellings of traditional tales. All feature characters faced with dilemmas. Demi is an author/illustrator whose books encourage readers to reflect on the behavior of the characters in the story. The story then becomes a springboard to reflect on your own actions and decisions. *The Greatest Power* and *The Hungry Coat* (which is featured in the section on Noodleheads above) are just two examples from Demi that can generate discussions about such topics as honesty, beauty, friendship, and what is important to you.

Two books from John J. Muth offer similar opportunities for reflection and discussion. *The Three Questions* and *Zen Shorts* are great choices for a response journal activity. Readers write their insights into the meaning of the questions or the short stories. Ed Young's *The Lost Horse*, which is another version of one of the stories in *Zen Shorts*, could also be used here (see the section on "Folktales from Six Continents" above).

In *Mr. Peabody's Apples*, lessons from the past are applied to the present. (Although the illustrations show an idyllic small town of a bygone era, they are more "present day" than the other stories in this section.) Actually opening a feather pillow to watch the feathers scatter really makes the connection about the danger of spreading rumors.

256 Demi * *The Greatest Power*
Illus. by the author * Scholastic, 2004 * 0-689-84503-0
ASIAN—CHINA * GRADES 2–6

In Demi's *The Empty Pot* (Holt, 1990), Ping's honesty was rewarded and he was chosen to be the next emperor. In *The Greatest Power* Ping is now the emperor and this time he sets the challenge for the children, asking them to find the greatest power in the world. After one year has passed, the children bring him a variety of interpretations of "power" including weapons, beauty, technology, and money. Only one little girl, Sing, brings him a lotus seed, which contains the power to be planted, grow, create more seeds, and begin again. The power of eternal life is "the greatest power" and Ping selects Sing to be his prime minister.

257 Madonna ✳ *Mr. Peabody's Apples*
Illus. by Loren Long ✳ Callaway, 2003 ✳ 0-670-05883-1
EUROPEAN AMERICAN ✳ GRADES 3–6

Mr. Peabody, an elementary school teacher, coaches a Little League team in Happville. His team does not win many games, but they enjoy playing. One day Tommy Tittlebottom watches Mr. Peabody walking home. Mr. Peabody walks by the fruit market, selects a beautiful apple, and continues on his way. Tommy tells his friends that Mr. Peabody is a thief. When it is time for another baseball game, no one comes to play. Billy Little comes to the baseball field and tells Mr. Peabody what Tommy has said.

Tommy goes to Mr. Peabody's home and Mr. Peabody explains that he is not stealing apples; he has paid for his apple earlier in the day. Tommy is chagrined and wants to make amends. Mr. Peabody asks Tommy to bring a feather pillow to the baseball field. They climb to the top of the bleachers, cut open the pillow, and shake all the feathers out. Then, Mr. Peabody tells Tommy to collect the feathers—a task that is as impossible as undoing the damage from the rumor Tommy started. The final picture shows a pillow that is nearly full of feathers and has been stitched back together, although there are still a few feathers floating in the air. An Author's Note describes how this story is based on a 300-year-old tale.

258 Muth, Jon J ✳ *The Three Questions: Based on a Story by Leo Tolstoy*
Illus. by the author ✳ Scholastic, 2002 ✳ 0-439-33911-1
UNIVERSAL ✳ GRADES 3–6

Nikolai is a boy who wants to do his best. He believes that the answers to his three questions—"When is the best time to do things?", "Who is the most important one?", and "What is the right thing to do?"—will help guide him. His friends the heron, the monkey, and the dog try to answer his questions but Nikolai is not satisfied. Finally he goes to Leo, the old turtle. While Leo thinks, Nikolai helps the turtle by digging in his garden. A storm rises and Nikolai rescues an injured panda and then retrieves her child from the forest. The next morning, the panda and her child leave. Nikolai still wants an answer to his three questions. Leo helps Nikolai understand that his actions with the pandas help answer the questions. What you do now is the most important time. The one you are with is the most important one. And doing good is the most important thing to do. An Author's Note describes how Jon J. Muth came upon this story and how it is connected to Zen philosophy and to the writings of Leo Tolstoy.

259 Muth, Jon J ✱ *Zen Shorts*
Illus. by the author ✱ Scholastic, 2005 ✱ 0-439-33911-1
UNIVERSAL ✱ GRADES 3–6

Three children discover they have a new neighbor—a panda named Stillwater. Each child goes to visit Stillwater and he tells a thought-provoking story. When Addy visits, she hears about "Uncle Ry and the Moon." In this story, Uncle Ry wishes he had more to give the robber who came to his home. Uncle Ry enjoys the beauty of the moon and appreciates the natural world. Next, Michael goes to visit and finds Stillwater high up in a tree. The story for Michael is "The Farmer's Luck." In this story, events happen that may seem lucky or unlucky, but the farmer is not impressed by the idea of luck. Finally, Karl goes to visit and learns about carrying "A Heavy Load." An Author's Note describes the Japanese tradition of meditation or Zen. The three stories in this book are meant to provoke thought and discussion and come from Zen Buddhist and Taoist literature. For another version of "The Farmer's Luck," see Ed Young's *The Lost Horse* (under "Folktales from Six Continents" above). *Zen Shorts* was a Caldecott Honor Book.

FABLES

READING LITERARY TEXTS IN MANY GENRES is a component of English and Language Arts standards, and children are expected to be familiar with fables. Jerry Pinkney's beautifully illustrated collection of *Aesop's Fables* and Doris Orgel's selections in *The Lion and the Mouse* can lead to a discussion of these stories and the moral lessons they are designed to teach. After reading stories from this collection, readers may want to explore the tales in *Doctor Coyote*. The preface to *Doctor Coyote* describes how the Aztec Indians were exposed to the traditional Aesop fables by the European explorers. The Aztec adapted these stories to reflect their own culture and made Coyote the central figure. Look for similarities between the Aztec and ancient Greek tales.

After reading *Doctor Coyote*, children can look at other Native American stories featuring Coyote, such as *Old Bag of Bones*. They can identify him as a trickster and then look for other trickster stories, such as those featuring Rabbit (*Rabbit Makes a Monkey of Lion*, for example), Anansi (*Ananse and the Lizard*), and Raven (*Raven*; see under "Folktales from Six Continents"). *Just a Minute* is a trickster tale from Mexico featuring an old lady who tricks a skeleton.

Christopher Wormell's *Mice, Morals, and Monkey Business* is a dramatic presentation of the morals of several fables from Aesop. Children could create their own illustrations using a variety of media or could even try wood cut/engraving like Wormell.

260 Aardema, Verna ∗ *Rabbit Makes a Monkey of Lion: A Swahili Tale*
Illus. by Jerry Pinkney ∗ Dial, 1989 ∗ 0-8057-0297-3
African—Swahili ∗ Grades 2–4

Rabbit follows a honey guide bird to the bees' nest and enjoys the sweet honey. Unfortunately, the nest belongs to Lion, who is angry with Rabbit and chases after her. Rabbit tricks Lion and escapes, but she cannot stay away from the honey. She returns to the nest only to have to use trickery to escape from Lion again. Jerry Pinkney's dramatic artwork for this book could connect with the paintings in *Aesop's Fables* and be part of an art study.

261 *Aesop's Fables*
Illus. by Jerry Pinkney * SeaStar Books, 2000 * 1-58717-000-0
GREEK, ANCIENT * GRADES 2–5

Nearly 60 Aesop's fables are presented here with outstanding illustrations from Jerry Pinkney. Readers will recognize many of these tales, but there are many that are less familiar. The morals are clearly presented; children would enjoy trying to "guess" the moral.

262 Bierhorst, John, reteller * *Doctor Coyote: A Native American Aesop's Fables*
Illus. by Wendy Watson * Macmillan, 1987 * 0-02-709780-3
NATIVE AMERICAN * GRADES 3–6

Read these fables and try to find the connection with the original Aesop's fables. When Coyote meets White Beard (the goat) and they jump into the well, readers could compare it to "The Fox and the Goat." The story about Coyote hunting with Puma and Donkey could be linked to "The Stork and the Cranes." How many other connections can you find?

263 Cummings, Pat, reteller * *Ananse and the Lizard: A West African Tale*
Illus. by the reteller * Henry Holt, 2002 * 0-8050-6476-1
AFRICAN—GHANA * GRADES 2–4

Ananse reads a notice posted on a tree and decides to try to guess the name of the Chief's daughter and win her hand in marriage. Ananse overhears the Chief's daughter and her servants talking and he learns her name. Lizard tricks Ananse into telling him the name. Lizard goes to the palace, tells the name, and marries the Chief's daughter. Ananse, the trickster, has been tricked!

264 Morales, Yuyi * *Just a Minute: A Trickster Tale and Counting Book*
Illus. by the author * Chronicle Books, 2003 * 0-8118-3758-0
MEXICAN * GRADES 1–3

Señor Calavera, a skeleton, has arrived at Grandma Beetle's door. He wants her to go with him. Grandma Beetle finds many things to do so that she does not have to go. She sweeps one/*uno* house, boils two/*dos* pots of tea, makes three/*tres* pounds of corn into tortillas, and so forth. She continues until she reaches ten/*diez*—the number of guests at her birthday party. Señor Calavera enjoys the party and he leaves without taking Grandma Beetle—but he promises to return for her next birthday party. This book received the Pura Belpré Award for Illustrations as well as an Américas Book Award and the Tomás Rivera Mexican American Children's Book Award.

265 Orgel, Doris, reteller ＊ *The Lion and the Mouse and Other Aesop's Fables*

Illus. by Bert Kitchen ＊ DK, 2000 ＊ 0-7874-2665-X
GREEK, ANCIENT ＊ GRADES 2–5

There are 12 fables in this collection. Some are familiar, such as "The Fox and the Goat," "The Hare and the Tortoise," and the title story. Others are less familiar. The introduction explains who Aesop was and what purpose the fables served. The moral lesson is not stated with each story, which will spur discussion. Readers will want to compare some of these with the stories in *Doctor Coyote*.

266 Stevens, Janet, reteller ＊ *Old Bag of Bones: A Coyote Tale*

Illus. by the reteller ＊ Holiday House, 1996 ＊ 0-8234-1215-6
NATIVE AMERICAN—SHOSHONI ＊ GRADES 2–4

Coyote is old. He asks Young Buffalo to share some of his youth and Young Buffalo agrees. Coyote is transformed into a young buffalo, and is now called "Buffote," but he remains a powerless coyote on the inside. "Buffote" promises to share his youth with Old Rabbit, Old Lizard, and Old Rat. Instead, they all remain old and "Buffote" is back to being Coyote, an old bag of bones.

267 Wormell, Christopher ＊ *Mice, Morals, and Monkey Business: Lively Lessons from Aesop's Fables*

Illus. by the author ＊ Running Press, 2005 ＊ 0-7624-2404-4
GREEK, ANCIENT ＊ GRADES 1–4

Beautiful engravings illustrate these fables from Aesop. Each double-page spread features a moral lesson from a fable and the title of the fable opposite a striking illustration of the moral. The bold lines of the engraving are enhanced with shades of color. For "The Lion and the Mouse," a large lion (shaded in brown, tan, and gold) dominates the page. The small brown mouse in the bottom corner of the illustration stands in front of a gnawed rope, proving that "Little friends may prove great friends." A brief retelling of the fable follows the illustrated collection of morals.

TELLING TRADITIONAL STORIES

Reflections

As an amateur storyteller myself, I find the hunt for the right story the most exciting part of the art. Sometimes I am looking for a particular kind of story to tell, sometimes I just stumble on a tale that seems perfect for telling. Each storyteller must find a satisfying method for learning the story. I dissect the story and learn each section of it as if were a photo in my mind. I can see the elements of each section and talk my way through them. When I'm confident about one section, I move on to the next "photo" and its ingredients. Somehow this method keeps me from being too nervous about remembering all the parts of the story when I am face-to-face with an audience.

Being a storyteller has many rewards. There is nothing like looking into the eyes of the audience and knowing that they are "hanging" on every word. That undivided attention is a thrill! It's as if you can see each person creating an image of what you are describing.

Storytelling is often restricted to children in school and library settings, but I have seen parents and families just as caught up in a story as any group of children. In fact, when telling stories at a Senior Center or a nursing home, the rapt looks of those listeners lets me know that each of them has a storyteller memory that has just been revived. Through storytelling, audiences experience the joy of hearing a tale of history, adventure, exaggeration, or fun through the oral tradition.

—Kathy East

IN MANY CULTURES AROUND THE WORLD, the storyteller is the person entrusted with preserving the meaning of rituals and celebrations. Most of what is known about the origins of many peoples has been handed down through "stories" that have been transcribed and preserved.

When a story is retold and passed on, many things happen. As in the old-fashioned game of telephone—in which one player whispers something to a neighbor, who passes it to another neighbor, and so on until the last person repeats what he or she has heard—storytellers inevitably change the stories they have heard. They add details that connect with their audience. They add characters and events that keep their listeners on the edge of their seats. Storytelling is both fascinating to the listeners and a rewarding experience for the teller.

Here are books that connect with the oral tradition and celebrate the tradition of telling stories. Children can be encouraged to learn stories or to tell stories about their own experiences. They might enjoy interviewing family members and collecting stories. Looking at family photographs—and they don't even have to be photos of your family—could spark a storytelling activity. Use props or puppets—anything to spark the imagination and enhance the performance.

268 Aliki ✶ *Marianthe's Story One: Painted Words; Marianthe's Story Two: Spoken Memories*
Illus. by the author ✶ Greenwillow, 1998 ✶ 0-688-15661-4
Greek American ✶ Grades 1–3

There are two stories in this book. In "Marianthe's Story One: Painted Words," Marianthe is starting school. She is worried because she is new—not only to the school but to America. She does not speak or understand English. Her teacher and classmates welcome her, and Mari adjusts to her classroom. During art time, Mari paints a picture of her family. She is able to communicate through her art. A boy named Patik calls Mari a dummy. Mari's next painting depicts her sadness and the teacher leads the class in a discussion. With each new day, Mari learns more about her new home, the language, and her classmates. Finally, using her drawings, she tells the story that goes with them.

To read the second story, turn the book over and the back cover becomes the front of "Marianthe's Story Two: Spoken Memories." Now Mari knows English well enough to participate in Life-Story Time in Mr. Petrie's class. She describes her childhood and the beauty of her homeland. She shares information about a war that happened before she was born and about the baby brother who died in the famine. Her own childhood was filled with joy. Her parents encouraged her to draw and she rejoiced in the arrival of twin brothers. Mari's parents decided to escape from the poverty of the village and travel to a new country. Papa left first and then the rest of the family joined him. As Mari finishes her story, her classmates are quiet. Her teacher touches her shoulder and says "Welcome to your new life." This book is not a traditional tale, but it has a strong connection to the oral tradition. After reading Mari's two stories, many children will want to share their own stories.

Joseph Bruchac

Joseph Bruchac is an author and storyteller whose work often reflects his Abenaki heritage as well as the customs and beliefs of other Native peoples. He has collections that explore animals, nature, sacred stories, folktales, games, and biographies. He writes poems, novels, and activity books. Librarians and teachers can use his books to encourage storytelling and creative dramatics.

Several of his books focus on months of the year, including *Thirteen Moons on Turtle's Back: A Native American Year of Moons* and *Seasons of the Circle: A Native American Year.* In the introduction to *Seasons of the Circle,* Bruchac suggests two Web sites for learning more about contemporary Native tribal nations. One is the National Museum of the American Indian (www.nmai.si.edu) and the other is Nativeculture.com (www.nativeculture.com). Select the link to Lisa Mitten's Native American Sites to find a list of useful links.

After reading these books, children could suggest their own names for the thirteen moons or describe their activities during the months of the year.

269 Bruchac, Joseph ✳ *Seasons of the Circle*

Illus. by Robert F. Goetzl ✳ BridgeWater, 2002 ✳ 0-8167-7467-6

NATIVE AMERICAN ✳ GRADES 2–5

Each month of the year is accompanied by a description and illustration of the activities of a group of native people. "January. Maliseet hunters follow the tracks of the moose through crusted snow." "November. Havasupai men build a winter home, its door open to the blessing of the rising sun." A note about each tribal nation includes the pronunciation along with details about its traditions, details of which are incorporated into the text and illustrations. For example, the O'odham women are shown weaving beautiful baskets using traditional patterns. There is also a map showing the locations of the tribal nations. The book concludes with examples of "Moon Names" from three tribes.

270 Bruchac, Joseph, and Jonathan London ✳ *Thirteen Moons on Turtle's Back*

Illus. by Thomas Locker ✳ Philomel, 1992 ✳ 0-399-22141-7

NATIVE AMERICAN ✳ GRADES 2–5

An Abenaki grandfather shows his grandson the thirteen "scales" on the turtle's shell and connects this to the thirteen moons that appear each year. Each moon has a story and different native people have different stories for the moons. Grandfather tells a story for each moon. For First Moon, he tells the story from the Northern Cheyenne about the "Moon of Popping Trees." Sixth Moon is the "Strawberry Moon" of the Seneca. Thirteenth Moon is "Big Moon" to the Abenaki. Bruchac and London add a note about the connection between understanding the natural world and survival for native peoples.

271 Lewin, Ted ✶ *The Storytellers*
Illus. by the author ✶ Lothrop, Lee & Shepard, 1998 ✶ 0-688-15179-5
AFRICAN—MOROCCO ✶ GRADES 1–4

Set in ancient Morocco, and richly illustrated in detailed watercolor, this book celebrates the beauty and importance of the "storyteller." Abdul and his grandfather head for the city's gate, where people gather, throw coins on the rug, and lean in to hear Grandfather's exciting and beautifully woven tales.

272 Morris, Ann ✶ *Grandma Lai Goon Remembers: A Chinese-American Family Story*
Photos and illus. by Peter Linenthal ✶ Millbrook Press, 2002 ✶ 0-7613-2314-7
CHINESE AMERICAN ✶ GRADES 2–5

Allyson and Daniel live in San Francisco. Their grandmother, Lai Goon, takes care of them before and after school. She speaks to the children in Chinese. She shows them pictures from her childhood in Dic Hoy, a small village in Canton, China, and she tells them stories about growing up there. She shows them how to write Chinese words, make toys, and play a pebble game. They help her cook *bow*, small dinner rolls made with potato dough. There is a glossary and suggested activities. On the last page, there is a family tree. Part of the series titled What Was It Like, Grandma?

273 Morris, Ann ✶ *Grandma Maxine Remembers: A Native American Family Story*
Photos and illus. by Peter Linenthal ✶ Millbrook Press, 2002 ✶ 0-7613-2317-1
NATIVE AMERICAN—SHOSHONI ✶ GRADES 2–5

Shawnee lives with her family on the Wind River Reservation in Wyoming. Her grandparents live nearby. Photographs show the beauty of the reservation and the activities of Shawnee and her siblings, including feeding the geese, ducks, chickens, and pigs. Shawnee loves to listen to her grandmother, Maxine, tell stories about childhood and the Shoshone people. She explains tribal customs and traditions. A recipe for Fry Bread and directions for making a God's Eye are included. There is a glossary and suggested activities. On the last page, there is a family tree. Part of the What Was It Like, Grandma? series.

274 Muten, Burleigh * *Grandmothers' Stories: Wise Woman Tales from Many Cultures*
Illus. by Sian Bailey * Barefoot Books, 1999 * 1-902283-24-4
MULTICULTURAL * GRADES 1–5

These eight stories represent all corners of the world, from Senegal to Ireland to Hawaii. The "old woman" in this collection refers to the qualities of the wise woman, known for compassion, kindness, and a willingness to work hard. Rich illustrations set the mood and mesmerize the reader.

275 Say, Allen * *Kamishibai Man*
Illus. by the author * Houghton Mifflin, 2005 * 0-618-47954-6
ASIAN—JAPAN * GRADES 1–5

Once upon a time, the storyteller man would arrive on a bicycle with a "Kamishibai" tied on the back—a box theater into which serialized story cards were placed. Many people gathered to experience the stories. However, this once-popular form of entertainment has been supplanted by television and other new technologies. One day, the storyteller returns to the city with his Kamishibai. His performance is received by an appreciative audience of workers who grew up with this storytelling tradition. Exquisite watercolor paintings by Allen Say further involve readers in this story.

CHAPTER FIVE

Exploring the Past in Diverse Communities

IN THIS CHAPTER, THE FOCUS IS ON THE PAST and the entries follow a general chronological order. In the section on Shakespeare, connect his plays to other experiences with theater and performing. Then look at experiences in America—of pioneers and protesters; of slaves and immigrants. Study how quilts and fabric art are used across cultures to depict important events—how quilts connect to the Underground Railroad, for example. The civil rights movement of African Americans connects to the protests led by Cesar Chavez and Nelson Mandela. Discuss the actions of brave men and women who faced prejudice and danger as they reached for freedom and equality. This chapter is filled with connections that encourage readers to explore and understand the impact of people and events in the past.

SHAKESPEARE AND THE THEATER

THE BOOKS FEATURED HERE INCLUDE INFORMATION about Shakespeare as well as about putting on a play. After reading Aliki's *William Shakespeare and the Globe*, look at books that feature his plays, including Mayer's *William Shakespeare's The Tempest* and Davidson's *All the World's a Stage*. Then, just for fun, read Aliki's *A Play's the Thing*. Why not choose a favorite classic book and story to "dramatize?" You might want to search databases and printed resources to see if this story has been done as a play. Or try script writing or reader's theater to bring the story to life.

After reading about Shakespeare, try other dramatic activities. *Pushing Up the Sky* is a collection of Native American plays based on traditional stories. *How and Why Stories for Readers Theaters* provides scripts and suggestions to encourage children to participate and perform.

276 Aliki ✳ *A Play's the Thing*
Illus. by the author ✳ HarperCollins, 2005 ✳ 0-06-074356-5
UNIVERSAL ✳ GRADES 2–4

> In comic-book format, Aliki takes an enthusiastic teacher and a creative class of children and helps them write, produce, and present their own rendition of the traditional "Mary Had a Little Lamb." Everyone has an important part to play. Miss Brilliant is all about spontaneity, interpretation, involvement, inclusion, surprises, and satisfaction as the production becomes meaningful. As a final accolade, the teacher recognizes talent and gives that talent responsibility. This title is the perfect book to share as a class tackles its own drama production. Miss Brilliant is truly inspirational—and brilliant.

277 Aliki ✳ *William Shakespeare and the Globe*
Illus. by the author ✳ HarperCollins, 1999 ✳ 0-06-027821-8
EUROPEAN—ENGLAND ✳ GRADES 3–6

> Aliki sets the tone for learning about the life and talent of William Shakespeare by saying, "Sooner or later, everyone learns that name. It belongs to one of the greatest storytellers who ever lived." Aliki uses five acts to tell her story: Shakespeare's childhood; the setting and

value of plays; theater groups and productions during his lifetime; the establishment of actual theaters in London; and the rebuilding of the famous Globe Theatre in London. The text is punctuated with charming drawings interspersed with quotes from Shakespeare's works. This combination of history, biography, and literature is a glorious feat.

Reflections

The year 2006 marked the 100th anniversary of the Shakespeare Round Table of Bowling Green, Ohio, a group of 20 women who examine two plays a year by William Shakespeare. To celebrate the centennial, we decided to visit the bard's home and theater. The highlight of the trip was a walking tour of Shakespeare's London, giving me an idea of what life was like in Elizabethan England. Walking the narrow streets it was easy to imagine the hustle and bustle of the 16th-century city—the traffic and trading along the river, the housing and water supply, the lack of sewage disposal, and the many everyday tasks. At the Globe Theatre, I felt the intimacy of the surroundings, the juxtaposition of royalty and commoners, and the excitement of hearing the stories presented by writers and actors including Shakespeare and his peers.

Our group attended "In Search of Shakespeare" at the National Portrait Gallery in London. The exhibit's focus was to decide which painting most accurately portrayed the bard (there are no known images of him). There were examples of dress and fabric from the period, archival documents such as marriage certificates, folios, and records of land holdings in Stratford. Later, walking the streets of Stratford-upon-Avon and visiting Anne Hathaway's Cottage, Trinity Church, and Shakespeare's birthplace brought the information from that exhibit to life. The trip was an inspiration to continue learning about the culture and history of the bard and his era.

—Kathy East

278 Bruchac, Joseph ✳ *Pushing Up the Sky: Seven Native American Plays for Children*
Illus. by Teresa Flavin ✳ Dial, 2000 ✳ 0-8037-2168-4
NATIVE AMERICAN ✳ GRADES 2–6

Represented in this collection are plays from the Abenaki, Ojibway, Cherokee, Cheyenne, Snohomish, Tlingit, and Zuni peoples. They feature tricksters and heroes and are filled with action, adventure, and humor. Each play is introduced with an overview about the native people, an identification of the characters, and suggestions for props, scenery, and costumes.

279 Davidson, Rebecca Piatt ✳ *All the World's a Stage*
Illus. by Anita Lobel ✳ Greenwillow, 2003 ✳ 0-06-029626-7
EUROPEAN—ENGLAND ✳ GRADES 4–6

Nine Shakespearean plays are introduced in this colorful picture book. On the left-hand pages, the words follow a pattern (as in "The House That Jack Built") as characters from each of the featured plays are introduced. On the facing page, there are scenes and quotations—"To be, or not to be . . . ," for example. Lobel's knowledge and love of the theater, staging, costumes, and set design add to the beauty of this introduction to these plays. The back of the book has pages highlighting and naming the characters depicted. Also included is a one-sentence summary of each play.

280 Mayer, Marianna ✳ *William Shakespeare's The Tempest*
Illus. by Lynn Bywaters ✳ Chronicle, 2005 ✳ 0-8118-5054-4
EUROPEAN—ENGLAND ✳ ALL AGES

This is a gorgeous prose presentation of the play. The magical tale is told with excitement, making it easy for young readers to become involved in the fate of Prospero, his daughter Miranda, and his magical sprite Ariel. The gouache paintings are magnificent, capturing the darkness of the storms and the beauty of the island landscape. Characters come to life in the words and the pictures. This volume encourages readers to learn more about Shakespeare and then read this play in the original. Follow up by seeing a production of *The Tempest*.

281 Wolfman, Judy ∗ *How and Why Stories for Readers Theatre*
Teachers Idea Press, 2004 ∗ 1-594690-06-5
MULTICULTURAL ∗ PROFESSIONAL

Forty scripts are based on multicultural folktales and Native American legends. Also included are suggestions for organizing and performing Reader's Theater.

282 *The World of Theater: The History of Actors, Singers, Costumes, Audiences, and Scenery*
Scholastic, 1993 ∗ 0-590-47642-4
UNIVERSAL ∗ ALL AGES

Part of the Scholastic Voyages of Discovery Music and Performing Arts series, this spiral-bound book is translated from French. Glossy pages—some with overlays, others with flip-out pages—give a concise history of the theater. Beginning with the ancient world of the Greeks and the Romans and progressing to opera houses, including the one in Sydney, Australia, this is a very appealing overview. The colorful illustrations include drawings, photos, and even some interactive pages with shadow puppets. This is a wonderful introduction to the theater.

PIONEERS AND THE WEST

MANY FORMER SLAVES BECAME PIONEERS, traveling to the West to build new lives as free men and women. Their efforts paralleled those of white settlers—they traveled in wagon trains, claimed land, built cabins, and began new lives. *I Have Heard of a Land* and *A Place Called Freedom* offer a look at the experiences of African American pioneers. *Black Cowboy, Wild Horses* is based on the life of Bob Lemmons, a legendary Texas cowboy. Read these books along with others about pioneers such as *Going West* and *Homesteading*.

Make a timeline of important events in the settlement of the West. Begin perhaps with the Lewis and Clark expedition from 1804 to 1806 and the role of York, a black slave who accompanied Captain William Clark. There are several books about him, including *American Slave, American Hero*. Look at the role of Sacagawea, a Native American who also aided the expedition. Mark the 1832 journey to freedom of the family depicted in *A Place Called Freedom*. Finally, feature the homesteading experiences of the late 1800s and the success of black cowboys such as Bill Pickett and Bob Lemmons.

283 Lester, Julius ✶ *Black Cowboy, Wild Horses: A True Story*
Illus. by Jerry Pinkney ✶ Dial, 1998 ✶ 0-8037-1787-3
AFRICAN AMERICAN ✶ GRADES 2–5

Bob Lemmons (ca. 1847–1947) was a former slave who became a cowboy in Texas. In this book, the author presents a fictionalized account of a hunt for wild mustangs. Riding Warrior, his black stallion, Lemmons follows the tracks until he catches up with the herd. He and Warrior mingle with the herd and then take it over. Now the mustangs follow Bob Lemmons across the plains to a corral. Jerry Pinkney's detailed illustrations convey the dramatic beauty of the wild mustangs and the western landscape.

284 Patent, Dorothy Hinshaw * *Homesteading: Settling America's Heartland*

Photographs by William Muñoz * Walker and Co., 1998 * 0-8027-8664-2

EUROPEAN AMERICAN * GRADES 3–6

The Homestead Act of 1862 opened the American prairie to settlers. The act allowed citizens to pay a small fee and claim 160 acres of land. The homesteaders had to grow crops, build a home, and, within five years, create an established farm. This book is illustrated with photographs of museums and re-created homesteads. There is information about building a home, survival, everyday life, schools, and recreation. A related book is *West by Covered Wagon: Retracing the Pioneer Trails* (Walker and Co., 1995).

285 Pinkney, Andrea D. * *Bill Pickett: Rodeo-Ridin' Cowboy*

Illus. by Brian Pinkney * Harcourt, 1996 * 0-15-200133-X

AFRICAN AMERICAN * GRADES 1–4

Willie M. Pickett (1871–1932) was the son of a former slave. Growing up in Texas, Bill watched the cowboys as they drove herds of cattle to the stockyards. At age 15, he worked as a cowhand and learned to lasso, ride, and bulldog. He became so skilled that he performed at rodeos throughout the West. After he married, he continued to travel and perform, returning home with tales of his success. Although many rodeo owners were against having a black cowboy performing for them, the Miller brothers knew he was a star attraction and hired him for their rodeo. Bill traveled around the world with the show until he decided to return home and work as a cowhand. Brian Pinkney's signature scratchboard illustrations show the energy and movement of a rodeo.

286 Pringle, Laurence ✳ *American Slave, American Hero: York of the Lewis and Clark Expedition*
Illus. by Cornelius Van Wright and Ying-Hwa Hu ✳ Calkins Creek
  Books, 2006 ✳ 1-590782-82-8
AFRICAN AMERICAN ✳ GRADES 3–5

This biography blends both information and speculation about the
life of York, a slave who participated in the 1804 expedition of Lewis
and Clark. The author documents information about the era and the
expedition while providing insights into what may have happened in
York's life. The author makes clear that very little is known about
York's personal life. The watercolor illustrations add to the drama of
the events on the expedition.

287 Sanders, Scott Russell ✳ *A Place Called Freedom*
Illus. by Thomas B. Allen ✳ Atheneum, 1997 ✳ 0-689-80470-9
AFRICAN AMERICAN ✳ GRADES 1–3

In 1832, young James Starman, 7, and his family were given their
freedom. They left the plantation in Tennessee and walked to Indiana where they worked to earn enough to buy land. Papa would
return to Tennessee to help other relatives reach freedom. Soon
there was a settlement of African Americans, with a church, a store, a
stable, and a mill. When the railroad built tracks through the village,
Mama and Papa named the village Freedom. A school was built and
the final page shows the young narrator writing.

288 Thomas, Joyce Carol ✳ *I Have Heard of a Land*
Illus. by Floyd Cooper ✳ HarperCollins, 1998 ✳ 0-06-023477-6
AFRICAN AMERICAN ✳ GRADES 2–5

A woman narrator describes the beauty and importance of staking a
claim, homesteading, and, finally, owning the land. In the Oklahoma
Territory in the late 1800s, many pioneers rushed to claim "free"

land. These pioneers included many former slaves. This poetic text repeats the phrase "I have heard of a land" while describing the hardships and hope of freedom and land ownership. Floyd Cooper uses muted shades of beige and brown to depict the pioneers. An Author's Note explains Thomas's personal connection to this story. *I Have Heard of a Land* was a Coretta Scott King Illustrator Honor Award.

289 Van Leeuwen, Jean ✳ *Going West*
Illus. by Thomas B. Allen ✳ Dial, 1992 ✳ 0-8037-1027-5
EUROPEAN AMERICAN ✳ GRADES 1–3

It is spring and the family is preparing for the long journey west in their covered wagon. Papa, Mama, Hannah (the narrator), Jake, and baby Rebecca are filling the wagon with essentials and saying goodbye to family and friends. They are traveling alone, not as part of a group of wagons and they face many challenges, including storms and crossing rivers. Finally, they reach the land they have been looking for. Papa and Mama build a house; they plant a garden, and adjust to their isolated home.

THE UNDERGROUND RAILROAD

IT IS IMPORTANT FOR CHILDREN TO UNDERSTAND and analyze significant events in history. They can compare the daily life of people in the past with that of the present. They can examine the impact of conflicts, such as slavery and the Civil War.

Many children are confused about the Underground Railroad. Was it a long tunnel? Was it really a train? Books such as *Freedom River*, *Night Boat to Freedom*, and *A Good Night for Freedom* will help them explore the people who assisted escaping slaves and the successful strategies employed. Raymond Bial's *The Underground Railroad* is a nonfiction book that provides historical documents and artifacts of this era. Reading about slavery in the United States can lead to a discussion of the slave trade. *The Village That Vanished* describes the experiences of one African village. Readers will see how these experiences paralleled those of the escaping slaves in America.

After exploring these resources, children can research the courageous people who took risks to help others, including Harriet Tubman and Levi Coffin. Visit the Web site of the National Underground Railroad Freedom Center at www.freedomcenter.org and select Speak, Listen, and Learn and then Underground Railroad to find a Timeline, along with information about People and Places.

290 Bial, Raymond ∗ *The Underground Railroad*
Illus. with photographs by the author and archival reproductions ∗
Houghton Mifflin, 1995 ∗ 0-395-69937-1
AFRICAN AMERICAN ∗ GRADES 3–5

> Readers seeking background information on the Underground Railroad will want to use this book. There are details about the laws regarding runaways, "conductors" like Harriet Tubman, "stationmasters" like Levi Coffin, and the hardships that escaping slaves had to endure. Photographs of wanted posters, slave auctions, safe houses, and more make this an excellent source for research.

291 Grifalconi, Ann * *The Village That Vanished*
Illus. by Kadir Nelson * Dial, 2002 * 0-8037-2623-6
AFRICAN—YAO * GRADES 3–6

The people of the African village of Yao know that the slave traders
are coming closer. Many of the men from the village have already
been captured. A young girl, Abikanile, worries that the slave traders
will return and take more people from her village. Her mother,
Njemile, has a plan. Njemile tells the people of the village that they
must disappear and take all evidence of their village with them. So,
stick by stick and stone by stone, they dismantle the village and walk
deep into the surrounding forest. Only Chimwala, Abikanile's grandmother, remains behind in her hut. The slave traders come and find
only one old woman, so they leave to look elsewhere.

292 Morrow, Barbara Olenyik * *A Good Night for Freedom*
Illus. by Leonard Jenkins * Holiday House, 2004 * 0-8234-1709-3
AFRICAN AMERICAN * GRADES 3–5

Hallie knows that Aunt Katy and Mr. Levi Coffin help runaway
slaves. She saw two girls hiding in the basement of the Coffins'
house. Hallie's father tells her not to meddle; Mr. Coffin talks about
following your conscience. When the slave catchers come to the
Coffins' house, Hallie makes a brave decision. An Author's Note
explains that this was based on historical facts about the home and
activities of Levi and Catherine Coffin in Fountain City (formerly
Newport), Indiana.

293 Rappaport, Doreen * *Freedom River*
Illus. by Bryan Collier * Hyperion, 2000 * 0-7868-0350-9
AFRICAN AMERICAN * GRADES 3–5

In Ripley, Ohio, John Parker assists escaping slaves. Parker was born a
slave and bought his own freedom. *Freedom River* describes the dangers he faced traveling back to Kentucky, a slave state, to escort
escaping slaves to the free state of Ohio. A historical Note provides
more biographical details. Parker's house in Ripley is now a museum.
Freedom River was a Coretta Scott King Illustrator Honor Award.

294 Raven, Margot Theis ✳ *Night Boat to Freedom*
Illus. by E. B. Lewis ✳ Farrar, Straus and Giroux, 2006 ✳ 0-374-31266-4
AFRICAN AMERICAN ✳ GRADES 5–6+

In the 1860s Granny has her 12-year-old grandson, Christmas John, row many passengers across the river from Kentucky to freedom in Ohio. Each night her question is, "What color is freedom?" Granny dyes thread and weaves cloth. She is making a quilt to honor the color of freedom. After many dangerous trips, John sees Granny's quilt as a rainbow bridge. Granny says when only two squares remain, their work will be done. Of course, those last squares represent the two of them. The tender text and rich watercolor artwork give a sense of the hard work and dangerous risks taken by those involved in the Underground Railroad. The story is laced with fascinating tidbits, such as Granny tying pouches filled with ground turnip around John's feet to protect him from the bloodhounds often roaming the river banks.

There are many other books about the Underground Railroad; consider using these:

295 Brill, Marlene Targ ✳ *Allen Jay and the Underground Railroad*
Illus. by Janice Lee Porter ✳ Carolrhoda, 1993 ✳ 0-87614-776-7
AFRICAN AMERICAN ✳ GRADES 3–5

A Quaker family provides help to runaway slaves. This book is based on actual events.

296 Edwards, Pamela Duncan ✳ *Barefoot: Escape on the Underground Railroad*
Illus. by Henry Cole ✳ HarperCollins, 1997 ✳ 0-06-027137-X
AFRICAN AMERICAN ✳ GRADES 3–5

An escaping slave is running through the night. The natural behaviors of the creatures of the forest help the runaway; for example, the croaking of a frog helps him find fresh water.

297 Lawrence, Jakob ✴ *Harriet and the Promised Land*
Illus. by the author ✴ Simon & Schuster, 1993 ✴ 0-671-86673-7
AFRICAN AMERICAN ✴ GRADES 3–5

A rhythmic text describes the bravery of Harriet Tubman. Inspiring paintings by the author accompany the text.

298 Ringgold, Faith ✴ *Aunt Harriet's Underground Railroad in the Sky*
Illus. by the author ✴ Crown, 1992 ✴ 0-517-58767-X
AFRICAN AMERICAN ✴ GRADES 3–5

This book uses a fantasy premise to provide information about Harriet Tubman. Cassie and Be Be fly into the sky and see Harriet Tubman conducting a train in the sky. Be Be rides the train but Cassie goes through the experiences of a runaway slave.

299 Winter, Jeanette ✴ *Follow the Drinking Gourd*
Illus. by the author ✴ Knopf, 1988 ✴ 0-394-89694-7
AFRICAN AMERICAN ✴ GRADES 3–5

An old sailor named Peg Leg Joe moves from plantation to plantation telling stories that provide information to slaves planning to escape along the Underground Railroad.

300 Wright, Courtni C. ✴ *Journey to Freedom: A Story of the Underground Railroad*
Illus. by Gershom Griffith ✴ Holiday House, 1994 ✴ 0-8234-1096-X
AFRICAN AMERICAN ✴ GRADES 3–5

Harriet Tubman leads a family of escaping slaves from Kentucky to Canada.

QUILTS AND FABRIC

MANY BOOKS FEATURE THE IMPORTANCE OF QUILTS in story-telling. Books such as *Show Way, Sweet Clara and the Freedom Quilt,* and *Under the Quilt of Night* focus on the experiences of African Americans in the years before and during the Civil War.

In Southeast Asia, the Hmong also tell stories with fabric designs. *The Whispering Cloth* describes the experiences of a Hmong refugee from Laos who is living in a camp in Thailand. *Dia's Story Cloth* is a similar story of refugees in Southeast Asia that also uses the design of a Hmong story cloth in the illustrations.

Using color and designs to represent events and emotions is also part of African traditions. *The Talking Cloth* and *The Spider Weaver* describe the symbolism in *adinkra* and *kente* cloth. *Fatuma's New Cloth* is another African story that connects.

All of these books could lead to activities with sewing—making cloth art that uses symbols, colors, and other design elements to communicate ideas and emotions.

301 Bulion, Leslie * *Fatuma's New Cloth*
Illus. by Nicole Tadgell * Moon Mountain Publishing, 2002 *
   0-9677929-7-5
AFRICAN—EAST AFRICA * GRADES 2–4

Set in modern-day East Africa, a mother and daughter visit the village market. Fatuma carries the empty basket for her mother as they walk. They plan to choose a new *kanga* cloth for Fatuma, then go home for cups of *chai* (tea). As they walk through the market, vendors call out to them. Each has something to sell to make the best chai. But Mama and Fatuma continue to the kanga shop where they pick a beautiful new cloth. On the cloth are the words "Don't be fooled by the color. The good flavor of chai comes from the sugar." Fatuma realizes that you can't see the sugar, it's inside and she learns that this is true for her as well. What is good about her is on the inside. An explanation of the bright cotton kanga cloth and a recipe for East African chai are also included at the end of the book.

302 Cha, Dia * *Dia's Story Cloth*
Stitched by Chue Cha and Nhia Thao Cha * Lee and Low, 1996 *
  1-880000-34-2
ASIAN—HMONG * GRADES 3–6

The author's aunt and uncle sent her a beautifully embroidered
cloth depicting their experiences as refugees in Thailand. Using
details from the story cloth, the author describes the experiences of
life in a refugee camp and the reasons why the Hmong people have
been displaced. A double-page spread in the middle of the book
shows the completed story cloth. Other illustrations are photographs
of smaller areas of the cloth. An Afterword describes the Hmong
people and their heritage.

303 Hopkinson, Deborah * *Sweet Clara and the Freedom Quilt*
Illus. by James E. Ransome * Knopf, 1993 * 0-679-82311-5
AFRICAN AMERICAN * GRADES 2–4

As a child, Clara was separated from her Momma and sent to work
in the fields on another plantation. She dreams about being reunited
with Momma. At the new plantation, an older woman called Aunt
Rachel teaches Clara to be a seamstress and she takes Clara to the Big
House to sew items for Missus and her daughter. In the Big House,
Clara overhears comments about runaways and maps. She realizes
that she could sew geographical details into a quilt. She begins talking to people in the Quarters and learning about the surrounding
area. When the quilt is finished, Clara leaves it on the plantation for
others to use; she has the memory of it in her head. She escapes with
Jack, another slave, and they travel to North Farm to get Momma
and Anna, Clara's little sister. Together, they travel to freedom. This
book also connects to the section on the Underground Railroad.

304 Hopkinson, Deborah * *Under the Quilt of Night*
Illus. by James E. Ransome * Atheneum, 2001 * 0-698-82227-8
AFRICAN AMERICAN * GRADES 2–4

A young girl runs north, escaping the cruelty of the slave master.
During the day, it is too dangerous to travel. At night, moving

through the darkness, she uses the stars and moon to guide her. Along the way, there are signs from those who want to help, including a quilt with deep blue squares that indicate a "safe" house. This book also connects with the section on the Underground Railroad.

305 Mitchell, Rhonda ✳ *The Talking Cloth*
Illus. by the author ✳ Orchard Books, 1997 ✳ 0-531-30004-8
AFRICAN AMERICAN; AFRICAN—GHANA—ASHANTI ✳ GRADES 2–4

Amber loves the many items her Aunt Phoebe has collected. Aunt Phoebe shows an adinkra cloth from the Ashanti people in Ghana. Aunt Phoebe explains the symbolism of the colors and designs, giving Amber a sense of pride in her African heritage.

306 Musgrove, Margaret ✳ *The Spider Weaver: A Legend of Kente Cloth*
Illus. by Julia Cairns ✳ Scholastic, 2001 ✳ 0-590-98787-9
AFRICAN—GHANA—ASHANTI ✳ GRADES 2–4

In Bonwire, an Ashanti village in Ghana, two men weave simple cloth for the people to wear. One night in the jungle, they discover a beautiful spider web but when they try to move it, it is destroyed. They decide to go back to the jungle and look for the spider that wove the web. Finding her, the men watch her and she teaches them how to create beautiful designs. They return to their village and begin to weave, creating cloth with colorful patterns. This kente cloth is still worn today. An Afterword describes the roots of this story and the importance of many of the patterns that are used in kente cloth.

307 Shea, Pegi Deitz ✳ *The Whispering Cloth: A Refugee's Story*
Illus. by Anita Riggio; stitched by You Yang ✳ Boyds Mills, 1995 ✳
1-56397-134-8
ASIAN—HMONG ✳ GRADES 3–6

Young Mai lives in a refugee camp in Thailand. She sits at the Widows' Store listening to Grandma and the other women tell stories while they sew *pa'ndau* story cloths. Mai learns how to create a cloth, making a beautiful design and then embroidering with careful stitches. Each pa'ndau tells a story, and Mai begins to create a beautiful story cloth that tells of her family. Her parents are gone, killed along with many Hmong people. Mai and her grandmother escape the violence but spend many years in the refugee camps. In her story cloth, Mai stitches her dream that they will fly away from the camp, join her cousins, and be safe. Mai realizes that she will not sell this cloth.

308 Woodson, Jacqueline ✴ *Show Way*
Illus. by Hudson Talbott ✴ Putnam, 2005 ✴ 0-399-23749-6
AFRICAN AMERICAN ✴ GRADES 3–5

A "Show Way" is a quilt designed to feature geographical elements and serve as a map for escaping slaves. This book focuses on generations of women in the author's family and describes the challenges they faced and the courage they displayed. The book begins with slaves helping each other to freedom and follows through the civil rights movement and concludes with images of the author and her daughter. Beautiful multimedia illustrations, which often feature a patchwork quilt motif, accompany this powerful tribute. *Show Way* was a Newbery Honor Book in 2006.

IMMIGRATION

WHAT WAS IT LIKE TO LEAVE YOUR HOME and journey to America? Why did so many people make this trip? What were the sacrifices and risks? What were the rewards? The books in this section explore the immigration experiences of people from diverse backgrounds—Chinese, Polish, Japanese, Russian, Italian, Irish, and more. They describe the emotional impact of arriving in America with few resources and a limited knowledge of English. They also explore the pride many immigrants came to feel for their new homeland.

There are books on this list that are part of the 2005–2006 We the People Bookshelf on Becoming American. Through a cooperative program between the American Library Association and the National Endowment for the Humanities, libraries across the country can receive free copies of books, a bookshelf as it were, on specific topics. In 2006, NEH Chairman Bruce Cole said, "The We the People Bookshelf reveals the many and varied influences that have shaped our nation's history and culture. These classics also provide another powerful lesson: that there are traits and values shared by all those who, by birth or choice, become American." Titles below marked with a 📖 were included in the 2005–2006 bookshelf. The others are appropriate for the subject.

A boxed section lists all We the People Bookshelf selections.

Picture Books

309 Bunting, Eve ✳ *A Picnic in October*
Illus. by Nancy Carpenter ✳ Harcourt Brace, 1999 ✳ 0-15-201656-2
ITALIAN AMERICAN ✳ GRADES 1–3

> This modern-day tale describes one family's annual October trip to Liberty Island, the home of the Statue of Liberty, to have a picnic. Tony has always thought the whole ritual was rather dumb. Singing "Happy Birthday" to Lady Liberty was embarrassing. Then he notices an immigrant family he had encountered earlier looking up with joy at the statue and it hits him. He realizes what it means to them and to his Italian grandmother to be in America.

310 ✎ **Garland, Sherry** ✳ *The Lotus Seed*
Illus. by Tatsuro Kiuchi ✳ Harcourt Brace Jovanovich, 1993 ✳ 0-15-249465-0
Vietnamese American ✳ Grades K–3

A young Vietnamese American girl describes the importance of a lotus flower to the people of Vietnam and to her family in the United States. When her grandmother was a young girl in Vietnam, she took a lotus seed from the garden of the emperor and brought it with her to America as she escaped the destruction of the war. Now the flower symbolizes the family's heritage as well as their hope for the future.

311 Lee, Milly ✳ *Landed*
Illus. by Yangsook Choi ✳ Farrar, Straus and Giroux, 2006 ✳ 0-374-34314-4
Chinese American ✳ Grades 4–6

Twelve-year old Sun is coming to America, planning to arrive at Angel Island in San Francisco harbor. Because of the 1882 Chinese Exclusion Act, he knows he must pass a difficult test to be admitted. He studies and memorizes facts about his family, his village, and so forth. Traveling with his father, who already has a store in San Francisco, Sun has been warned that he might be detained for days or even weeks while his father would be allowed to disembark. After several interrogations he is permitted to enter the country. He is met at the waterfront by his father and three grown men he hardly recognizes. They are his brothers, who made the same journey when they were 12. The story is based on the experiences of the author's father-in-law.

312 Levinson, Riki ✳ *Soon, Annala*
Illus. by Julie Downing ✳ Orchard, 1993 ✳ 0-531-08644-5
Polish American ✳ Grades K–3

In this sequel to *Watch the Stars Come Out*, Anna Sarah anticipates the arrival from Poland of her two younger brothers. She has been in America for nearly a year and she is eager to share her knowledge of her new country. When her brothers finally arrive, they are given their first lesson in English by their proud big sister.

313 📘 Levinson, Riki ✳ *Watch the Stars Come Out*
Illus. by Diane Goode ✳ Dutton, 1985 ✳ 0-525-44205-7
POLISH AMERICAN ✳ GRADES K–3

The young narrator of this book remembers the stories she has heard from her grandmother about the family's journey to America. Although this is a brief account, the story is just enough for a young child to understand what "immigrating to another country" might mean. The joy of being reunited as a family is enhanced by the satisfaction of being "connected" by knowing that wherever you are you can watch the stars come out.

314 📘 Say, Allen ✳ *Grandfather's Journey*
Illus. by the author ✳ Houghton Mifflin, 1993 ✳ 0-395-57035-2
JAPANESE AMERICAN ✳ GRADES K–3

This Caldecott-winning book recounts the simple yet poignant experience of a Japanese immigrant to America as told by his grandson. As a young man, Grandfather loved all the things he saw and experienced in the New World but still longed for what he remembered of his homeland. Yet, when he returned to Japan, he missed America. Beautiful watercolor paintings add to the family history feeling of this tender reflection on loving two countries.

315 Woodruff, Elvira ✳ *The Memory Coat*
Illus. by Michael Dooling ✳ Scholastic, 1999 ✳ 0-590-67717-9
RUSSIAN AMERICAN ✳ GRADES K–3

A young Russian girl, Rachel, and her orphaned cousin, Grisha, make the treacherous journey to America. Their story focuses on the fear at the inspection station at Ellis Island. They know almost anything could cause them to be rejected and sent back to the old country. When Grisha doesn't pass inspection because of an injury to his eye, Rachel cleverly gets him to turn his coat inside out and leads him to a different line with a kinder inspector who recognizes the eye injury as just a scratch. The story of the tattered coat and the love associated with it has been passed on to every succeeding generation.

Novels

316 📖 Lord, Bette Bao ∗ *In the Year of the Boar and Jackie Robinson*
Illus. by Marc Simont ∗ HarperCollins, 1984 ∗ 0-06-440175-8
Chinese American ∗ Grades 4–6

Shirley Temple Wong migrates from China to Brooklyn, New York, arriving in 1947. She is overwhelmed by her new land and has a hard time learning English and making friends. Then she finds out about baseball and the player Jackie Robinson. Shirley's teacher combines lessons on immigration, integration, social issues, and baseball to assist her students and help Shirley understand her new country. This humorous tale teaches many lessons and opens the door for open discussion.

317 Moss, Marissa ∗ *Hannah's Journal: The Story of an Immigrant Girl*
Illus. ∗ Scholastic, 2000 ∗ 0-439-31233-7
Russian American ∗ Grades 3–6+

This work of fiction is based on the stories of the author's family as they migrated from Russia to America, coming past the Statue of Liberty and through Ellis Island. The conditions in Russia that forced the decision to make the difficult journey are described. In America, the family is motivated to get jobs, learn English, and save their money so other members of the family will be able to join them. This book is designed to look like a hand-written journal on a lined yellow pad, with drawings, doodles, and Yiddish sayings that add to the charm of the story. Readers may want to read some of the other journals by Moss including *Rachel's Journal: The Story of a Pioneer Girl* and *Emma's Journal: The Story of a Colonial Girl*.

WE THE PEOPLE BOOKSHELF

The We the People Bookshelf is a cooperative effort from the National Endowment for the Humanities and the American Library Association Public Programs Office. According to the ALA Web site (www.ala.org/wethepeople), this initiative was established "to encourage young people to read and understand great literature while exploring themes in American history."

Libraries that wish to participate in this program must complete a grant application that is available on the Web site. Libraries that are selected to receive the Bookshelf must plan programs to use the books with young people in the community.

In 2006–2007, the theme was "Pursuit of Happiness"; in 2005–2006, the theme was "Becoming American," which connects with the experience of immigrants; in 2004–2005, the theme was "Freedom"; and in 2003–2004, it was "Courage." Many of the titles that have been selected for these Bookshelf themes reflect diverse experiences.

Here is a complete list of the We the People Bookshelf titles:

2006–2007: Pursuit of Happiness

Grades K–3
Aesop's Fables by Aesop
Mike Mulligan and His Steam Shovel by Virginia Lee Burton
Mike Mulligan y su máquina maravillosa by Virginia Lee Burton (translated by Yanitzia Canetti)
Stopping by Woods on a Snowy Evening by Robert Frost

Grades 4–6
Tuck Everlasting by Natalie Babbitt
Tuck para siempre by Natalie Babbitt (translated by Narcis Fradera)
The Great Migration by Jacob Lawrence

These Happy Golden Years by Laura Ingalls Wilder

Journal of Wong Ming-Chung by Laurence Yep

Grades 7-8

Carry On, Mr. Bowditch by Jean Lee Latham

A Wrinkle in Time by Madeleine L'Engle

Esperanza Rising by Pam Muñoz Ryan

Esperanza renace by Pam Muñoz Ryan (translated by Nuria Molinero)

Grades 9-12

Kindred by Octavia Butler

O Pioneers! by Willa Cather

Pioneros by Willa Cather (translated by Gema Moral Bartolomé)

The Great Gatsby by F. Scott Fitzgerald

Common Sense by Thomas Paine

Leaves of Grass by Walt Whitman

Bonus CD

Happy Land: Musical Tributes to Laura Ingalls Wilder performed by various artists

2005-2006: Becoming American

Grades K-3

The Lotus Seed by Sherry Garland

Watch the Stars Come Out by Riki Levinson

Grandfather's Journey by Allen Say

Grades 4-6

Immigrant Kids by Russell Freedman

The People Could Fly: African Black Folktales by Virginia Hamilton

Rip Van Winkle by Washington Irving

In the Year of the Boar and Jackie Robinson by Betty Bao Lord

Grades 7–8

Rifles for Watie by Harold Keith
The Glory Field by Walter Dean Myers
A Tree Grows in Brooklyn by Betty Smith
Dragonwings by Laurence Yep

Grades 9–12

Death Comes for the Archbishop by Willa Cather
Autobiography of Benjamin Franklin edited by Louis P. Masur
Barrio Boy by Ernesto Galarza
Giants in the Earth: A Saga of the Prairie by Ole Edvart
   Rølvaag

2004–2005: Freedom

Grades K–3

Sam the Minuteman by Nathaniel Benchley
The Girl Who Loved Wild Horses by Paul Goble
Paul Revere's Ride by Henry Wadsworth Longfellow
The Tale of Peter Rabbit by Beatrix Potter

Grades 4–6

The House of Dies Drear by Virginia Hamilton
Ben and Me by Robert Lawson
To Be a Slave by Julius Lester
The Complete Chronicles of Narnia by C. S. Lewis

Grades 7–8

Fahrenheit 451 by Ray Bradbury
Across Five Aprils by Irene Hunt
The Witch of Blackbird Pond by Elizabeth George Speare

Grades 9–12

Miracle at Philadelphia by Catherine Drinker Bowen
My Ántonia by Willa Cather
Animal Farm and *1984* by George Orwell
One Day in the Life of Ivan Denisovich by Alexander
Solzhenitsyn

2003–2004: Courage

Grades K–3

The Cabin Faced West by Jean Fritz
Anansi the Spider by Gerald McDermott
Sylvester and the Magic Pebble by William Steig

Grades 4–6

The Matchlock Gun by Walter D. Edmonds
My Side of the Mountain by Jean Craighead George
The Dream Keeper and Other Poems by Langston Hughes
Little House on the Prairie by Laura Ingalls Wilder

Grades 7–8

Narrative of the Life of Frederick Douglass by Frederick
Douglass
Johnny Tremain by Esther Forbes
The Hobbit by J. R. R. Tolkein

Grades 9–12

The Red Badge of Courage by Stephen Crane
Invisible Man by Ralph Ellison
Profiles in Courage by John F. Kennedy
To Kill a Mockingbird by Harper Lee
Adventures of Huckleberry Finn by Mark Twain

318 Russell, Barbara Timberlake ✳ *Maggie's Amerikay*
Illus. by Jim Burke ✳ Farrar, Straus and Giroux, 2006 ✳ 0-374-34722-0
IRISH AMERICAN ✳ GRADES 3–6

Maggie McCrary and her family have come from Ireland to settle in New Orleans in 1898. Their new life is difficult—the baby is sick and Mother can't work. Maggie wants to help the family even though her father says the reason he brought her to this new land was so she could get a good education. Maggie is able to earn money by listening to and writing down the stories of Daddy Clements, a black man who describes his life story—beginning in Africa where he was captured and forced to come to America and following through his years as a slave and later as a free man. Maggie and Daddy Clements see a connection in their stories, both having experienced hardships and finding joy from music in their lives.

Nonfiction

319 🗎 Freedman, Russell ✳ *Immigrant Kids*
Illus. with photographs ✳ Dutton, 1980 ✳ 0-525-32538-7
EUROPEAN AMERICAN ✳ GRADES 3–6+

Sepia historical photographs chronicle the lives of children arriving in the United States from Europe and being quickly transferred, along with their parents, to Ellis Island. Many poor families lived in tenements in New York City and other major cities, where they believed they would find jobs. There are pictures of children in overcrowded two- and three-room apartments; trying to play on the fire escapes, rooftops, and in the streets; attending school and learning trades; and taking jobs to help their families. These "new" Americans demonstrated the hope and promise of this New World country.

320 Hoobler, Dorothy and Thomas ✳ *We Are Americans: Voices of the Immigrant Experience*
Illus. ✳ Scholastic, 2003 ✳ 0-439-16297-1
MULTICULTURAL ✳ GRADES 5–6+

This thorough history of immigration begins with the premise that all Americans are immigrants or descendants of immigrants. Beginning with the crossing of the ice barrier in prehistoric times to the constant flood of people seeking a new country even today, readers find stories of what is described as the "push factor" and for America, the "pull factor." Included are historical photographs, paintings, documents, and boxes of compelling personal tales.

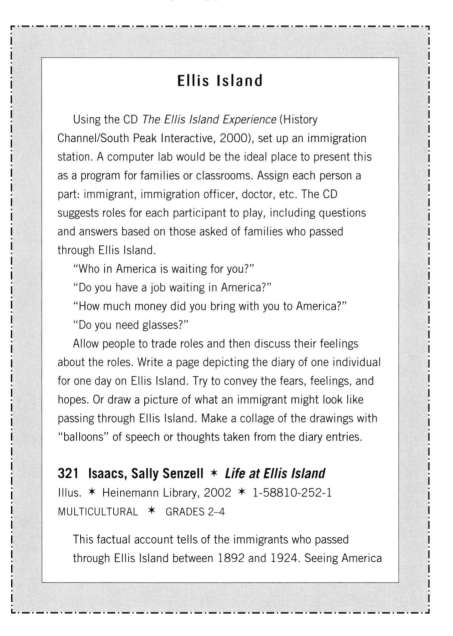

Ellis Island

Using the CD *The Ellis Island Experience* (History Channel/South Peak Interactive, 2000), set up an immigration station. A computer lab would be the ideal place to present this as a program for families or classrooms. Assign each person a part: immigrant, immigration officer, doctor, etc. The CD suggests roles for each participant to play, including questions and answers based on those asked of families who passed through Ellis Island.

"Who in America is waiting for you?"
"Do you have a job waiting in America?"
"How much money did you bring with you to America?"
"Do you need glasses?"

Allow people to trade roles and then discuss their feelings about the roles. Write a page depicting the diary of one individual for one day on Ellis Island. Try to convey the fears, feelings, and hopes. Or draw a picture of what an immigrant might look like passing through Ellis Island. Make a collage of the drawings with "balloons" of speech or thoughts taken from the diary entries.

321 Isaacs, Sally Senzell ✳ *Life at Ellis Island*
Illus. ✳ Heinemann Library, 2002 ✳ 1-58810-252-1
MULTICULTURAL ✳ GRADES 2–4

This factual account tells of the immigrants who passed through Ellis Island between 1892 and 1924. Seeing America as the land of plenty, people left their homes and journeyed, often under very poor conditions, to be accepted or rejected by the inspectors on Ellis Island. Maps, graphs, photographs, and drawings illustrate the conditions on the ships, the waiting and fears while detained on the island, the anxiety of separation from family and homeland, the difficulties of not knowing the language, and the jobs and lifestyle available to these immigrants.

322 Quiri, Patricia Ryon ✶ *Ellis Island*

Illus. with photographs ✶ Children's Press, 1998 ✶ 0-516-20622-2
MULTICULTURAL ✶ GRADES 2–4

This early reader describes with words and photographs the history of Ellis Island and the way it served as a gateway for millions of people to enter the United States. In less than 50 pages, the reader gains insight into the experience of immigration through this island in New York Harbor.

323 Raatma, Lucia ✶ *Ellis Island*

Illus. ✶ Compass Point Books, 2003 ✶ 0-7565-0302-7
MULTICULTURAL ✶ GRADES 4–6

Although the majority of this book describes the immigration center known as Ellis Island as it appeared and worked in the early 1900s, the book also describes the continued connections of this island with immigration into the United States. With the start of World War I, the rules were made much harder and limits were set for the numbers of people from individual countries. In 1945 the immigration station was closed. In the 1960s the island was designated an historical park and the buildings were restored to house a museum.

324 Strom, Yale * *Quilted Landscape: Conversations with Young Immigrants*
Illus. with photographs * Simon & Schuster, 1996 * 0-689-80074-6
MULTICULTURAL * GRADES 4–6+

Readers meet 26 young immigrants to the United States during the 1990s, learning briefly about their countries of origin and about each person's life in the United States through their words and photos. The honesty of their expectations, experiences, and goals for themselves is very revealing. Readers quickly reflect on their own lives and appreciate what they have.

325 Testa, Maria * *Something About America*
Candlewick, 2005 * 0-7636-2528-0
YUGOSLAV AMERICAN * GRADES 4–6+

This series of poems tells of a young Yugoslav family's shattered dreams and flight from Kosovo to America. Settling in in the new country is easiest for the young girl writing the poems. When the war at home is over, she fears her family will want to return, especially after an ugly incident in Lewiston in which protesters say there are too many people coming into their town! Her father's efforts to lead a rally make her proud and prompt her to a saying of her own, "If you can't find the welcome mat when you arrive, put one out yourself." This sensitive collection will be most appreciated by older readers and writers of poetry in particular.

FLIGHT

ANGELA JOHNSON'S NEW PICTURE BOOK *Wind Flyers* celebrates the spirit of a man who loved to fly and who served as a member of the Tuskegee Airmen. The poetic language and Loren Long's rich acrylic paintings take the reader on a soaring journey where childhood dreams become reality. Pair this with a nonfiction book about the Tuskegee Airmen to extend the reader's understanding of the history of these soldiers. Then look at other books that celebrate flight and flying, such as Chris Demarest's book about Charles Lindbergh.

The African American men who served in the Tuskegee Airmen faced many prejudices. So did many women. Elizabeth "Bessie" Coleman had to overcome a series of obstacles as she tried to achieve her dream of being a pilot. *Talkin' About Bessie* is a unique book that combines historical information with imagined monologues to provide insights into the life of this intrepid woman. Books about other female flyers, including David Adler's biography of Amelia Earhart and Julie Cummins's book about Blanche Stuart Scott, will add to the study of those who triumphed over adversity.

326 Adler, David A. ✳ *A Picture Book of Amelia Earhart*
Illus. by Jeff Fisher ✳ Holiday House, 1998 ✳ 0-8234-1315-2
EUROPEAN AMERICAN ✳ GRADES 1–3

> Amelia Earhart was a pioneer. In an era where women were limited in their opportunities, she challenged the barriers and is best known for her achievements as a pilot, including being the first woman to fly solo across the Atlantic Ocean. Her disappearance on a flight around the world is described.

327 Brooks, Philip ✳ *The Tuskegee Airmen: African American Pilots of World War II*
Compass Point, 2005 ✳ 0-7565-0683-2
AFRICAN AMERICAN ✳ GRADES 3–5

> This nonfiction book provides information about the Tuskegee Airmen. Although many African Americans were accomplished pilots, the segregated military allowed them no opportunities to serve

except in support positions. Finally, the 332nd Fighter Group was formed, giving these airmen the chance to participate in leadership positions. There is a glossary, as well as lists of important dates, people, and additional resources.

328 Cummins, Julie ✱ *Tomboy of the Air: Daredevil Pilot Blanche Stuart Scott*
HarperCollins, 2001 ✱ 0-06-029243-1
EUROPEAN AMERICAN ✱ GRADES 3–6

Blanche Stuart Scott was driving a car when she was 13 and flying planes when she was 26. Her life was filled with firsts—the first woman pilot in the United States, the first woman test pilot, and the first woman stunt flyer. Born in 1886, she challenged the barriers that women faced.

329 Demarest, Chris L. ✱ *Lindbergh*
Illus. by the author ✱ Crown, 1993 ✱ 0-517-58718-1
EUROPEAN AMERICAN ✱ GRADES 2–4

When Charles Lindbergh was a child, automobiles were a novelty and airplanes were still being developed. As a young man, he "barn-stormed" around the Midwest, often walking out on the wings of a plane to call down to people on the ground and encourage them to come for a ride. Backed by a group of businessmen from St. Louis, he decided to try to win a prize for flying nonstop from New York to Paris. On May 21, 1927, he made history, becoming the first aviator to make a solo nonstop flight across the Atlantic Ocean.

330 Grimes, Nikki ✱ *Talkin' About Bessie: The Story of Aviator Elizabeth Coleman*
Illus. by E. B. Lewis ✱ Scholastic, 2002 ✱ 0-439-35243-6
AFRICAN AMERICAN ✱ GRADES 2–5

This is an award-winning "fictionalized" biography. An introduction provides the facts about Bessie Coleman, who was born in Texas in 1892 and endured prejudice as an African American and as a woman. The rest of the book takes place in 1926 as friends and family gather for Coleman's funeral. Their reminiscences are presented in poetic vignettes. Gorgeous full-color watercolor paintings accompany the reflections. This book received a Coretta Scott King Author Honor Award as well as the Coretta Scott King Illustrator Award.

331 Johnson, Angela ✳ *Wind Flyers*
Illus. by Loren Long ✳ Simon & Schuster, 2007 ✳ 0-689-84879-X
A<small>FRICAN</small> A<small>MERICAN</small> ✳ G<small>RADES</small> 1–4

Angela Johnson has written a poetic tribute to the Tuskegee Airmen. During World War II, the military was segregated. The U.S. Army Air Force created all-black squadrons that trained in Tuskegee, Alabama, and came to be known as the Tuskegee Airmen. The text focuses on Great-Great Uncle, who dreamed of flying. As a child, he flew with a barnstormer and he was filled with wonder and joy at the vision of the world from up in the clouds. He joined the 332nd Fighter Group and served in World War II. As an old man, he reminisces about his love of flying and his pride in his accomplishments. Loren Long's lush paintings are beautiful, filled with color and light.

THE HOLOCAUST

WORLD WAR II IS A FAMILIAR TOPIC IN CHILDREN'S BOOKS, many of which describe the experiences of Jewish characters faced with prejudice and violence. Readers can explore the emotions of Daniel in *Daniel Half Human and the Good Nazi*. They can be encouraged to create an artistic interpretation and then examine the embroideries in *Memories of Survival*. Another book that features the importance of the arts is *The Cat with the Yellow Star*, in which the adult prisoners of Terezin teach the children of the camp to perform the Czech opera *Brundibar*. And, of course, the picture book *Brundibar* is a natural connection.

Secrets in the Fire describes the impact of another war, the civil war in Mozambique. Readers will want to research this conflict and discuss the connections to the issues arising in World War II.

There are many stories of bravery and courage during times of such oppression. *The Flag with Fifty-Six Stars* describes the horrors of the Mauthausen concentration camp and the hopes of those imprisoned there. Several recent books explore the heroic efforts of ordinary people to help those in danger, such as *The Greatest Skating Race* and *The Cats of Krasinski Square*. Josephine Poole's biography of Anne Frank is another book that could be shared, as is Patricia Polacco's *The Butterfly*, which is based on an experience of the author's family.

Many of these books provide examples of bravery. Readers could be asked to develop a list of books that feature characters facing danger. A chart could be created listing the book title, the character's name, the danger or difficulty, and the response to it.

332 Borden, Louise ✴ *The Greatest Skating Race*
Illus. by Niki Daly ✴ Simon & Schuster, 2004 ✴ 0-689-84502-2
JEWISH—EUROPEAN—NETHERLANDS ✴ GRADES 3–6

In 1941 the German soldiers occupied Holland. Piet Janssen, a young Dutch boy, dreams of skating the Elfstedentocht—the Eleven Towns Race. As the years of occupation continue, Piet's skating skills are put to a different test. He must skate from Sluis to Brugge escorting two Jewish children to the safety of their aunt's home. The dangerous journey tests not only their skating skills but also their bravery as they pass German soldiers along the way.

333 Chotjewitz, David ✳ *Daniel Half Human and the Good Nazi*

Translated by Doris Orgel ✳ Atheneum, 2004 ✳ 0-689-85747-0

JEWISH—EUROPEAN—GERMANY ✳ GRADES 5–6+

In 1945, Daniel returns to Hamburg, Germany. The war is over and as he visits his former neighborhood, now in rubble, he remembers events before the war. He and his friend Armin participate in the Hitler Youth during the 1930s but Daniel's future is threatened when his parents reveal that his mother is Jewish. Daniel copes with his own feelings of racism even as he fears that his secret will be discovered. Armin knows Daniel's secret and struggles with his loyalty to the Nazi agenda and the truth about his friend. This book was a Mildred L. Batchelder Honor Book and received the Sydney Taylor Book Award Honor Award for Older Readers.

334 Hesse, Karen ✳ *The Cats in Krasinski Square*

Illus. by Wendy Watson ✳ Scholastic, 2004 ✳ 0-439-43540-4

JEWISH—EUROPEAN—POLAND ✳ GRADES 3–6

A young girl helps smuggle food to the Warsaw Ghetto. The German soldiers threaten to use dogs to find the food and stop it from being delivered. Cats are gathered from all around the city and released at the train station, distracting the dogs and the soldiers. This book received the Sydney Taylor Book Award Honor Award for Older Readers.

335 Krinitz, Esther Nisenthal, and Bernice Steinhardt ✳ *Memories of Survival*

Illus. with embroideries ✳ Hyperion, 2005 ✳ 0-7868-5126-0

JEWISH—EUROPEAN—POLAND ✳ GRADES 4–6+

Through a series of 36 gorgeous embroideries, Esther Nisenthal describes growing up in rural Poland. When she was 12, she and her sister Mania ran from the Gestapo. Through many hardships they survived the Holocaust. To remember the family she lost she told stories to her daughters, filled notebooks with reminiscences (written in English and Yiddish), and created these embroideries.

The Conquerors

336 McKee, David * *The Conquerors*

Illus. by the author * Handprint, 2004 * 1-59354-078-7
UNIVERSAL * GRADES 3–6

Do you remember the Caldecott-winning *Drummer Hoff* adapted by Barbara Emberley and illustrated by Ed Emberley (Simon & Schuster, 1967)? In it, soldiers build a cannon, which Drummer Hoff fires off. After a huge explosion, the final illustration of the book shows the cannon covered with vines in a field of flowers. Birds have built a nest in it and spiders have woven a web. Perhaps, peace has finally come. *The Conquerors* is another picture book with a lesson about war and conflict.

It begins with the sentence: "There was once a large country that was ruled by a General." The general and his army attack all the surrounding countries and conquer them despite resistance. Finally, there is only one small country left. The general and his army are surprised by the citizens, who do not resist. They welcome the soldiers and treat them like guests. The soldiers join in the activities of the country— singing, telling stories, playing games. The general sends for new soldiers—conquerors—but they, too, adapt to the ways of the small country.

The general returns home, leaving only a few soldiers behind. But, his homeland has changed. The food, games, and even the clothes are different. They are from the small "conquered" country. And when the general sings his child a bedtime song, he sings a song from the little country.

*

> After sharing *The Conquerors*, children can discuss the impact of nonviolent resistance—Gandhi's achievements in India and the American civil rights movement, led by Dr. King. They can even relate this issue to peer mediation programs in their schools. *The Conquerors* should lead to lively discussions.

337 Mankell, Henning ✳ *Secrets in the Fire*
Annick Press, 2003 ✳ 1-55037-801-5
AFRICAN—MOZAMBIQUE ✳ GRADES 4–6

This is a novel of Maria and Sofia, young sisters whose lives are shattered by the tragedy of civil war and the horror of landmines in their homeland of Mozambique. While innocently walking along a path between fields, Sofia loses her balance and falls, landing on a mine. Maria is killed; Sofia survives but loses both legs. Her pain and loneliness give readers insight into the way a life can change in just a moment. The book also illustrates how war destroys the simple joys of childhood, so taken for granted by the reader. This is a riveting story full of emotion and is based on the real-life experiences of a friend of the author. Although the civil war in Mozambique ended in the early 1990s, the danger from landmines continues. At the conclusion of the story there is information about efforts to remove landmines.

338 Polacco, Patricia ✳ *The Butterfly*
Illus. by the author ✳ Philomel, 2000 ✳ 0-399-23170-6
JEWISH—EUROPEAN—FRANCE ✳ GRADES 3–6

Monique discovers that her family is hiding a young Jewish girl—Sevrine. Now Monique must help keep the secret as the Nazi soldiers search the village and "remove" the Jewish citizens. Monique observes the violence of the soldiers, first as they attack and drag

Reflections

After the ILFA meeting in Berlin, Germany, in 2003, my husband and I traveled to Poland. It was a bit of a family history touchstone for me as my father had emigrated from Poland as a young man in the early 1900s. My father died when I was 10 years old, so the stories of his homeland were sparse, mostly consisting of tales of the Russians taking over Poland and forcing families to change their Polish names to a Russian variation. Since the conference brought me so close to my father's homeland, I felt I should at least set foot in the country.

On the advice of some neighbors with a Polish heritage, we decided to visit Krakow. That sounded wonderful as I was familiar with the Newbery winner *The Trumpeter of Krakow* (Macmillan, 1928), which tells the story of a brave young trumpeter's efforts to save his town from invading Tartars. Also, I knew that the city of Krakow had not been bombed during World War II so the historic aspects of the visit were very attractive. After a few days there, we arranged for a tour of Auschwitz and Birkenau, concentration camp sites that are now national memorials. The trip was very sobering.

Our tour guide took us to Birkenau first. We viewed the railroad tracks leading to the crematoriums. Even though much of the camp was dismantled at the end of the war, what remains is still very powerful. The three-hour tour of Auschwitz was even more compelling. Many, many people of all nationalities were touring, but the crowd was silent. The atmosphere was very somber. The tour ended at the torture chambers. We left with feelings of shock, disbelief, and deep sadness. The impact of this visit is always within me, and it influences every book that I read or discuss about this era.   —Kathy East

away a local merchant and then as a soldier crushes a beautiful butterfly in his gloved hand. When a neighbor sees Sevrine and Monique looking out the window, Monique's mother arranges for Sevrine to be taken to another hiding place. This story is based on events in the author's family history.

339 Poole, Josephine ✷ *Anne Frank*
Illus. by Angela Barrett ✷ Knopf, 2005 ✷ 0-375-83242-4
JEWISH—EUROPEAN—GERMANY ✷ GRADES 3–6

While many readers are familiar with Anne Frank's life from her diary, they may not know about her early life. She was born in 1929 in Frankfurt, Germany at a time when Germany was recovering from the devastation of World War I. Anne's father was successful, but as Adolf Hitler became more powerful, the Franks and other Jewish families became the targets of bigotry and hatred. To escape the violence, the family moved to Amsterdam in the Netherlands, but the influence of Hitler and the Nazis came there, too. The Franks made arrangements to go into hiding in an annex of an old building. Anne's life in hiding was lonely; writing in her diary provided her an outlet for her fears and dreams. In 1944, the German soldiers raided the annex and captured the eight people who had been hiding there, sending them to concentration camps. At the end of the war, only Mr. Frank survived. Miep Gies, who had helped the family while they were in hiding, gave Anne's diary to Mr. Frank.

340 Rubin, Susan Goldman ✷ *The Flag with Fifty-Six Stars: A Gift from the Survivors of Mauthausen*
Illus. by Bill Farnsworth ✷ Holiday House, 2005 ✷ 0-8234-1653-4
EUROPEAN—AUSTRIA ✷ GRADES 5–6+

When a U.S. Army unit liberated the Mauthausen concentration camp in Austria, the soldiers received a gift: a flag made by the prisoners from scraps of fabric. They had worked from memory and the replica of the U.S. flag had an extra row of stars! That flag was proudly flown over the camp as a symbol of the prisoners' faith and joy.

This book describes the horrible experiences of prisoners at Mauthausen. It was the last concentration camp to be built and was planned by Heinrich Himmler, one of Hitler's most ruthless officers. This is a difficult book to read, yet it balances the terrible details of torture and death with the hopes of the prisoners as they listened to the engines of American planes flying over Austria. When the 11th Armored Division finally entered Mauthausen, a band of prisoners played "The Star-Spangled Banner." Several days later, a group of prisoners presented to the American commander the flag they had made in secret. The final image in this book is a photograph of the flag, which is now exhibited in the Simon Wiesenthal Center in Los Angeles, California. Wiesenthal was a prisoner at Mauthausen.

341 Rubin, Susan Goldman with Ela Weissberger * *The Cat with the Yellow Star: Coming of Age in Terezin*
Illus. with photographs and artifacts * Holiday House, 2006 *
0-8234-1831-6
JEWISH—EUROPEAN—CZECHOSLOVAKIA * GRADES 4–6

This touching biography recounts Ela Weissberger's life in the Terezin concentration camp with other Czech Jews. Even in the dire conditions of their camp, many talented individuals kept everyone's spirits alive, especially those of the children who were secretly given lessons. Ela recounts the effort and delight she and her friends felt as they prepared and presented the children's opera *Brundibar*. Ela and the other children performed more than 50 secret performances, which not only brought joy to the other prisoners, but also served as a powerful resistance to the Nazis.

Since being liberated in 1945, Ela has kept in contact with many of her friends from Terezin. She has traveled extensively, relating her experiences during the Holocaust. Many photos are included in this volume—of Ela and her family, historical photographs of the concentration camp, numerous reunion pictures of Ela and her friends from "Room 28" as their tiny space was called, and even one picture of the cast of the opera. Of course, after reading *The Cat with the Yellow Star*, share Tony Kushner's *Brundibar*. This retelling of the Czech opera connects with the story of Ela and her fellow prisoners who used music, drama, and art to confront tyranny.

342 Kushner, Tony * *Brundibar*
Illus. by Maurice Sendak * Hyperion, 2003 * 0-7868-0904-3
EUROPEAN—CZECH * GRADES 3–6

Brundibar is based on a Czech opera; the title means "bumblebee." Two young children try to earn money to buy milk for their sick mother. They meet an organ grinder, Brundibar, who hates children and even threatens them. The youngsters find allies in a cat, a dog, some sparrows, and hundreds of schoolchildren who join together to sing a beautiful lullaby. The townspeople throw coins, but Brundibar tries to steal the money. Brundibar is chased out of town and the children can buy milk. Although this ending seems happy, there is the threat of danger as Brundibar insists he will return. Sendak's pictures include some recognizable characters from earlier works along with political overtones that adults are more likely to understand.

WORLD WAR II IN AMERICA

WORLD WAR II ALSO IMPACTED PEOPLE in the United States. Many Japanese Americans were forced to leave their homes and enter internment camps. *Baseball Saved Us* and *So Far from the Sea* are among the many books that explore this experience and provide another opportunity to discuss what it means to be courageous.

Nim and the War Effort describes one girl's determination to help the war. It also could be compared with *Baseball Saved Us* and *So Far from the Sea*. Nim and her family are of Chinese descent. Her grandfather even wears a pin of the Chinese flag. Children could analyze the reasons for the concern that Nim's family feels about their heritage. They could discuss the issues of the internment of Japanese Americans and research other instances of discrimination.

Coming on Home Soon gives another perspective on the experiences of families during the war. *Dirt on Their Skirts* includes a note about the many contributions that American women made during World War II.

343 Bunting, Eve ✱ *So Far from the Sea*
Illus. by Chris K. Soentpiet ✱ Clarion, 1998 ✱ 0-395-72095-8
Japanese American ✱ Grades 3–6

> Laura Iwasaki and her family are moving from California to Boston. As they begin their journey, they take time to visit the grave of Laura's grandfather. He died while he was interned at the Manzanar War Relocation Center. Following the attack on Pearl Harbor, thousands of Japanese Americans were sent to camps like Manzanar. Laura's father, who was also in the camp, shares his memories of the fear, mistrust and hysteria that influenced the decision to put American citizens into custody.

344 Lee, Milly ✶ *Nim and the War Effort*
Illus. by Yangsook Choi ✶ Farrar, Straus and Giroux, 1997 ✶ 0-374-
 35523-1
CHINESE AMERICAN ✶ GRADES 3–5

> Nim lives with her parents, siblings, and grandparents in San Francis-
> co. It is 1943 and the United States is involved in World War II. Nim
> and her family are careful to demonstrate that they are loyal Ameri-
> cans. Grandfather even wears a special pin with the American flag
> and the Chinese flag to show his heritage. Nim collects all the news-
> papers that she can, hoping to win the paper drive at her school. A
> classmate, Garland Stephenson, always seems to be just ahead of her.
> Although this is forbidden, Nim decides to go out of Chinatown to
> look for more papers and she finds an apartment building on Nob
> Hill that has a room filled with papers. Nim finds a creative way to
> get the papers to her school and she wins the contest. Later, she
> must face the disapproval of her grandfather and explain her disobe-
> dient behavior.

345 Mochizuki, Ken ✶ *Baseball Saved Us*
Illus. by Dom Lee ✶ Lee & Low, 1993 ✶ 1-880000-01-6
JAPANESE AMERICAN ✶ GRADES 2–4

> During World War II, "Shorty" and his family have been relocated
> into a desolate camp. As Japanese Americans, their loyalty has been
> questioned. The camp is hot and dusty; there is no privacy and little
> to do. Shorty's dad helps organize baseball games to occupy the days
> and provide respite from the tedium. A field is built, uniforms are
> made, and friends from home send bats, gloves, and balls. Kids and
> grown-ups practice and play games and Shorty, who has not been a
> very good player, hits a home run to win the championship. Finally,
> Shorty and his family return home, and there is still discrimination
> and distrust. Once again, Shorty's experiences on the baseball field
> help him deal with the cruelty. An Author's Note at the beginning of
> the book explains the internment of Japanese Americans during
> World War II. At that time, the government of the United States
> feared that these citizens might be disloyal and act on behalf of the

Japanese, although there was no evidence of this. The Note states, "In 1988, the U.S. government admitted that what it did was wrong."

346 Rappaport, Doreen, and Lyndall Callan * *Dirt on Their Skirts: The Story of the Young Women Who Won the World Championship*
Illus. by E. B. Lewis * Dial, 2000 * 0-8037-2042-4
EUROPEAN AMERICAN * GRADES 2–4

It is 1946 and Margaret is at the championship game for the All-American Girls Professional Baseball League. The league was formed during World War II. With so many men fighting in the war, women took on jobs and responsibilities that used to be done by men, including playing baseball. This book features a fictional child and her family watching their team, the Racine Belles, win the championship against the Rockford Peaches. A Box Score of the game and an Author's Note about the league are included.

347 Woodson, Jacqueline * *Coming on Home Soon*
Illus. by E. B. Lewis * Putnam, 2004 * 0-399-23748-8
AFRICAN AMERICAN * GRADES 2–4

Because so many men are fighting in World War II, Mama leaves Ada Ruth with Grandma so she can take advantage of the newly available jobs in Chicago. Ada Ruth and Grandma miss Mama. When a small black kitten comes to their home, Ada Ruth cares for the kitten even though Grandma says they cannot keep it. A letter from Mama includes money and the best news: Mama will be "coming on home soon." E. B. Lewis's evocative watercolor illustrations received a Caldecott Honor Medal. They are the perfect accompaniment to Woodson's sparse, poetic text.

Boxes for Katje

348 Fleming, Candace ∗ *Boxes for Katje*

Illus. by Stace Dressen-McQueen ∗ Farrar, Straus and Giroux,
2003 ∗ 0-374-30922-1

EUROPEAN AMERICAN; EUROPEAN—NETHERLANDS ∗ GRADES
3–5

At the end of World War II, Katje and her family and neighbors
still suffered from the effects of the war. In the small town of
Olst in Holland, food was scarce, clothes were tattered,
supplies were limited. One day, Katje received a box from the
Children's Aid Society in America. In the box was soap, socks,
and chocolate. Katje writes a note of thanks to her American
benefactor, Rosie Johnson from Mayfield, Indiana. When
Rosie gets the letter, a project begins. Rosie's school, church,
and the local businesses send boxes of supplies and treats.
Katje shares them with the people in her town, brightening the
winter months in her war-torn homeland. In the spring, the
people of Olst send a box to Rosie filled with tulip bulbs from
Holland. This book is based on events that happened to the
author's mother.

★

After reading *Boxes for Katje*, encourage children to work on a
community service project. They could collect money or supplies
to assist people in a natural disaster; they could collect books for
a shelter; they could plant bulbs or seeds to bring beauty to an
area. As children feel empathy for the needs of others, it is
important for them to be empowered to provide assistance.

VIETNAM WAR

WALTER DEAN MYERS'S BOOK *Patrol* describes the fear and uncertainty of a young African American soldier in Vietnam. Readers are drawn into the dramatic circumstances through the first person narration. *Patrol* can be read aloud to students who are beginning a study of the Vietnam War. Before reading this book, the teacher or librarian can create a KWL chart asking: What I *Know*. What I *Want to Know*. What I *Learned*. The children can then add to the chart after hearing the book, and be encouraged to do research about the war in Vietnam. *The Journal of Patrick Seamus Flaherty* is another book that would add to the discussion.

The Wall by Eve Bunting provides another perspective on the impact of the Vietnam War. This book shows a boy and his father looking for a name on the wall. Learning more about the Vietnam Veterans Memorial will extend the reader's understanding of this era in history.

349 Bunting, Eve ✳ *The Wall*
Illus. by Ronald Himler ✳ Clarion, 1990 ✳ 0-395-51588-2
EUROPEAN AMERICAN ✳ GRADES 2–6

A boy and his father visit the Vietnam Veterans Memorial to find a name. They are looking for the name of the boy's grandfather—his father's father. There are so many rows of names, each one a soldier killed in the war. Finally they find the name. His father's pride is tempered by the boy's sense of longing for the grandfather that he will never know.

350 Stone, Amy ✳ *Maya Lin*
Illus. with photographs ✳ Raintree, 2003 ✳ 0-739-86863-2
CHINESE AMERICAN ✳ GRADES 3–6

After reading Eve Bunting's *The Wall*, children may want to research the Vietnam Veterans Memorial. A competition was held to select a design for this memorial. While still a student at Yale, Maya Lin submitted an entry. Her design for a Wall of Names was selected as the winner of the competition. Carved into the wall are the names of those who lost their lives as a result of the Vietnam War.

351 Myers, Walter Dean ∗ *Patrol: An American Soldier in Vietnam*
Illus. by Ann Grifalconi ∗ HarperCollins, 2002 ∗ 0-06-028363-7
AFRICAN AMERICAN ∗ GRADES 5–6+

> A poetic text describes the experiences of a young American soldier
> in Vietnam. His squad of nine men is deep in the forest looking for
> the enemy. The soldier wonders—how near is he? The soldier real-
> izes—I am here to kill him. The soldier's fear grows as he senses that
> the enemy is near. He hears shots, then silence and the agony of wait-
> ing. Bombs are dropped to clear the way and the patrol moves on.
> They secure a village, filled with women, children, and old men, but
> are they the enemy? As the patrol moves on into the rice paddy, there
> are more shots and there is the enemy. The two soldiers freeze and
> stare, feeling each other's fear. The sound of a chopper distracts them
> and the enemy slips away. The patrol returns to the base camp and
> the young soldier writes home, expressing his loathing for the war.

352 White, Ellen Emerson ∗ *The Journal of Patrick Seamus*
Flaherty: United States Marine Corps, Khe Sanh, Vietnam 1968
Scholastic, 2002 ∗ 0-439-14890-1
EUROPEAN AMERICAN ∗ GRADE 6

> Even though he has a football scholarship, Patrick Seamus Flaherty
> has chosen to enlist in the Marine Corps. As he prepares to leave for
> Vietnam, his father gives him a journal in which to record his
> thoughts. As a soldier during World War II, Patrick's father kept jour-
> nals himself. Now, in Vietnam, Patrick writes about his experiences.
> In Khe Sahn, Patrick is overcome by the constant attacks by the
> North Vietnamese. At first he makes friends, but he becomes more
> distant as his friends are killed or wounded. He begins to question
> the war and his own involvement. There are vivid details of fighting
> and death. The entry for February 11, 1968, chronicles the death of a
> 17-year-old soldier, Mooch, who is shot in the stomach and dies
> before he can be evacuated. Patrick is overcome with grief. In April,
> Patrick is wounded and sent home. An Epilogue describes what
> Patrick experienced when he returned home. As with other books in
> this series (Dear America: My Name Is America), historical informa-
> tion follows the text.

CIVIL RIGHTS

CHILDREN MAY WONDER WHAT IT WAS LIKE to be young during the civil rights movement. There were marches and speeches. Many people left the segregation, "Whites Only" signs, and poverty in the South seeking better opportunities in the North. Several of the picture books featured here provide an introduction to the civil rights movement and serve as preparation for reading a longer novel such as *The Watsons Go to Birmingham, 1963* or *Abby Takes a Stand*.

After reading these books, children can study other important people and events, learning that the struggle for civil rights occurs throughout the world. *A Dream of Freedom* is an excellent nonfiction book for research. They can also read about the struggle against apartheid in South Africa. *The Day Gogo Went to Vote* describes the importance of open elections in South Africa; a biography of Nelson Mandela connects with the study of other leaders seeking equality.

Picture Books

353 Harrington, Janice N. * *Going North*
Illus. by Jerome Lagarrigue * Farrar, Straus and Giroux, 2004 *
    0-374-32681-9
AFRICAN AMERICAN * GRADES 3–6

In the South during the 1960s, many African American families lived in poverty with few opportunities. *Going North* describes how one family leaves Alabama and moves to Nebraska hoping to find work and prosperity. Jessie and her family say good-bye to family and friends and start out in their yellow station wagon. Their trip is more difficult because they can only go to "Negro stations" and "Negro stores." This book is based on the author's experiences.

354 Johnson, Angela * *A Sweet Smell of Roses*
Illus. by Eric Velasquez * Simon & Schuster, 2005 * 0-689-83252-4
AFRICAN AMERICAN * GRADES 2–4

Two girls slip unnoticed out of their house and join a march led by Dr. King. They hear his words and march along. They also hear the taunts of people in the crowd. The girls keep marching, knowing they are participating in a part of history. Arriving home, they face their worried mother who hugs them close while they talk about their dramatic day. Eric Velasquez has illustrated the book in black-and-white charcoal drawings that lend a realistic tone to the story. A touch of red on many of the pages connects with the author's use of the image of roses in the text.

355 Sisulu, Elinor Batezat ✶ *The Day Gogo Went to Vote: South Africa, April 1994*
Illus. by Sharon Wilson ✶ Little, Brown, 1996 ✶ 0-316-70267-6
AFRICAN—SOUTH AFRICA ✶ GRADES 2–4

Thembi loves her great-grandmother, Gogo. Gogo is old and she shares her memories of the past. When black South Africans are finally allowed to vote, Gogo announces that she will participate. The family is worried about her—is she strong enough for the long journey and the crowds of people? A wealthy neighbor drives Gogo to the voting office and she casts her ballot. Back home, there is a celebration. When the results are known, Nelson Mandela has been elected president of South Africa.

356 Wiles, Deborah ✶ *Freedom Summer*
Illus. by Jerome Lagarrigue ✶ Atheneum, 2001 ✶ 0-689-83016-5
AFRICAN AMERICAN ✶ GRADES 3–6

Two boys, one black (John Henry) and one white (Joe), are friends in a rural southern town. John Henry's mother, Annie Mae, works for Joe's mother. The boys spend their days together playing marbles and swimming in the creek. The town has a swimming pool, but John Henry is not allowed to swim there. Nor is John Henry allowed in the front door of the general store. Then a new law comes into force. When the town swimming pool is opened, everyone will be allowed in. John Henry and Joe race to the pool only to find that county dump trucks have delivered asphalt and it has been poured into the pool. In an ironic twist, John Henry's older brother is on the work crew that closes the pool. Joe comes to understand the emotional impact that segregation has had on John Henry. As the story ends, the two boys are walking through the front door of the general store together.

357 Woodson, Jacqueline ✻ *The Other Side*
Illus. by E. B. Lewis ✻ Putnam, 2001 ✻ 0-399-23116-1
AFRICAN AMERICAN ✻ GRADES 3–6

A fence divides Clover's town: on her side are the black people and on the other side are the whites. Clover has been told to stay on her side of the fence. Clover can see a white girl on the other side and she keeps her distance, but she begins to wonder why. Clover watches the girl until one day, they introduce themselves through the fence. The two girls decide to sit on the fence together and talk. One day, they leave the fence and join a group of Clover's friends jumping rope. Then all the girls sit on the fence and think about how one day the fence will come down. E. B. Lewis's watercolor illustrations are an outstanding complement to Jacqueline Woodson's poetic text.

Novels

358 Curtis, Christopher Paul ✻ *The Watsons Go to Birmingham, 1963*
Delacorte, 1995 ✻ 0-385-32175-9
AFRICAN AMERICAN ✻ GRADES 4–6+

Kenny, Joetta, Byron, and their parents live in Flint, Michigan. It is 1963. The first eight chapters are humorous, as Kenny, the narrator, describes the family's life in Michigan. Of course, Kenny tells several stories involving himself and his older brother Byron. The family's nickname is "the Weird Watsons." In the opening chapter, Byron is admiring himself in the sideview mirror of the car. It is freezing, but By loves to see himself. He is so enamored of his appearance that he kisses the mirror and his lips become stuck. The family's reactions and their attempts to release him are hilarious. Then there is the chapter in which Byron gets his hair processed. The chapters become more serious when the family decides to visit relatives in Alabama. Momma plans the trip carefully, knowing they will be traveling through the segregated South. In Alabama, they stay with Grandma

Sands. Kenny nearly drowns in a whirlpool but By rescues him; the brothers, who usually argue, are united, albeit briefly. Then it is Sunday. Kenny stays home while the rest of the family goes to church. There is an explosion at the church and Joetta is missing. She is found, but four girls are killed in the bombing. Kenny withdraws, reliving his fear of the whirlpool and the violence. Back home in Michigan, his family, especially Byron, help him recover. After reading *The Watsons Go to Birmingham, 1963* readers can research the historical events in Birmingham in a nonfiction book such as *A Dream of Freedom* by Diane McWhorter. *The Watsons Go to Birmingham, 1963* received a Coretta Scott King Author Honor Award and a Newbery Honor Award.

359 McKissack, Patricia C. ✳ *Abby Takes a Stand*
Illus. by Gordon C. James ✳ Viking, 2005 ✳ 0-670-06011-9
AFRICAN AMERICAN ✳ GRADES 3–6

The book opens "In Gee's Attic." Gee is Grandma and the cousins are Mattie Rae, Aggie, and Trey. They love going into the attic and finding items that spark Grandma's memories of the past. When they find a menu, Grandma begins a story about when she was a young girl named Abby.

It is 1960 in Nashville, Tennessee. Abby is ten. She and her best friend Patsy enjoy going to movies, eating snacks, and buying special stuff for school. Despite court rulings, many of the businesses in Nashville are still segregated, including the Monkey Bar Grill at Harveys Department Store. Blacks can shop at the store but not eat in the restaurant.

Abby makes the mistake of going into the Monkey Bar; she is publicly embarrassed and told to leave. Abby's Mama is so angry that she agrees to attend a protest meeting. The group decides to organize sit-ins at the downtown lunch counters. The sit-ins continue for several months; the protestors are arrested and the house of the lawyer helping them is bombed. Finally, there is victory and Mama takes Abby to the Monkey Bar. The novel returns to the present time and Gee promises more stories in the future. This is the first book in the Scraps of Time series.

Nonfiction

360 Cooper, Floyd * *Mandela: From the Life of the South African Statesman*
Illus. by the author * Philomel, 1996 * 0-399-22942-6
African—South Africa * Grades 2–6

From his birth in 1918 in the South African village of Mvezo to his election as the first black president of South Africa, this book celebrates the life and accomplishments of Nelson Mandela. Readers learn about the impact of apartheid and the punishment that Mandela endured as a leader of the African National Congress. Floyd Cooper's illustrations use muted shades of brown and gold to depict the details of Mandela's life.

361 McDonough, Yona Zeldis * *Peaceful Protest: The Life of Nelson Mandela*
Illus. by Malcah Zeldis * Walker, 2002 * 0-8027-8821-1
African—South Africa * Grades 4–6

When he was born in 1918, his family named him Buti. His father, a ruler of the Thembu people in the village, refused to accept the restrictions of the English officials. As a result, he lost his land but he set an important example for young Buti. At school, the teacher assigned English names and Buti became Nelson Mandela. Throughout his childhood, he experienced segregation and prejudice, yet he followed his father's example and maintained his convictions despite the consequences.

As a young man in Johannesburg, Mandela studied law and joined others who wanted change. In the African National Congress, he organized protests against apartheid—the policies that continued white supremecy in South Africa. In 1963, Nelson Mandela was arrested and sent to prison. He could only have one visitor and receive one letter every six months. Even from prison, he continued his protest and the anti-apartheid movement grew. Finally, in 1990, after 27 years in prison, Mandela was released. Four years later he was elected president of South Africa. A chronology, bibliography, and pronunciation guide are included.

362 McWhorter, Diane * *A Dream of Freedom: The Civil Rights Movement from 1954 to 1968*
Illus. with photographs * Scholastic, 2004 * 0-439-57678-4
AFRICAN AMERICAN * GRADES 5–6+

Chapters begin in 1954 with *Brown* v. *the Board of Education of Topeka* and continue chronologically through 1968 and the assassination of Dr. Martin Luther King, Jr., in Memphis. Key events such as the Montgomery Bus Boycott, Freedom Rides, the March on Washington, and Black Power are presented. Boxed inserts cover related topics including lynching, Jim Crow, Gandhi and nonviolence, Ruby Bridges, Marian Anderson, Marcus Garvey, and more. There is information about sit-ins, riots, boycotts, and the political agendas of Malcolm X, the Black Panthers, and Dr. King. This is a thorough presentation that provides background information for readers from later elementary through high school. Numerous photographs depicting the events and the chronological arrangement make this very user-friendly.

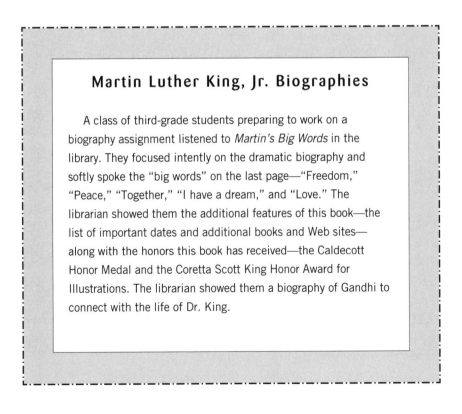

Martin Luther King, Jr. Biographies

A class of third-grade students preparing to work on a biography assignment listened to *Martin's Big Words* in the library. They focused intently on the dramatic biography and softly spoke the "big words" on the last page—"Freedom," "Peace," "Together," "I have a dream," and "Love." The librarian showed them the additional features of this book—the list of important dates and additional books and Web sites— along with the honors this book has received—the Caldecott Honor Medal and the Coretta Scott King Honor Award for Illustrations. The librarian showed them a biography of Gandhi to connect with the life of Dr. King.

She then showed them three other recent books about Dr. King and asked, "Since this is such a great book, why do we need others?" The third graders commented:

* The books might contain different facts
* The teacher wants at least two sources
* One book is from his sister and she would know more about his childhood
* You need books for little kids and books for us
* Lots of kids want to know about Dr. King, so you need lots of books

After the discussion the children went to the biography section to look for their resources.

363 Demi ✳ *Gandhi*

Illus. by the author ✳ Simon & Schuster, 2001 ✳ 0-689-84149-3

ASIAN—INDIA ✳ GRADES 3–6

Dr. Martin Luther King was influenced by the teachings of Mohandas Gandhi. This biography will help children understand the struggle for freedom in India and Gandhi's commitment to nonviolence.

364 Farris, Christine King ✳ *My Brother Martin: A Sister Remembers Growing Up with the Reverend Dr. Martin Luther King, Jr.*

Illus. by Chris K. Soentpiet ✳ Simon & Schuster, 2003 ✳ 0-689-84387-9

AFRICAN AMERICAN ✳ GRADES 2–6

As the subtitle states, this is a sister's memoir about the early years with the brother who grew up to be one of the world's greatest activists for civil rights. An Illustrator's Note follows the text and adds insights into the development of this book.

365 King, Martin Luther, Jr. * *I Have a Dream*
Scholastic, 1997 * 0-590-20516-1
AFRICAN AMERICAN * GRADES 1–6

Fifteen Coretta Scott King Award and Honor Book artists illustrate the text of Dr. King's famous speech. Biographical information about Dr. King follows the speech and there is a Foreword by Coretta Scott King.

366 Myers, Walter Dean * *I've Seen the Promised Land: The Life of Martin Luther King, Jr.*
Illus. by Leonard Jenkins * HarperCollins, 2004 * 0-06-027703-3
AFRICAN AMERICAN * GRADES 3–6

This book emphasizes Dr. King's role as a civil rights leader. Marches, boycotts, arrests, and bombings are described along with Dr. King's commitment to nonviolence and the teachings of Mohandas Gandhi.

367 Rappaport, Doreen * *Martin's Big Words: The Life of Dr. Martin Luther King, Jr.*
Illus. by Bryan Collier * Hyperion, 2001 * 0-7868-0714-8
AFRICAN AMERICAN * GRADES 2–6

From the endpapers showing stained glass windows to the inspiring text and outstanding collage illustrations, this is a beautiful book to share with children. Quotes from Dr. King extend the text. His words are inspirational and the imagery in the illustrations heightens their impact. Scenes showing Dr. King speaking from a pulpit or a lectern add drama to the powerful language in the text. *Martin's Big Words* received a Coretta Scott King Illustrator Honor Award and a Caldecott Honor Award.

MIGRANT WORKERS
AND PROTESTS

THE CIVIL RIGHTS MOVEMENT GENERALLY REFERS to the efforts of African Americans in the 1950s and 1960s to receive equal rights and opportunities. However, many groups have sought equal rights. The migrant farm workers endured many of the same conditions and experiences as the African Americans. Cesar Chavez and the National Farm Workers Association helped improve the treatment and pay of the farm workers in the western states, primarily California.

Read *Harvesting Hope: The Story of Cesar Chavez* and then read a biography of Rosa Parks. How are their stories similar and how are they different? *Gathering the Sun* is an alphabet book that features the experiences of Hispanic American farm workers. Look also at the lives of the Chinese workers on the Transcontinental Railroad as described in *Coolies* and make connections with the experiences in the other books featured here.

368 Ada, Alma Flor; English translation by Rosa Zubizarreta ✳
  Gathering the Sun: An Alphabet in Spanish and English
Illus. by Simón Silva ✳ Lothrop, Lee & Shepard, 1997 ✳ 0-688-
  13903-5
Hispanic American ✳ Grades 2–6

Spanish words representing the letters of the Spanish alphabet are accompanied by brief descriptive poems that explore the experiences of migrant workers. The English translation of the words and poems is printed next to the Spanish text. A bright, colorful illustration accompanies each word and letter. From Árboles—trees that bear the fruit for migrant workers to harvest—to the Lluvia—rain that waters the fields—to the Zanahoria—carrot that is harvested by the workers—this book celebrates the hard work and spirit of a farmworker's family. A note explains that Ch and Ll will no longer be considered separate letters of the Spanish alphabet, but they are included as such here.

369 Giovanni, Nikki ★ *Rosa*
Illus. by Bryan Collier ★ Henry Holt, 2005 ★ 0-8050-7016-7
AFRICAN AMERICAN ★ GRADES 2–6

Rosa Parks was a pioneer in the civil rights movement. Her dignity and courage made her the focal point for one of the most celebrated events in American history. This biography of Rosa Parks describes the events in Montgomery, Alabama, that led to the Montgomery Bus Boycott. In 1955, Mrs. Parks worked as a seamstress. After work on December 1st, she finished work and waited to board a city bus for the ride home. In Montgomery, blacks would pay in the front of the bus, then get off the bus and board through the back door and ride on designated seats in the back. Blacks could use a few seats in the middle until a white person needed the seat. On this day, Rosa Parks sat in the "neutral" seats and when the bus driver ordered her to move, she did not. She was arrested and the news of her arrest spread through the black community. Citizens began to boycott the buses in support of her defiance. Dr. Martin Luther King, Jr. came to Montgomery to join their cause. For almost a year, many people did not ride the buses and in November 1956, the Supreme Court of the United States ruled that the segregation of the buses was illegal. *Rosa* received the Coretta Scott King Illustrator Honor Award and was selected a Caldecott Honor book.

370 Krull, Kathleen ★ *Harvesting Hope: The Story of Cesar Chavez*
Illus. by Yuyi Morales ★ Harcourt, 2003 ★ 0-15-201437-3
MEXICAN AMERICAN ★ GRADES 2–6

This biography of Cesar Chavez describes his childhood and the experiences that helped him become an inspiring civil rights leader. Chavez grew up on a ranch in Arizona, part of a large extended family. At school, Cesar was shy but his mother encouraged him to study and learn. She also urged Cesar and his siblings to avoid using force to solve problems. Following a drought in Arizona and the loss of their ranch, the family moved to California looking for work. All of the children now worked in the fields with their parents and they lived in the poor quality housing provided by the owners for the field. Many communities excluded the Hispanic workers with "White Trade Only" signs and mocked them for their limited knowledge of English. The migrant workers received wages so low it was hard to survive; those who complained faced violence. Cesar Chavez began to try to organize the workers for better pay and working conditions, stressing nonviolence. He founded the National Farm Workers Association and his movement was called *La Causa*. In 1965, Chavez organized a march to Sacramento to seek government support. The marchers left the fields, where ripe produce waited to be picked. They faced police and hostile property owners. They also received help from supporters along the way. The march began to receive attention from the media and more and more people joined in. By the time the marchers reached Sacramento, there were more than 10,000 people. The National Farm Workers Association, led by Cesar Chavez, became the representative for thousands of workers and negotiated better working conditions, pay, and treatment. An Author's Note describes Chavez's continued nonviolent protests until his death in 1993. *Harvesting Hope* was a Pura Belpré Award Honor Book for illustration.

371 Pérez, L. King * *First Day in Grapes*
Illus. by Robert Casilla * Lee & Low, 2002 * 1-58430-045-0
MEXICAN AMERICAN * GRADES 2–4

Chico and his family are migrant workers, traveling across California to pick vegetables and fruits. Right now, they are picking grapes. Chico will be going to school while his parents work and he is apprehensive about being the new kid once again. The bus driver seems mean but his teacher and new classmates are welcoming. Chico wants to please his new teacher and his math skills attract her attention. She encourages him to be in the Math Fair. Later at lunch, two bullies bother him but Chico finds the courage to stand up to them. On the bus ride home, Chico introduces himself to the bus driver and he looks forward to staying in this school for a while—at least until the grapes have been picked. *First Day in Grapes* was a Pura Belpré Award Honor Book for illustration.

372 Yin * *Coolies*
Illus. by Chris K. Soentpiet * Philomel, 2001 * 0-399-23227-3
Chinese American * Grades 4–6

A grandmother, Paw Paw, celebrates Ching Ming Festival with her grandson. They honor their ancestors, especially two men who left China in 1865 to come to America and work on the Transcontinental Railroad. The bosses ridiculed the Chinese laborers and called them Coolies. They were made to work long hours doing heavy, often dangerous construction. The brothers, Shek and Little Wong, stayed together. When the Chinese workers tried to protest because their pay was lower that the pay of the non-Chinese workers, the bosses refused to give them food or water. The Chinese workers were forced to return to work.

For four years, the brothers endured the hardships of building the railroad. They sent money home to help their family in China and saved for the future. When the railroad was completed, the brothers settled in San Francisco and brought their family to America.

As Paw Paw finishes the story, she and her grandson celebrate the memory of these brave ancestors. An Author's Note describes the historical events that inspired this story. *Coolies* received an Asian/Pacific American Award Honorable Mention for Illustration in Children's Literature.

CHAPTER SIX

Knowing Today's World

AT THE BEGINNING OF THIS CHAPTER ARE BOOKS about America and the role of our country in the world. Other sections feature books about the global economy—how people around the world earn and use money; how and where they spend it. As children mature, they become more aware of the problems in the world and they need opportunities to discuss the questions they are asking. What is it like to be a refugee—to leave your home and, perhaps, your homeland to escape the impact of a war, like the characters in *Gleam and Glow*? What happens if you stay and endure the conflict, hoping to survive and protect the things that are important to you as in *The Librarian of Basra*? Discussing events in today's world helps prepare children to value and respect the differences among the people of the world.

AMERICA AND THE WORLD

AMERICA IS . . . BY LOUISE BORDEN celebrates the United States of America. It is an emotional, patriotic salute to America. Sharing this book with children can lead to a discussion of what each child thinks America is and what it means to be an American. A chart of their responses could be created. Young people are expected to learn about citizenship and democracy. *America Is . . .* could be the focus of an activity that expands to connect across cultures and promote a discussion of global issues.

After reading *America Is . . .*, a teacher or librarian could bring in books that focus on countries around the world. *If the World Were a Village* and *How People Live* examine the global society. In both books, facts about the world are presented as if the global village contained only 100 people. Information about languages, religions, food, and more could lead to a discussion of the distribution of people, beliefs, and resources of the world. *Respecting Cultural Differences* is another book with a global perspective.

Let's Eat! and *Wake Up, World!* describe foods and daily life of children around the world. After reading these books, conduct a survey of the foods and routines of the children. Use math skills to create graphs and charts of statistics. *Hello World!* can be used to promote a discussion of foreign languages. A group of children could select other words or phrases and make their own book full of ways to say "thank you," "please," or "good-bye." Even the illustrations from *Hello World!* can be used as a model for the finished book.

373 Borden, Louise ✶ *America Is . . .*
Illus. by Stacey Schuett ✶ Simon & Schuster, 2002 ✶ 0-689-83900-6
MULTICULTURAL ✶ GRADES 2–6

This book celebrates the diversity of the United States. The people, the land, the symbols, the history, and the ideals are presented in the poetic text and colorful illustrations.

374 Hollyer, Beatrice * *Let's Eat! What Children Eat Around the World*
Illus. with photographs * Henry Holt, 2003 * 0-8050-7322-1
MULTICULTURAL * GRADES 1–3

South Africa, Mexico, Thailand, France, and India are the featured countries in this book, which was published in association with Oxfam, the charity that combats hunger around the world. Each chapter describes a child and his or her family. The focus is on foods—Luis from Mexico enjoys tortillas, oranges, and tacos with tuna fish or cheese; Yamini from India eats rice, *chapatis*, chickpea *dal* and *paneer*. There is a recipe for a favorite dish from each child. A Food Glossary is included.

375 Hollyer, Beatrice * *Wake Up, World! A Day in the Life of Children Around the World*
Illus. with photographs * Henry Holt, 1999 * 0-8050-6293-9
MULTICULTURAL * GRADES 1–3

What is a child's day like in Vietnam? How are everyday activities different in Ghana or Brazil? The arrangement of this book features an activity, such as "Wake Up!" or "At School," along with captioned photographs explaining what eight children are doing. For "Helping Others," Anusibuno from Ghana sweeps the rooms and fetches firewood while Paige from the United Kingdom cleans her hamster's cage. The endpages at the back of the book provide additional information about the countries. This book was published in association with Oxfam.

376 *How People Live*
Illus. with photographs * DK, 2003 * 0-7894-9867-7
MULTICULTURAL * ALL AGES

This coffee-table style book of the world is a massive and gorgeous photoessay on all the peoples of the world. After an introduction that tries to put the term "global village" into perspective by saying "if the world was a village of 100 people," then breaking down this village by food, education, nationality, religion, language, and air and water conditions, the book moves through the six inhabited continents to highlight the unique features of the people who live there and their lifestyles. This is a fascinating collection of delectable tidbits of information.

377 Smith, David J. ✳ *If the World Were a Village: A Book About the World's People*
Illus. by Shelagh Armstrong ✳ Kids Can Press, 2002 ✳ 1-55074-779-7
MULTICULTURAL ✳ GRADES 4–6

As in *How People Live*, the global village is presented as if there were only 100 people there. Information about nationalities, languages, ages, religions, food, and more are included. Literacy, resources, and electricity are also examined. There is an essay about "Teaching Children About the Global Village," which encourages educators to use maps, discussions, Web sites, and other activities to develop world-minded citizens.

378 Stojic, Manya ✳ *Hello World! Greetings in 42 Languages Around the Globe*
Illus. by the author ✳ Scholastic, 2002 ✳ 0-439-36505-4
MULTICULTURAL ✳ GRADES PRESCHOOL–2

This book is just what the subtitle says—how to say "hello" in 42 languages. The phonetic spelling and origin accompany each greeting. The illustrations are colorful paintings of the faces of children—one close-up face for each greeting. When you share this with a group, it looks as if each child in the book is right there saying "hello!" An index lists the 42 origins from Amharic to Zulu. Older children can research where each greeting is used. All children will enjoy learning to say some of the greetings.

379 Watson, Susan ✴ *Respecting Cultural Differences*
Smart Apple Media, 2004 ✴ 1-58340-400-7
MULTICULTURAL ✴ ALL AGES

This factual book helps to define what it means to be a global citizen. Issues discussed include environments, religions, types of families, racial backgrounds, styles of communication, political systems, standards of living, cultural celebrations and accepting others. The outline format is helpful in opening doors to further discussion among students, families, and groups of youngsters or adults who seek a better understanding of the people around us and in our world.

THE GLOBAL ECONOMY

THE STANDARDS FOR SOCIAL STUDIES PROMOTE LEARNING about people, places, and environments. Children are expected to examine the distribution of resources and develop an understanding of the global economy, learning about such terms as supply and demand, bartering, trading, currency, and resources.

In *Beatrice's Goat*, readers learn about a family that becomes self sufficient through a program that provides families with a goat. Parallel the experiences in Africa with those of Juan Quezada in *The Pot That Juan Built*. Learn about bartering in *Saturday Sancocho* and about honesty and responsibility in *A Day's Work* and *Bikes for Rent! Ryan and Jimmy and the Well in Africa That Brought Them Together* shows the determination of one child to earn money and make a difference in the world.

The importance of education is also featured in *Beatrice's Goat* and *Babu's Song*. These could be connected with books in Chapter One, including *Ruby's Wish* and *Running the Road to ABC*.

380 Andrews-Goebel, Nancy ✶ *The Pot That Juan Built*
Illus. by David Diaz ✶ Lee & Low, 2002 ✶ 1-58430-038-8
MEXICAN ✶ GRADES 2–4

> There are two texts in this book. The main text has a rhythmic pattern like "The House That Jack Built." For example, "This is the pot that Juan built." Details about the artistic process of making a pot and the materials used are added on with each new page. In smaller print on every page there is information about Juan Quezada, a professional potter who researched a pottery process from the Casas Grandes people who lived in Mexico more than 600 years ago. He uses that process to make his pots and his pottery business has grown to include many other residents in his village. An Afterword explains the economic impact of pottery making and includes photographs of Juan Quezada and his village, Mata Ortiz.

381 Bunting, Eve ✳ *A Day's Work*
Illus. by Ronald Himler ✳ Houghton Mifflin, 1994 ✳ 0-395-67321-6
Mexican American ✳ Grades 2–4

Francisco waits with his grandfather in the parking lot where day laborers are offered work. Grandfather, *Abuelo*, does not speak English. When a man looks for a gardener for the day, Francisco claims his grandfather is a fine gardener. At the job site, Francisco and Grandfather work under the hot sun, but they remove the plants and leave the flowering chickweeds. Grandfather realizes that Francisco has lied and arranges to repair the damage. Francisco learns a lesson about being honest and taking pride in your work and in your reputation.

382 McBrier, Page ✳ *Beatrice's Goat*
Illus. by Lori Lohstoeter ✳ Atheneum, 2001 ✳ 0-689-82460-2
African—Uganda ✳ Grades 2–4

The people of the village of Kisinga in Uganda often struggle to survive. Beatrice and her family plant in the fields and take their produce to the market to sell. There is never any extra money—certainly not enough to buy the materials needed for Beatrice to go to school. Beatrice's family is selected by a charitable organization to receive a goat and Beatrice is given the job of caring for the goat, which she names Mugisa. The goat delivers two kids and provides milk for them and the family. The extra milk is sold and the money that is saved is enough to send Beatrice to school. An Afterword by Hillary Rodham Clinton describes the real Heifer International, a program that provides resources to promote self-sufficiency.

383 Mollel, Tololwa M. ✳ *My Rows and Piles of Coins*
Illus. by E. B. Lewis ✳ Clarion, 1999 ✳ 0-395-75186-1
African—Tanzania ✳ Grades 1–3

In a rural village in Tanzania, Saruni is saving his money to buy a bicycle. With a bicycle, he will be able to help his mother do more errands, thus earning more money for his family. Months pass and Saruni keeps counting his rows and piles of coins. When he finally goes to buy a bicycle, the man laughs at him and his meager savings. Saruni's father, Murete, buys a motorbike and sells his old bicycle to Saruni for the exact amount that Saruni has saved. Now Saruni can help his mother with all she has to carry. This book received a Coretta Scott King Illustrator Honor Award.

384 Olaleye, Isaac * *Bikes for Rent!*
Illus. by Chris Demarest * Orchard, 2001 * 0-531-30290-3
AFRICAN—NIGERIA * GRADES 3–6

In western Nigeria, Lateef passes the rental bicycle stall every day. Oh, to have enough money to rent a bike and ride with all the other boys! Lateef decides to sell firewood and mushrooms he can collect from the rain forest and save his money. Eventually he hopes to rent a bike and learn to ride. One day he rents the only new bike in the stall. The other boys challenge him to ride and take his hands off the handlebars! He does and it is disastrous. Lateef has to work a long time to repay the damage. But he likes the work and continues to save for his own bicycle. Sometimes good things can come out of near-disasters! And new skills can be learned as well.

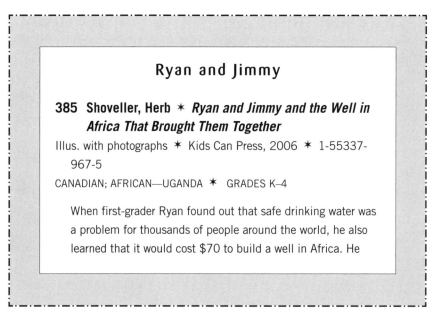

Ryan and Jimmy

385 Shoveller, Herb * *Ryan and Jimmy and the Well in Africa That Brought Them Together*
Illus. with photographs * Kids Can Press, 2006 * 1-55337-967-5
CANADIAN; AFRICAN—UGANDA * GRADES K–4

When first-grader Ryan found out that safe drinking water was a problem for thousands of people around the world, he also learned that it would cost $70 to build a well in Africa. He thought his parents would give him the money. However, his parents thought he should earn the money by being paid for chores. It took four months. Then came disappointing news— the $70 would only buy a hand pump. Building an entire well would cost $2000! Ryan's determination to proceed is described in great detail in this photoessay. Ryan even traveled to Uganda in 2000 to visit the village where the well had been built. While he was there, he met Akana Jimmy, a young orphan who thanked him for this wonderful gift. The two boys bonded immediately. After Ryan returned home to Canada, he learned that war had erupted in Uganda. Life was now difficult and dangerous for Jimmy. Eventually Jimmy was brought to Canada. When he was about to enter 9th grade, his visa was going to expire and the war in Uganda was still a real issue. The family decided the dangers in returning were too great and they applied for Convention Refugee status for the Jimmy. He quickly became a permanent member of the Hreljac family.

★

Jimmy's courage is so evident. And for such a young man! Children can discuss the meaning of courage and list books that demonstrate determination like Jimmy's. What fundraising efforts have youngsters been involved in? How much money did they raise? How does that compare with the money raised by Ryan? What made Ryan decide to stay with the project? Why is helping people abroad important? What lessons did Ryan and Jimmy learn? What lessons did you learn?

386 Stuve-Bodeen, Stephanie ★ *Babu's Song*
Illus. by Aaron Boyd ★ Lee & Low, 2003 ★ 1-58430-058-2
AFRICAN—TANZANIA ★ GRADES 3–6

Done in a picture-book format, this story of economics in modern
Tanzania tells of the joint efforts of Bernardi and his mute grandfather, Babu, and how they manage to make a living. Babu is a toy
maker and on market day Bernardi sells the toys. Bernardi also loves
to play soccer, but his only chance is when the schoolboys need an
extra player at recess as Bernardi cannot afford to attend school.
When a tourist gives Bernardi many dollars for a lovely music box
made by Babu, Bernardi is thrilled and dreams of buying the soccer
ball he saw in a store window. However, he realizes he probably
should not have sold the music box and confesses to Babu and hands
him all the money. Babu uses the money for a school uniform and
arranges for Bernardi to attend school. And Babu makes him a soccer
ball from leftover scraps as well. This is a lesson on hard work and
setting priorities as well as being honest.

387 Torres, Leyla ★ *Saturday Sancocho*
Illus. by the author ★ Farrar, Straus and Giroux, 1995 ★ 0-374-36418-4
SOUTH AMERICAN ★ GRADES 1–3

When Maria Lili visits her grandparents on Saturdays, they make
chicken sancocho, a thick stew. This week there is no food and no
money, but Mama Ana has a plan. She trades eggs with the vendors
in the market and she accumulates the necessary ingredients for the
stew. The setting is a rural village in South America and a recipe is
included. This book can also lead to a discussion of bartering.

MARKETS AROUND THE WORLD

READERS CAN LOOK AROUND THEIR OWN COMMUNITIES for different marketplaces. There may be supermarkets and department stores. They may notice a farmers' market or a roadside stand. And what about an ice cream truck? The books in this section depict the activity at markets in Ireland, Mexico, and Haiti. Two books by Ted Lewin show markets around the world.

Look at the creative illustrations in Lois Ehlert's *Market Day*. They are photographs from the author/illustrator's collection of items from around the world. Make a display of similar items from children in your classroom or library group. Or bring in items from your own travels.

Think about ordering small items—pencils, cute erasers, bookmarks—and selling them in the school or at the public library. Where will you get the money to start the business? How much will you charge for each item? How many items will you need to sell to make a profit? And what will you do with the profit? Kids will enjoy selecting and ordering the items to be sold and making posters to advertise them.

388 Bunting, Eve ✳ *Market Day*
Illus. by Holly Berry ✳ HarperCollins, 1996 ✳ 0-06-025368-1
EUROPEAN—IRELAND ✳ GRADES 1–3

On the first Thursday of every month it is Market Day. Tess and her friend, Wee Boy, love to watch the street fill up with vendors. There is lace from Donegal, honey, pots and pans, and many animals. There is Baba-Ali, the sword swallower, and a man who walks on red-hot coals. A gypsy looks into her crystal ball and tells Wee Boy about his future. The setting seems to be a rural Irish village in the early 1900s.

389 Ehlert, Lois ✳ *Market Day: A Story Told with Folk Art*
Illus. by the author ✳ Harcourt, 2000 ✳ 0-15-202158-2
MULTICULTURAL ✳ GRADES PRESCHOOL–2

A simple rhyming text describes a family's preparations for market day. They pack up their truck with their wares and head for the town square. They sell what they have and buy from other vendors.

Finally, they pack up and return home. The illustrations for this book are spectacular. They are photographs of folk art and textiles (most are from the author/illustrator's collection). The items are staged to depict the events in the story. At the back of the book, there is a double-page spread showing the individual items and where they came from, like an appliqué of a farm house from Colombia, a beaded bull from Africa, and painted clay figures from Mexico.

390 Grossman, Patricia ✳ *Saturday Market*
Illus. by Enrique O. Sánchez ✳ Lothrop, Lee & Shepard, 1994 ✳ 0-688-12176-4
Mexican ✳ Grades 1–3

Every Saturday, this market in Mexico is filled with families from the surrounding farms hoping to sell their goods. Carmen sells her beautiful *rebozos* (shawls) and Rosa has made 200 *huaraches* (sandals). Pedro's family has woven rugs; Juan has baked cookies and breads; Ana sells *tortillas*. A glossary of terms follows the text.

391 Lewin, Ted ✳ *How Much? Visiting Markets Around the World*
Illus. by the author ✳ HarperCollins, 2006 ✳ 0-688-17553-8
Multicultural ✳ Grades K–3

How do people sell their products? In Bangkok, Thailand, there is a floating market. Vendors maneuver small boats through the canals. The boats are filled with a variety of items—fruit, fish, and other foods. There is even a vendor selling fried bananas. In Madras, India, there is a flower market. Near Machu Picchu in Peru, people set up stalls to sell textiles. Also featured is a camel market in Egypt and a flea market in New Jersey. Evocative watercolor illustrations depict the diversity of the experience of buying and selling. This is a companion book to Lewin's *Market!*

392 Lewin, Ted ✳ *Market!*
Illus. by the author ✳ HarperCollins, 1996 ✳ 0-688-12161-6
MULTICULTURAL ✳ GRADES K–3

Six diverse marketplaces are featured in this book. Readers learn
about markets in Ecuador, Nepal, Ireland, Uganda, the United States,
and Morocco. They sell spices, vegetables, flutes, horses, fruit, meat,
fish, and animals. They are urban and rural—the Fulton Fish Market
in New York City and a market near the desert in Rissani in Morocco. This is a companion book to Lewin's *How Much?*

393 Williams, Karen Lynn ✳ *Painted Dreams*
Illus. by Catherine Stock ✳ Lothrop, Lee & Shepard, 1998 ✳ 0-688-
  13901-9
CARIBBEAN—HAITI ✳ GRADES 1–3

Ti Marie has a dream—to be an artist—and she draws pictures
whenever she can. A mysterious neighbor, Msie Antoine, lives in a
compound of houses that are brightly colored and decorated with
carvings and sculptures. Ti Marie's family is too poor to buy her supplies, so she sifts through the trash from Msie Antoine. One day, Ti
Marie helps her mother at the market. She notices that the wall
behind their stall is large and empty and she begins to fill it with
bright, colorful paintings. The people in the market come to see Ti
Marie's paintings and they buy her mother's vegetables. The family
realizes the importance of Ti Marie's art.

SOUTHERN AFRICA

MANY STORIES SET IN SOUTH AFRICA FEATURE NATIVE ART.
Two books, *Elsina's Clouds* and *My Painted House, My Friendly Chicken, and Me* focus on the tradition of decorating houses. After reading these books to a group of children, an art activity inspired by their content is a natural extension. Use watercolors to paint bright, geometric designs on cinder blocks or concrete patio stones. Put the finished blocks outdoors and allow the rain to wash the paintings away. See this as a good omen and be thankful for the rainy weather.

Additional books about Africa can be displayed with this program. *Galimoto* by Karen Lynn Williams demonstrates how children in Malawi use often-limited resources to create toys and art. And *Over the Green Hills* describes the importance of music to a South African family.

394 Angelou, Maya ✳ *My Painted House, My Friendly Chicken, and Me*
Photographs by Margaret Courtney-Clarke ✳ Clarkson Potter, 1994 ✳
AFRICAN—SOUTH AFRICA—NDEBELE ✳ GRADES 1–4

Color photographs capture the beauty of the people, their homes, and the artistic designs used to decorate them in this Ndebele village in South Africa.

395 Isadora, Rachel ✳ *Over the Green Hills*
Illus. by Rachel Isadora ✳ Greenwillow, 1992 ✳ 0-688-10509-2
AFRICAN—SOUTH AFRICA ✳ GRADES K–2

Zolani lives in a village by the sea on the east coast of South Africa. He and his mother travel inland to visit Zolani's grandmother. When they reach her house, she is not there. But they can hear the sound of her pennywhistle. At the end of the book, Zolani and his grandmother are making music together. Included are details about the Transkei homeland of South Africa.

Reflections

In November 1996, I had the pleasure of traveling to South Africa as an ambassador with the People to People Program, established by President Eisenhower. This trip was just two years after the country became a democracy. The joy and pride expressed by people from all walks of life in acquiring freedom—combined with great faith in the future—so impressed all the delegates. Life was very different now!

The Crèches of Soweto

On a spring morning our group visited a child care center within the township of Soweto—a place where between 2 million and 3 million people live in poverty on the outskirts of Johannesburg. The center was immaculate. The children—there were between 15 and 20—were clean and dressed in little blue smocks. Brightly colored children's art decorated the walls.

Beyond the charm of these youngsters was the determination of the women there, who were being trained to run crèches (day or child care centers) of their own, so badly needed within this township. These women recognize the importance of education and want to provide it to the children, the future of South Africa. Some women were making simple dolls using toilet paper tubes and fabric scraps; others were creating large books with pictures taken from magazines. Stimulation for the mind through imagination and picture reading skills! Another woman was planning to teach sewing as the center had acquired three industrial machines. Any products would be sold.

The center and its association had a motto that read:

> Forward   YES
> Backward   NEVER

And then (translated from their Sotho language):

> "When women do something, they have no fear
> and deal with the problem"

Truly inspirational!

—Kathy East, Journal Entry, Tuesday, Nov. 5, 1996

396 Williams, Karen Lynn ∗ *Galimoto*
Illus. by Catherine Stock ∗ HarperCollins, 1990 ∗ 0-688-08789-2
AFRICAN—MALAWI ∗ GRADES K–2

Despite his older brother Ufulu's doubts, Kondi goes from place to place to collect enough scrap wire to make a "galimoto," a type of push-toy made by children. Through his resourcefulness and persistence, Kondi achieves his goal. This story is set in Malawi, a country in southeast Africa. A Note explains how galimotos are made and the possible origin of the the Chichewa word—from the English "motor car."

397 Winter, Jeanette ∗ *Elsina's Clouds*
Illus. by the author ∗ Farrar, Straus and Giroux, 2004 ∗ 0-374-32118-3
AFRICAN—SOUTH AFRICA—BASOTHO ∗ GRADES K–3

In the Basotho tradition, young Elsina has brightly painted the outside walls of the house's new addition as a plea to the ancestors to bring rain. Finally rain comes and washes away her designs. Long droughts have traditionally allowed South African villagers to paint beautiful pictures on their houses and they are happy to see them disappear when the rain finally arrives.

KOREA

Reflections

South Korea is a country full of tradition and, at the same time, cutting-edge progress. Attending the IFLA conference there in August 2006 introduced me to the "old" country and culture I learned about in so many children's books and also exposed me to the high-tech environment of the modern country. The capital city of Seoul has a population of more than 14 million people. The huge city is divided by the very wide Han River, crisscrossed by numerous bridges. Sidewalks are wide, which is good because people park on them, ride their motorbikes on them, and hold night markets there on weekend evenings. The city pulsates with music, lights, and huge signs and many street corners feel like Times Square in New York City. All this bustle contrasted with the storytelling sessions in the libraries I was fortunate to visit.

Most storytelling follows the "old" tradition. Children come into the room—often a separate, small, intimate space—take off their shoes, sit down on their mats, and listen attentively to the storyteller in front of the room, sitting straight with hands in the lap, telling the story in a gentle voice with few inflections and no dramatic movements. This style makes it difficult for a listener who does not know the language to understand the story. But it is still a beautiful experience, just to hear the language. I also met a special group of storytellers who called themselves "Beautiful Grannies." These grandmothers decided to "act out" some of the traditional Korean tales for their audiences. What a delight as they donned animal ears and tails, crawled around on the floor "speaking" their parts and interacting with other grannies, while the narrator kept the story moving. I wanted to be a "beautiful granny!"

It was a memorable experience to celebrate that cultural heritage and to appreciate both styles of presentation. Once again, the power of words so carefully crafted for passage from generation to generation reinforces the need for those special times when the human voice captures the attention and imagination of the listeners, no matter their age.

—Kathy East

398 Balgassi, Haemi ✳ *Peacebound Trains*
Illus. by Chris K. Soentpiet ✳ Clarion, 1996 ✳ 0-395-72093-1
ASIAN—KOREA ✳ GRADES 3–6

Sumi likes to perch on a large rock and watch the trains below wind through the valley as she imagines all the places they go. She is hoping her mom, who is in the Army will soon return. When a birthday package with a doll made by her mom arrives, she dashes off to the rock where she can privately cry and miss her mom. Before long, her grandmother arrives. Grandmother tells of her memory of riding on a train roof with her two children as she escaped from Seoul during the civil war in Korea. She remembers her final moments with her husband, whom she never saw again. She shares her successful escape to Pusan and her reunion with friends. Sumi and her grandmother reflect and then plan the day they will go down to the valley to meet the train that brings her mother home. Short chapters capture this emotional story. The watercolor pictures dramatically illustrate the impact of war on the ordinary people of a country.

399 Choi, Yangsook ✳ *Peach Heaven*
Farrar, Straus and Giroux, 2005 ✳ 0-374-35761-7
ASIAN—KOREA ✳ GRADES 2–5

This picture book relives the summer of 1975 when heavy rainstorms threatened the peach harvest in Puchon, South Korea. While doing a homework assignment to write about the best thing in her town, Yangsook wrote, peaches! Her house was surrounded by peach orchards and she loved the big, sweet fruit. Her grandmother interrupted her to come look at the heavy rain and the hail. The hail turned out to be peaches knocked off the trees and blown onto the homes. Yangsook said, "This is peach heaven!" When the rain stopped, everyone gathered the peaches. The next day, they thought of the poor farmers who relied on this crop. They packed up the fruit and pushed the carts up the hills and hung them with yarn on the trees! The simple illustrations celebrate the mythology of the culture, which regards the peach as a magical fruit, symbolizing peace.

400 Han, Oki. S., and Stephanie Habousch Punkett ✳ *Kongi and Potgi: A Cinderella Story from Korea*
Illus. by Oki S. Han ✳ Dial, 1996 ✳ 0-8037-1572-2
ASIAN—KOREA ✳ GRADES 2–5

In the tradition of the original fairy tale, Kongi is treated badly by her new stepmother and stepsister. But when the prince is seeking a bride, Kongi is assisted by hundreds of little sparrows who help winnow the grain so the rainbow of radiant angels can dress her for the party, right down to her lovely embroidered shoes. The tale runs true, but the Korean version includes spirits in the form of animals who assist Kongi in meeting the challenges and hardships given her. Han's illustrations capture the traditional costumes, the countryside, and the brilliance of color of this culture and land. Also, Kongi's qualities of kindness and forgiveness are emphasized. Comparing this with Cinderella stories from other cultures (such as those discussed in Chapter Four) would be a wonderful extension activity.

401 Park, Linda Sue ✳ *The Firekeeper's Son*
Illus. by Julie Downing ✳ Clarion, 2004 ✳ 0-618-13337-2
ASIAN—KOREA ✳ GRADES 1–4

This picture book brings to life the bonfire signal system long used in Korea to let the king know that all parts of the country were safe from enemy approach. In this simplified retelling, Sang-hee's father tells of the importance of their meager village because they live in the valley between many of the "humps" of the landscape of Korea. Each night the father climbs to the top of the mountain carrying a little brass pot filled with live coals to start the first fire that will signal to the next mountaintop that all is safe. One night Sang-hee notices the fire has not been started. Does that mean something is wrong? He looks and sees only seagulls. No enemies. No trouble; but still no fire. Sang-hee finds his father injured. He is told to go start the fire. Tempted to see what will happen if the fire is not lighted, he has trouble with the coals, but he hears his father's voice saying "a time of peace," which is very important to all the people of the kingdom. The fire catches! The gentle watercolors give a sense of tranquility, and leave room for the imaginative play and dreams of Sang-hee as he learns this important tradition of his village.

SCHOOLS

MANY BOOKS EXPLORE CHARACTERS AND EVENTS in a school setting. By reading about the school experiences of children around the world, young people can reflect on their own experiences and explore similarities and differences. They can compare and contrast the way they get to school, what their school looks like, what clothes they wear to school, what subjects they study, what free time activities are available, and what goals they have for their future. Education aims to develop young people into citizens of the world, and technology brings everyone closer together as a global family.

The books featured here will help readers have a better understanding of what going to school may mean in other countries of the world. They range from humorous stories (*A Book of Coupons*) to more serious books (*The Gold-Threaded Dress* and *Rickshaw Girl*). The nonfiction *Going to School in India* adds a perspective on the experiences of Naima in *Rickshaw Girl. Danitra Brown, Class Clown* is a poetic exploration of friends at school and *The Year of Miss Agnes* describes the impact of a new teacher on the children in an Alaskan village. A boxed feature describes the experiences of a first-grade class reading about going to school in Japan.

An activity to connect with any of these books would be to ask children what is important to them about their school. Each child could make a list. The teacher or librarian could compile the responses and then organize a discussion. For one group of third-graders, computers were cited as the most important aspect, but as the children discussed each other's suggestions, they began to focus on the importance of other elements, including their teachers, the books and other materials, their classrooms, and even the heat in the building (it was a cold day)!

402 Grimes, Nikki ✶ *Danitra Brown, Class Clown*
Illus. by E. B. Lewis ✶ Amistad, 2005 ✶ 0-688-17290-3
AFRICAN AMERICAN ✶ GRADES 3–5

Zuri Jackson and Danitra Brown are best friends who have appeared in two previous books—*Danitra Brown Leaves Town* (2002) and *Meet Danitra Brown* (1994). In this book, the girls are starting a new school year and Zuri is apprehensive about doing well. She is also worried about her mother's illness. Danitra distracts her—and their class and the teacher—by being silly when Zuri is struggling in the classroom. The rhyming poems connect to tell the story of these two likeable friends.

403 Heydlauff, Lisa ★ *Going to School in India*
Illus. by Nitin Upadhye ★ Charlesbridge, 2005 ★ 1-57091-666-7
ASIAN—INDIA ★ GRADES 4–6+

This book gives inspiring accounts of children seeking an education throughout the provinces of India. The children face many challenges including geography, population, language, disability, calamity, transportation, and lack of materials. For example, there are the children who get to school by sliding across a river gorge on a swing attached to a pulley. Others have classes held in the shade of a mango tree. When it's lunch time all kinds of lunch boxes and containers appear and they are filled with many different foods, such as soups thickened with rice so children can roll the mixture into balls with their fingers. There are children who work during the day and go to school at night in buildings that are powered by solar lights casting an eerie blue glow. Other children who belong to wandering tribes have little formal instruction but learn survival skills as their tribe moves from place to place finding food, understanding the plant and animal life surrounding them, learning traditional stories, and enjoying the freedom of learning in an outdoor classroom. In Old Delhi, some children gather once a week to create a newspaper that they paste on the walls. There is even an outdoor school on the platform of the train station. There are poignant reflections from children sharing their dreams. Madrasa says, "When I grow up, I will make paper flowers. I will wear them in my hair and make garlands around my neck." Amina says, "E-mails move by magic." And Lobzang declares, "I will travel to teach Buddhism. . . ." All of this reinforces the need for good education in every hamlet in the world, in every country in the world.

    Photo collages, pen-and-ink drawings, and a backdrop of colorful, swirling Indian designs enhance the energy and determination of the 12 children featured here.

404 Hill, Kirkpatrick ✶ *The Year of Miss Agnes*
Simon & Schuster, 2000 ✶ 0-689-82933-7
Multicultural ✶ Grades 3–6

Miss Agnes, the new teacher from England, arrives in a small Alaskan village in the late 1940s and changes the lives of all the children. Fred (Frederika), who is 10, narrates the story. Miss Agnes is unlike any of the former teachers who have come to this Athapascan village. She wears pants, drinks tea with sugar and milk, and puts the desks in a circle. She packs up all the old textbooks and gets out lots of colored pencils and paints. This eccentric teacher reads good literature aloud and helps Fred's deaf sister learn sign language. She has everyone singing and dancing and studying maps and science. Then she decides she is lonesome for England and needs to return. This is a wonderful book to promote a discussion of favorite teachers who really help students learn.

405 Marsden, Carolyn ✶ *The Gold-Threaded Dress*
Candlewick Press, 2002 ✶ 0-7636-1569-2
Thai American ✶ Grades 4–6+

Oy is adjusting to being in the fourth grade in a new school. Not only is she the "new kid," but she is also teased about her Thai heritage. Some girls in her class have a club, but Oy is not included. The leader of the group, Liliandra, shows an interest in Oy when she sees a photograph of Oy in a beautiful pink silk dress. Liliandra decides that Oy can be in the club if she brings the dress to school and allows all the other girls in the club to try it on.

Oy's desire to belong leads her to bring the dress to school. At recess, the girls go to a secluded area on the playground and begin to try on the dress. It is damaged as the girls struggle to stretch the delicate fabric over their larger bodies. The playground monitor finds the girls and they are taken to speak to the principal.

At home, Oy confesses to her mother, who is understanding and helps her repair the dress. Back at school, Oy reaches out to a boy who has been tormenting her, only to find that he has a Chinese grandmother and has also been teased. Oy's story continues in *The Quail Club* (Candlewick, 2006).

406 Morgenstern, Susie * *A Book of Coupons*
Illus. by Serge Bloch * Viking, 1999 * 0-670-89970-4
EUROPEAN—FRANCE * GRADES 3–5

At Marie Curie School, there is a new teacher. He is Monsieur Hubert Noël. The students had been looking forward to having a "new" teacher for their final year of elementary school. However, Monsieur Noël is not what they anticipated. Although he is a new teacher, he is an old man. His teaching style is also not what they expected. He gives each student a "Book of Coupons" that includes coupons for skipping a day of school, losing your homework, eating in class, dancing in class, and even giving the teacher a kiss on the cheek. At first, his students used many coupons, but as the year progressed, they found his class too interesting to miss. Unfortunately, the school principal, Incarnation Perez, does not share their enthusiasm. She finds Monsieur Noël's teaching methods to be totally unsatisfactory and she refuses to renew his contract. Although his students are devastated, Monsieur Noël reminds them that there is a time for everything, including his retirement. He gives them each a blank book for "telling your life story" and they give him 26 *wild card* coupons and an oversized coupon with the words "One coupon for a happy and well-deserved retirement." This delightful book was an Honor Book in 2002 for the Mildred Batchelder Award, which, according to the Web site of the American Library Association, is "awarded to an American publisher for a children's book considered to be the most outstanding of those books originally published in a foreign language in a foreign country, and subsequently translated into English and published in the United States."

407 Perkins, Mitali * *Rickshaw Girl*
Illus. by Jamie Hogan * Charlesbridge, 2007 * 1-58089-308-2
ASIAN—BANGLADESH * GRADES 3–5

Naima wants to help by earning money for her family. However, since she is a girl, she is restricted to doing chores around the house and designing *alpana*, the traditional patterns for special celebrations. Naima's family can no longer pay her school fees so Naima decides to take action. She disguises herself as a boy and drives her father's rickshaw, but later crashes it and must face the consequences for her disobedience. Readers will connect with this story of a girl whose life is different from theirs but whose personality and energy will be recognizable and familiar.

Japan

When a first-grade class visited the library, they were introduced to a variety of books about Japan. The focus of the visit was the book *The Way We Do It in Japan* and after hearing it the children made a list of the differences between their school and the school in the book. "We don't wear uniforms." "We don't wash the windows and sweep the classroom." "Our school does not meet on Saturdays." The librarian showed them other books, including *I Live in Tokyo* and they looked at books featuring the Japanese language.

A serendipitous addition was that one student had been born in Japan! Some of his relatives still live there and for the next library visit he brought in items from his home, including a stiff black leather book bag like the one Gregory uses in *The Way We Do It in Japan*. What began as a thematic story session turned into an opportunity to discuss family backgrounds and cultures.

408 Amery, Heather ✳ *First Thousand Words in Japanese*

Illus. by Stephen Cartwright ✳ Usborne, 1995 ✳ 0-7945-0480-9

ASIAN—JAPAN ✳ GRADES 3–6

Learning about other cultures should include information about the language. In this picture dictionary, readers see words grouped by topic—home, backyard, playground, city, animals, vehicles, and more. An Introduction explains *kana* signs and provides some pronunciation guides. Accessing the

Usborne Internet site provides additional resources including audio activities. The word list includes the Japanese and English words for the illustrations.

409 Iijima, Geneva Cobb ✳ *The Way We Do It in Japan*
Illus. by Paige Billin-Frye ✳ Albert Whitman, 2002 ✳ 0-8075-7822-3
JAPANESE AMERICAN ✳ GRADES 2–4

Gregory's mother was born in America; his father in Japan. The family relocates to Japan and Gregory describes what he observes as he adjusts to living in Tokyo. The living room in the new apartment is furnished with a low table and pillows. When it is time for bed, Gregory's father shows him the mattresses that are stored in a closet and are taken out at night and spread on the floor. Gregory continues to adjust . . . to the bathroom, school, the food, and language. Just when he feels alienated and alone, his classmates surprise him with a lunch of peanut butter and jelly sandwiches. After the story there is a descriptive Note about Japan. Japanese words are used in the text and the pronunciation is included.

410 London, Jonathan ✳ *Moshi Moshi*
Illus. by Yoshi Miyake ✳ Millbrook Press, 1998 ✳ 0-7613-0110-0
ASIAN—JAPAN ✳ GRADES 1–4

Moshi moshi means hello in Japanese. And these are the words that the narrator and his brother Elliot speak to Kenji when they arrive in Tokyo. The two apprehensive American boys are there to meet pen pal Kenji. They find living in Japan has many positive sides as they learn to eat strange foods, to speak new words, and some of the traditional art of sword fighting. After the trip, the boys await Kenji's turn to visit America the next summer.

411 Takabayashi, Mari ✳ *I Live in Tokyo*

Illus. by the author ✳ Houghton Mifflin, 2001 ✳ 0-618-07702-2

ASIAN—JAPAN ✳ GRADES 1–3

Mimiko, 7, describes her life in Tokyo. Each month of the year is presented in double-page spreads. There is a brief text and numerous illustrations featuring common activities. In January, the new year is celebrated with special foods and gifts. In April, Mimiko begins second grade. The illustrations depict Japanese writing and show Mimiko and her brother Kenta in their school clothes. There is an illustrated list of Mimiko's top ten favorite meals. She describes everyday activities with her friends and at school. Japanese words are included throughout the text and the final page includes simple phrases and pronunciations.

412 Takahashi, Peter X. ✳ *Jimi's Book of Japanese: A Motivating Method to Learn Japanese*

Illus. by Yumie Toka ✳ PB & J Omnimedia, 2002 ✳ 0-9723247-0-4

ASIAN—JAPAN ✳ GRADES 3–6

Forty-six *hiragana* and more than 100 words are presented in this lively book. Three characters help explain each page—Jimi, a monkey; Robotto-san, a robot; and Akiko, a character resembling an alligator. Large illustrations of the *kana* (symbols) demonstrate how to form each sign. A description of a word using the symbol explores an aspect of Japanese culture.

ISLAM

AS CHILDREN'S KNOWLEDGE OF THE WORLD WIDENS, so does their interest in other people's lives and cultures. Religion plays an important role in societies around the world, and the recognition of the right to worship varies from place to place. The books listed here introduce the traditions and practices of Islam and will prompt discussion of religious freedom and tolerance.

Using David Macaulay's *Mosque*, begin a study of the Muslim religion by exploring their house of worship. Then read about Salaam and Bilal, two Muslim American boys who face prejudice and hostility for their heritage. Eve Bunting's *One Green Apple* features a Muslim girl in a similar situation. The ongoing conflict in the Middle East makes it important to understand the beliefs of people from that area and not accept that being "different" is the same as being "dangerous." Demi's biography, *Muhammad*, adds more information about Islam and the Muslim religion as does *A Faith Like Mine*.

413 Brown, Tricia ✷ *Salaam: A Muslim American Boy's Story*
Photographs by Ken Cardwell ✷ Henry Holt, 2006 ✷ 0-8050-6538-5
MUSLIM AMERICAN ✷ GRADES 1–3

> Imran is a Muslim American boy living in the San Francisco area. He enjoys activities such as playing with his dog and going to birthday parties. He goes to school and plays with his friends. He worries about the hostility that his family has experienced, such as the upsetting phone call his mother received from a stranger. When his friend Trevor asks him about his beliefs, Imran provides information about Islam. The black-and-white photographs show a loving family. A glossary is included along with an explanation of "The Five Pillars of Islam." Use this book to start a discussion about similarities and differences in religions.

414 Buller, Laura ✳ *A Faith Like Mine: A Celebration of the World's Religions Through the Eyes of Children*
Illus. with photographs ✳ DK, 2005 ✳ 0-7566-1177-6
MULTICULTURAL ✳ GRADES 4–6

Hinduism, Buddhism, Sikhism, Judaism, Christianity, Islam, and five other faiths are described in this photoessay. Children speak to the meaning of their faith and through photographs describe many of the traditions of their religion—costumes and dress, images, writings, and so forth. Children from the various countries where the religion is practiced tell of traditions in their culture. Each child's words make evident their innocence, knowledge, and involvement in their religion's teachings at that particular age. This book is a wonderful way for a family to become more aware and sensitive to the many different religions practiced around the world.

415 Bunting, Eve ✳ *One Green Apple*
Illus. by Ted Lewin ✳ Clarion, 2006 ✳ 0-618-43477-1
MUSLIM AMERICAN ✳ GRADES 2–4

Farah tells of her experiences at her new school in a new country. She feels alienated because she cannot speak or understand English. She wears a *dupatta*—a scarf that covers her head and shoulders. The class goes on a field trip to an apple orchard. One girl, Anna, introduces herself and Farah smiles. At the orchard, the children each pick one apple. Most of the children pick bright red apples, but Farah picks a small green apple. All of the apples are put into a cider mill and the children help turn the handle to crush the apples. Anna encourages Farah to join her as they push the handle. The children drink the cider that was made from their apples. On the way home, another child introduces himself and Farah repeats the new word that she has learned—"App-ell." The metaphor of the one green apple blending with the other red apples to make a cider can be connected to Farah's experience.

416 Demi ✳ *Muhammad*
Illus. by the author ✳ Simon & Schuster, 2003 ✳ 0-689-85264-9
MUSLIM ✳ GRADES 1–4

This beautifully illustrated biography explores the life of Muhammad, a prophet who experienced revelations that declared him to be a Messenger of God. Muhammad's name means "often praised" or "praiseworthy." Born in 570 A.D., he spent his childhood years in the desert, where he helped with the sheep and goats. After the death of his parents (his father died before he was born and his mother died when he was 6 years old), Muhammad was raised by his grandfather and, after his death, by his uncle. From each new experience, Muhammad learned about the world.

As a young man, he was known for being fair and trustworthy and he was sought out to deal with conflicts. After his marriage, Muhammad experienced his first revelation when the angel Gabriel revealed the first verses of the Koran to him. Muhammad began to advocate the tenets of Islam and convinced many people around him to convert. He experienced many more revelations until the Koran was complete.

Yet even as many converted to Islam, there were those who persecuted Muhammad and his followers. In 620 A.D., Muhammad experienced a revelation that transformed him. With the angel Gabriel he journeyed to paradise and then prayed in Jerusalem before reaching the Seventh Heaven and the presence of God. As he shared this story with his followers, Muhammad knew that the danger from his enemies was increasing. He escaped from Mecca to Medina, where he gave a sermon about brotherhood. He led his followers into a battle against their enemies and, although outnumbered, Muhammad and his people won.

Now, more converts were turning to Islam, following the teachings of the Koran (sacred writings) and the Sunnah (less sacred writings). Muhammad died in Medina having truly served as a Messenger of God. A brief Note after the text provides more information about Islam and there is a map of Muhammad's world.

417 Macaulay, David ∗ *Mosque*
Illus. by the author ∗ Houghton Mifflin, 2003 ∗ 0-618-24034-9
Muslim ∗ Grades 5–6+

Using the basic form of the sixteenth-century Ottoman mosque, Macaulay creates a fictional building complex to describe and examine the required prayer hall, the covered portico, the arcaded courtyard, the fountain, the minarets, etc., and how they were constructed. His detailed drawings show plans, cutaways to illustrate the depth and placement of columns, etc. and his careful description of how the pieces and sections were made by blacksmiths, stone masons, carpenters, and other guild members is fascinating reading. The uses for each part of the building are clearly defined. The reader feels a part of the design decisions and has a sense of ownership as the structure takes shape and begins to loom overhead. The three years of work involved in building the mosque are truly appreciated by the end of the book. Youngsters will enjoy examining the tools used, and comparing them with today's tools and also trying to project how the construction might have progressed differently with modern tools.

418 Mobin-Uddin, Asma ∗ *My Name Is Bilal*
Illus. by Barbara Kiwak ∗ Boyds Mills, 2005 ∗ 1-59078-175-9
Muslim American ∗ Grades 4–6+

Bilal's family has moved from Chicago and he and his sister Ayesha are going to their new school. In Chicago, many Muslim children attended their school. Here, he and Ayesha are the only Muslims. When some boys taunt his sister, Bilal stands back; he does not help her. Later, Bilal decides to alter his identity—he will be Bill. His teacher, Mr. Ali, who is also Muslim, tries to counsel Bilal. Mr. Ali gives Bilal a book to read about Bibal Ibn Rabah, the first person to give call to prayer during the time of the Prophet Muhammad. After reading the book, Bilal is proud of his heritage and he is able to defend himself and his sister against the bullies. He is even able to reach out to his tormentors when he asks one of the boys to play basketball with him. His gesture begins to break down the barriers that religious misunderstanding produced.

419 Morris, Ann ✳ *Grandma Hekmatt Remembers: An Arab-American Family Story*
Photographs and illus. by Peter Linenthal ✳ Millbrook Press, 2003 ✳
  0-7613-2864-5
ARAB AMERICAN ✳ GRADES 2–5

This photoessay features an Arab American family living in New Jersey. The three girls often visit their grandparents and listen to stories about growing up in the Middle East. Their grandparents share memories of Cairo and there are photographs in the family album showing their grandmother, Hekmatt, with her family in Egypt. Both grandparents help the girls learn cultural traditions. They help them learn Arabic words and the Arabic alphabet. School, religion, and holidays are also featured along with a glossary and suggested activities. On the last page, there is a family tree. Part of the series What Was It Like, Grandma?

COPING WITH CONFLICT

AS CHILDREN GROW UP, THEY BECOME MORE AWARE of the wider world and the crises facing other populations. Iraq, Sudan, Bosnia, and Southeast Asia have all been prominent in the news in recent years. The books featured here provide opportunities for research and discussion.

Before reading any of these books, ask your group what they already know about the conflict. For example: Where is Bosnia? Why was there a war there? What is happening there now? Find out what they know about the world and then read the story. After reading, encourage them to get accurate information. Use this as an opportunity to look at reference books, including encyclopedias. If possible use both the print copy and use the online version.

Compare the ways in which characters face the conflict. In *Brothers in Hope*, Garang became the leader of a group of boys trying to escape the danger and destruction. In *The Librarian of Basra*, Alia saved 30,000 books by taking action on her own. Make a word wall of terms that describe the behaviors of the characters in these stories and then search for other books where the characters cope with conflict.

420 Bunting, Eve ✴ *Gleam and Glow*
Illus. by Peter Sylvada ✴ Harcourt, 2001 ✴ 0-15-202596-0
EUROPEAN—BOSNIA-HERZEGOVINA ✴ GRADES 3–6

> Viktor, his little sister Marina, and their mother must leave their home to escape the approaching enemy. As they leave, they release two pet fish into the pond. Marina has named them Gleam and Glow. The family walks to the border and lives in a refugee camp, where they are joined by Papa, who has been in the underground. After many months, they return to their village, where all of the homes have been destroyed. The children run to the pond, which they find teeming with golden fish. This book was inspired by a true story from a small village in Bosnia-Herzegovina, where a family left their home in 1990, releasing two golden fish into a lake. Returning in 1995, they found lake full of golden fish.

421 Shea, Pegi Deitz ✳ *The Whispering Cloth: A Refugee's Story*
Illus. by Anita Riggio; stitched by You Yang ✳ Boyds Mills, 1995 ✳ 1-
56397-134-8
ASIAN—HMONG ✳ GRADES 3–6

> Young Mai lives in a refugee camp in Thailand. She sits at the Wid-
> ows' Store listening to Grandma and the other women tell stories
> while they sew *pa'ndau* story cloths. Mai learns how to create a
> cloth, making a beautiful design and then embroidering with careful
> stitches. Each pa'ndau tells a story, and Mai begins to create a beauti-
> ful story cloth that tells of her family. Her parents are gone, killed
> along with many Hmong people. Mai and her grandmother escape
> the violence but spend many years in the refugee camps. In her story
> cloth, Mai stitches her dream that they will fly away from the camp,
> join her cousins, and be safe. Mai realizes that she will not sell this
> cloth.

**422 Williams, Mary ✳ *Brothers in Hope: The Story of the Lost Boys
of Sudan***
Illus. by R. Gregory Christie ✳ Lee & Low, 2005 ✳ 1-58430-232-1
AFRICAN—SUDAN ✳ GRADES 3–6

> Garang, 8, was born in Sudan and grew up on his family's farm.
> Then the war came to his village. His family was gone and Garang
> began to walk away from the destruction. Other boys were walking,
> too. Hundreds of boys, then thousands. The older boys organized the
> group, deciding to go to Ethiopia, walking at night and sleeping in
> the forest. Older boys carried younger boys. Garang was chosen to
> lead a group of 35 boys and he helped them stay together and find
> food and water. When there was no water, they drank their own
> urine. All of Garang's boys made it to Ethiopia, where they were
> taken to a refugee camp. From that camp, they went to a camp in
> Kenya. They were there for years, until a resettlement program
> brought many of the Lost Boys to the United States. An Author's
> Note before the text and an Afterword provide additional informa-
> tion about the Lost Boys and the foundation that provides them
> with assistance. Christie's acrylic paintings portray the danger and
> drama of this moving story.

423 Winter, Jeanette ✳ *The Librarian of Basra: A True Story from Iraq*
Illus. by the author ✳ Harcourt, 2005 ✳ 0-15-205445-6
MIDDLE EASTERN—IRAQ ✳ GRADES 2–6

A librarian in Iraq, Alia Muhammad Baker, listens to the people in Basra and worries that the bombing and fighting from the war will destroy the library where she works. Many of the books are ancient and irreplaceable. With no support from the government, she decides to save some of the books. Every night she takes books to her home. She fills a restaurant near the library with books. The library is destroyed and, as the fighting subsides, Alia hires a truck and moves 30,000 books to her home and to the homes of her friends. For now, the books are safe. But the war continues. An Author's Note shares information about the facts behind this story.

CHAPTER SEVEN

Parent-Child Book Discussion Groups

BOOK DISCUSSION GROUPS CAN BE A VERY GOOD AVENUE for opening conversations between parents and young people. As their desire for independence and trust grows, preteens and teens tend to move away from their parents or caregivers and to avoid deep discussions with them. They view many questions as nosy—"Where are you going?" "Who will you be with?" "How long will you be gone?"—and expect conversations to become confrontational. Yet parents want to talk to their children about everything from everyday life to issues of global concern. Books can serve as an excellent way to break the ice and stimulate dialogue.

A library program called Novel Chit-Chats is designed for the 9- to 13-year-old age group. The program pairs young people with adults (a parent or other adult reading partner). It is usually held every five or six weeks during the school year, and lasts about an hour. (One summer there was a session using a book that complemented the summer reading program.) New pairs can join the group at any time.

The program is promoted through handouts to selected grade levels in public and parochial schools, prominent displays and flyers in the library, inclusions on the library calendars and Web sites, and press releases to local newspapers.

Usually the first session features a picture book—often a wordless book—so the group can discuss the "reading" of pictures. This is also a time for everyone to get to know each other and to hear each other's voices. At the end of the session, the next book for discussion—usually a novel—is handed out. Phone calls a week to 10 days before the next session remind participants and alert those who missed the previous session to the title of the next book.

In most cases, the pairs read the book before the group gets together. They do not always talk about the book themselves, but this has not been a problem. In fact, many pairs say they discussed the book more or even reread it *after* the session at the library.

The discussion itself takes many formats. It is not meant to be a quiz or a test about the story, and it does not always include a complete review of the story. That can be left for the pairs to do.

When a group of pairs met to discuss the wordless picture book *A Circle of Friends* by Giora Carmi, someone volunteered to give a quick synopsis of the story of the little boy who gets some money, buys a muffin, and starts a chain of events involving a homeless man, a bird, and generous actions. The story makes a circle. The intent of the author became the subject of a lively discussion. Some felt the author was calling attention to the problem of homelessness while others thought the reason for the story was to make us aware of how much we take for granted and how little attention we pay to the world around us—to people who may be in need of food or a friend, or simply to the birds, the little animals, or even the plants. The conclusion was: "We need to slow down and appreciate what we have and what is happening around us. And pay attention to each other." Additional discussion began when the pairs considered how their eyes were directed to the most important part of the story. The drawings are done in sienna ink with highlights in color—the muffin, for example. Everyone agreed that the color helped to focus the eye on the important part of a page, but also that the reader must pay attention to the other parts of the illustration, which make the story come alive. Everyone had a chance to identify their favorite double-page spread and explain why. The materials needed to create similar artwork were also discussed.

When the group discussed *The Witch of Blackbird Pond* by Elizabeth George Speare, they looked at four themes: the book as a story of an orphan, a story of colonial America, a story of matchmaking (which made the boys groan!), and a story of friendship. The group discussed the culture and beliefs of Puritans and Quakers in the late 1600s and the views of various characters in the story. How did individual views of Hannah Tupper, the suspected witch, differ? What is the turning point of the story? All this led to the declaration of a favorite character and a least favorite character. The group talked about this book as a Newbery-winning title (1959) and explored its outstanding features.

When the Afghan novel *The Kite Runner* by Khaled Hosseini (Riverhead, 2003) was selected as the title for the adult Community Reads program, two books appropriate for young people and set in Afghanistan were selected for Novel Chit-Chats: *The Breadwinner* and *Parvana's Journey*, both by Deborah Ellis. The Chit-Chats group had a serious discussion on Afghanistan and the imposition of religious views after the Taliban takeover. The events befalling a normal family—an issue not frequently covered in newspapers and on television—touched a very gentle and concerned part of the hearts of all the readers. Readers found it amazing to follow young Parvana's brave efforts to take on the role of provider, her decision to remain behind in case her father is released and comes looking for his family, and her concerns when she finds out that the very city to which her mother and the rest of the family are headed has been captured by the Taliban. Everyone in the group began to understand how much decisions by people in the government, people you do not know, can really change your life!

The second book, *Parvana's Journey*, begins with Parvana burying her father. Her subsequent difficult journeys and experiences—before her eventual reunion with her family—made the readers admire her and empathize with her situation even more. A long discussion centered on one of Parvana's statements: "I didn't create this world, I only have to live in it." After talking about loyalty, survival, families, and friendship, the group said that reading these two books made them sad. Sad for the world. Even though they knew the books were fiction, the emotions depicted struck close enough to recognize they were based on real possibilities. This was truly one of the most heartfelt book discussions of all!

Overall, the program has been very satisfying. One of the young readers said, "We have a great time talking about the characters and what they do in the books we read." And a parent said, "I like reading the same books as my son and hearing the kids' insights." Words of recognition far outweigh any test scores!

Although this particular program is set in a public library, it could work equally well in a school/public library collaboration. Perhaps the school librarian could be joined by the public librarian, and home-schooled students could also participate. And if the students were all encouraged to extend the activity to their own families as well, the beginning goal—of creating opportunities for parents or caregivers and children to read and have real conversations—would be met!

Kathy East
Head of Children's Services
Wood County District Public Library
Bowling Green, OH 43402

Books Mentioned in the Overview

424 Carmi, Giora ✳ *A Circle of Friends*
Illus. by the author ✳ Star Bright Books, 2003 ✳ 1-93206-500-8
Universal ✳ Grades K–4

425 Ellis, Deborah ✳ *The Breadwinner*
Groundwood Press, 2000 ✳ 0-88899-419-2
Asian—Afghanistan ✳ Grades 4–6+

426 Ellis, Deborah ✳ *Parvana's Journey*
Groundwood Press, 2002 ✳ 0-88899-514-8
Asian—Afghanistan ✳ Grades 4–6+

427 Speare, Elizabeth George ✳ *The Witch of Blackbird Pond*
Houghton Mifflin, 1958 ✳ 0-395-07114-3
European American ✳ Grades 3–6

Additional Books to Consider

428 Burns, Khephra ✶ *Mansa Musa: The Lion of Mali*
Illus. by Leo and Diane Dillon ✶ Harcourt, 2001 ✶ 0-15-2000375-4
AFRICAN—MALI ✶ GRADES 5–6+

> This flowing, fictionalized account of the history of 14th-century
> Mali, in Africa, focuses on young Kankan Musa, who discovers that
> he is from a family of former rulers of this kingdom. Kankan's father
> died when the boy was quite young. Kankan was not aware of his
> heritage, and he lacked training in the traditions of his people. Dur-
> ing a grueling trip across the desert to the land of Egypt and back,
> Kankan comes to know himself and to understand the importance of
> his homeland. Encounters with slave traders, the mysteries of the
> desert, the beauty and uncertainty of mirages and dreams, and expo-
> sure to a variety of cultures and peoples—all these become part of
> the growth and education of a boy who was to become a document-
> ed leader. The Dillons have captured in pictures and design the rich-
> ness and grandeur of majestic Mali history. The rich colors, the
> golden highlights, the traditional mosaic designs all give the reader a
> sense of presence in the journey. *Coming-of-age rituals of cultures
> throughout the world were a natural subject for discussion. Why should
> a young person prove, at a predetermined age, that he or she is capable of
> certain skills or judgments? What in our American tradition compares to
> these historical rituals?*

429 Creech, Sharon ✶ *Granny Torrelli Makes Soup*
HarperCollins, 2003 ✶ 0-06-029291-1
ITALIAN AMERICAN ✶ GRADES 3–6

> Granny loves to make soup and she is also a good person to talk to.
> Rosie is mad at her best friend and neighbor, Bailey, who is blind.
> Through this story sprinkled with Italian phrases that need no trans-

lation, readers see how much easier it is to talk about problems and relationships when your hands are busy doing something else, especially when there is a wise mentor, sharing her stories and getting you to solve your own predicaments. *Discussion soon centered on the importance of families spending time sharing a meal together in a relaxed atmosphere. What bonding and what joy! Our group made pretzels and ate them together in the library staff room at the end of this discussion. We used Italian phrases and laughed a lot!*

430 Curtis, Christopher Paul ✴ *Bud, Not Buddy*
Delacorte Press, 1999 ✴ 0-385-32306-9
AFRICAN AMERICAN ✴ GRADES 4–6+

Bud, 10, is alone, but not alone. Since the death of his mother, he has been living in a home for boys. The caseworker announces that he is moving to a temporary-care home with Mr. and Mrs. Amos and their son Todd. Todd torments Bud and then whines to his parents, who decide to return Bud to the home. Instead, Bud escapes from the Amoses and begins his life "on the lam" searching for his father.

As soon as Bud feels he is safe, he opens up his suitcase and checks his belongings. In addition to a picture of Momma, there is a small bag of rocks and there are flyers featuring a performance of "Herman E. Calloway and the Dusky Devastators of the Depression." Bud believes that Herman E. Calloway must be his father, but when he finally catches up with the band, Bud finds out that he is wrong—Calloway is his grandfather.

The Depression era setting (1936) in Michigan provides a backdrop for Bud's adventures. His collection of "Rules and Things to Have a Funner Life and Make a Better Liar Out of Yourself" are funny and poignant. Bud is a survivor whose story will touch many readers.

This book is the first to win both the Newbery Medal and the Coretta Scott King Award for Writing. *What would you do if you had to go looking for your family, for the father you have never met? In a book discussion of* Bud, Not Buddy *readers explored issues of identity and choices. They empathized with Bud's search for his father and his desire to be independent but still belong.*

431 Hickman, Janet ✶ *Zoar Blue*
Macmillan, 1978 ✶ 0-02-743740-X
GERMAN AMERICAN ✶ GRADES 4–6+

Being part of a German Separatist group brings conflict into the lives
of Barbara, an orphan, and John, a boy who wants to be a volunteer
in the Union Army. They both leave their community to go their
separate ways. Life beyond the community proves much harsher
than either anticipated, especially the impact of the Civil War, and
they both return to Zoar, welcomed beyond their wildest expectations. They feel they are home. *Because Zoar Village, a historic site, is
in Ohio, much discussion centered on that setting and the lessons we can
learn from the period. Other communities, like the Shakers and the
Amish, became a part of the discussion, too. Many readers wondered
what it would be like to live in a restrictive society today. Not having television, cell phones, computers, and iPods would be a hardship for some
of them!*

432 Johnson, Angela ✶ *Heaven*
Simon & Schuster, 1998 ✶ 0-689-82229-4
AFRICAN AMERICAN ✶ GRADES 5–6+

Marley, 14, lives in Heaven, Ohio, with her Momma, Pops, and
brother Butchy. She receives letters from Uncle Jack, who is Pops's
twin brother, and his dog, Boy. Heaven is a small town but there is a
Western Union service at Ma's Superette. From the Western Union,
Marley can send money to Uncle Jack. With her friend Shoogy, Marley enjoys her life in Heaven. Then, Momma gets a letter. The letter
is from Deacon James David Major of the First Mission Church. It
asks for a copy of the birth certificate of Monna Floyd, the niece of
Momma and Pops. Monna Floyd is actually Marley. Marley is devastated to learn that the people she thought were her parents are really
her aunt and uncle. Her real father is "Uncle Jack"; and her real
mother is dead. Marley feels that her life is a lie and that everyone
around her is a liar. She withdraws from her family and searches to
understand who she really is.

With the help of her friends and the love and support of Momma,
Pops, and Butchy, Marley realizes "It's going to be okay. I mean—

sooner or later." She meets Jack and she comes to accept that she still has a loving family, but some of the roles have been changed.

Heaven received the Coretta Scott King Award for Writing. *As a group began to discuss* Heaven, *they focused on certain questions: What would you do if you suddenly realized that the people you loved and trusted had been keeping a secret from you? Who can you trust and love if you feel you have been betrayed? They explored Marley's alienation from her family and her eventual acceptance of their decision to keep the truth about her real parents from her.*

433 Johnston, Tony ∗ *Any Small Goodness: A Novel of the Barrio*
Scholastic, 2001 ∗ 0-439-18935-5
Mexican American ∗ Grades 3–6

Eleven-year-old Arturo Rodriguez gives the reader personal insight into his quirky but loving family, his Mexican heritage, and the ups and downs of life in his home, school, and neighborhood in Los Angeles. Arturo shares joys—being a part of a barrio of basketball-playing maniacs—and sadnesses—mean-spirited bullying by gang members and injustices like the loss of the school's great librarian because she had no proper credentials. This is a quick read peppered with Spanish words and phrases. *Concepts from the book—"the poor, but decent come to LA to get on with their dream," "love each other, help each other," "if you do not find enough of the good, you must create it— any small goodness is of value"—spurred discussion of human values and aspirations.*

434 Konigsburg, E. L. ∗ *The View from Saturday*
Atheneum, 1996 ∗ 0-689-80993-X
Multicultural ∗ Grades 4–6+

The View from Saturday tells the stories of the members of Mrs. Olinski's Academic Bowl team and how and why she chose them. The team proves to be a healing experience for her—she is a paraplegic as a result of an automobile accident. Members of the team represent various cultures, including Julian Singh, who is Indian, and Noah Gershom, who is Jewish. The team's success brings these diverse youngsters together. This book received the Newbery Medal in 1997. *A tea party was the perfect setting for the Novel Chit-Chats discussion of this book. Each attendee was given a strip of paper with a quote and a character's name typed on it. Working in their pairs, they needed to identify the character and his or her contribution to the story.*

435 Lin, Grace ✳ *The Year of the Dog*
Illus. by the author ✳ Little, Brown, 2006 ✳ 0-316-06000-3
CHINESE AMERICAN ✳ GRADES 3–6

The opening chapter is called "A Sweet New Year" and introduces the Lin family. There is Grace, whose nickname is Pacy, her mom and dad, her older sister Lissy, and her younger sister Ki-Ki. They are preparing to celebrate the Chinese New Year, and the details about this event will interest readers. At school, Grace makes friends with a new girl, Melody Lin, who is also Chinese American. The two girls enjoy sharing secrets and participating in the science fair; they even like the same boy. Grace sometimes struggles with her heritage; when she wants to try out for the part of Dorothy in *The Wizard of Oz*, for example, a classmate tells her that "Dorothy's not Chinese," and Grace is crushed. She decides to write her own book and she wins fourth place in a national writing contest. Grace realizes she wants to be an author and illustrator, which, of course, she already is. Throughout the book there are family stories—such as "How Grandpa Got Rich" and "Mom's First Day of School." They help Grace understand the importance of her heritage and how it connects to her present. The book is illustrated with small, charming drawings. *Readers discussed how relationships with family and friends are universal, cutting across cultures. They especially enjoyed the family stories that were interspersed throughout the book. This gave an opportunity for the parent-child pair to spend some time telling a favorite family memory to each other.*

436 Lord, Bette Bao ✳ *In the Year of the Boar and Jackie Robinson*
Illus. by Marc Simont ✳ HarperCollins, 1984 ✳ 0-06-440175-8
CHINESE AMERICAN ✳ GRADES 4–6

Shirley Temple Wong, a new arrival from China in the late 1940s, has trouble fitting in at her new school in Brooklyn, New York. But her interest in sports makes the transition easier, and parallels between her own problems and those of Jackie Robinson are illuminating. *This funny story easily prompted discussions about tolerance and friendship. Questions about Jackie Robinson provided an opportunity to use other library resources to find more information.*

437 Oppenheim, Joanne ∗ *Dear Miss Breed: True Stories of the Japanese American Incarceration During World War II and a Librarian Who Made a Difference*
Scholastic, 2006 ∗ 0-439-56992-3
JAPANESE AMERICAN ∗ GRADES 6+

Clara Breed was a children's librarian at the San Diego Public Library. At the library, she advised and befriended many Japanese American children and young adults. When many of these patrons were taken to internment camps, Miss Breed continued to communicate with them and serve them. She sent books, gifts, and mail. She encouraged them to be patient and to plan for a better time. This book is a collection of historical documents and interviews with many of those who were served by Miss Breed. It documents how the hysteria of the time impacted innocent families whose only crime was their heritage. *The importance of library work was an obvious topic here, in addition to racial prejudice. There were also questions about the internment. What generated the most discussion was the impact that one person could have on the lives of others. You don't have to be famous to make a difference!*

438 Park, Linda Sue ∗ *The Kite Fighters*
Clarion, 2000 ∗ 0-395-94041-9
ASIAN—KOREA ∗ GRADES 3–6

In 15th-century Korea, the New Year Festival includes a kite competition. Two brothers—Kee-sup, oldest son of the privileged Lee family, and Young-sup—have individual talents when it comes to building and flying kites. Kee-sup takes great care in measuring, planning, and painting his kite, which is a beautiful object. But it won't fly. Young-sup, on the other hand, feels the wind speak to him, guiding him to a successful launch every time. As the younger brother must show respect to his older brother, Young-sup's patience is often tested. The two brothers work well together, however, when the king needs a kite for a competition. This book gives beautiful insight into family traditions, celebrations, respect, and honor of a culture. *Sibling rivalry was the focus of discussion after reading this book, and many pairs left with plans to create their own kites.*

439 Park, Linda Sue ∗ *Project Mulberry*
Clarion, 2005 ∗ 0-618-47786-1
KOREAN AMERICAN ∗ GRADES 3–6+

Julia, a Korean American, and her friend Patrick look for a good project for their after-school club. When Julia's mom suggests growing silkworms, Julia says, "It's too Korean!" But Patrick loves the idea and starts searching the Internet to find a place to buy the worms. Complications arise with the search for a mulberry tree. *Discussions centered not only on cultural differences, but also on the unusual presentation, in which the author has conversations with her young heroine.*

440 Park, Linda Sue ∗ *A Single Shard*
Clarion, 2001 ∗ 0-395-97827-0
ASIAN—KOREA ∗ GRADES 4–6+

The dream of an orphan boy in 12th-century Korea is to learn the craft of the master potter named Min. Min's specialty is celadon pots. Tree-Ear, the orphan, lives with the lame and elderly Crane-Man, who encourages the boy to learn and achieve. The greatest honor for a potter is to create a piece for the palace. Min's desire for perfection, Tree-Ear's daring journey to take Min's pot to the palace, and the continuing inspirational adages of Crane-Man keep the reader emotionally involved in this book. This book won the Newbery Medal in 2002. *It was rewarding to discuss the meaning of this book's title. A piece of celadon pottery and the fragments of a shattered pot brought meaning to the word "shard." Everyone also had a chance to share what they saw as the funniest, saddest, bravest, and most inspirational moments in the book.*

441 Slote, Alfred * *Finding Buck McHenry*
HarperCollins, 1991 * 0-06-021653-0
African American * Grades 4–6

Jason, 11, loves baseball and collecting baseball cards. When Jason is cut from the Little League team and joins an expansion team, there is one problem—the team needs a coach. Jason convinces himself that the school janitor, Mack Henry, is really the famous Negro League pitcher Buck McHenry and persuades him to become coach. Mr. Henry is eventually recognized as an experienced player in the pre-integration South, and he succeeds in inspiring many young players. *Discussion initially centered on being recruited for a team. Then we turned to planning the highlights of this book as a movie for TV.*

442 Taylor, Theodore * *The Cay*
Delacorte, 1987 * 0-3850-7906-0
Multicultural * Grades 5–6+

Eleven-year-old Phillip is on his way home to Virginia with his mother when their ship is torpedoed in 1942. Phillip survives but loses his sight and finds himself stranded on a deserted island with a black man and a cat. *When the book discussion pairs arrived at the library, the kids were blindfolded and the adults were not. Then another adult, not from the "pair," led them as "Phillip" on a scenic tour through the children's area of the library, ending up in the book discussion room, where they remained blindfolded and discussed what they had learned from this exercise. They also examined how what they were feeling and saying reflected the themes of survival, independence, and race that are part of* The Cay. *The dedication was consulted to establish the reason for the book.*

443 Taylor, Theodore * *Maria: A Christmas Story*
Harcourt Brace Jovanovich, 1992 * 0-15-217763-9
Mexican American * Grades 3–6

In the San Joaquin Valley of California, a Christmas tradition is a parade of floats. But until now there has never been a Mexican American float. Young Maria is determined to participate despite the disparity between her community's resources and their wealthy ranching neighbors. *The emotional reaction to this story shows that it is more than a simple Christmas story; it is a story that breaks down barriers through love and beauty.*

444 Wyss, Thelma Hatch * *Bear Dancer: The Story of a Ute Girl*
Simon & Schuster, 2005 * 978-1-4169-0285-0
NATIVE AMERICAN—UTE * GRADES 3–6

Based on a true story, this is a fictionalized account of Elk Girl, proud sister of Ute chief Ouray, who was captured by Cheyenne warriors in the Rocky Mountains during the 1860s and forced to become a slave. Elk Girl has many bad experiences during her time with Native Americans but she fears most the White Man. *This fast-moving adventure captured everyone's interest. Readers wanted to discuss the Native American traditions as well as Elk Girl's feelings of vulnerability toward both her own peoples and the settlers.*

CHAPTER EIGHT

Literature Circles

LITERATURE CIRCLES ARE DISCUSSION GROUPS. They are similar to parent/child book groups and to teacher-directed book discussions. However, literature circles are led by children. In a classroom (typically) or as part of a public library program, children meet in groups to talk about selected books. For this overview, a school classroom model will be presented.

In one third-grade classroom, the teacher uses literature circles as a way to encourage his students to interact with books. To begin the activity, the librarian gathers a selection of issue-themed picture books and the teacher gives a brief overview of each book. The students select their top three choices, writing the titles on squares of paper. The teacher divides the class into groups of five or six students per book. The librarian requests extra copies of the chosen books from every school, so that, if possible, each child can have a copy.

As the books are being selected and the groups assigned, the teacher gives an overview of the structure he uses for literature circles. Within each group, each child has a defined role. The roles shift each time the group meets so that each child experiences each role. There are many possible roles; one Web site lists 12 suggestions. In the beginning, this third-grade class used five:

Discussion Director
Literary Luminator
Cool Connector

Word Wizard

Artsy Artist

The Discussion Director prepares questions for the group to discuss. It may take several days (or weeks for a longer book) for the group to discuss an individual book. The Literary Luminator brings the group's attention to interesting passages in that day's reading. The Cool Connector finds links between the reading and other experiences, subjects, or books. The Word Wizard focuses on vocabulary, making a list of words that are unusual or difficult. The Artsy Artist creates an artistic interpretation of the passage.

After experiencing several literature circles, the teacher made some changes. First, he encouraged the Artsy Artist to do an illustration that shows a sequence of the action—perhaps the beginning, the middle, or the end. Then, two more roles were created:

Sam the Summarizer

Story Mapper

Sam the Summarizer does retelling, which connects to the standards for English and Language Arts. The Story Mapper also evolved from the standards. This role presents information using graphic organizers, such as Venn diagrams and sequence charts.

As the children experience each role, they demonstrate different types of learning and use different domains. They develop organizational skills; they use their creative talents; they focus on vocabulary, characters, and themes; they link books to real life. Literature circles allow students choices.

In this third-grade class, the students focused on picture books to learn the process. Then they moved on to novels, informational books, poetry, biographies, and other genres of literature. For their first experience, the teacher used *Freedom Summer* by Deborah Wiles to introduce the process and help the children formulate thinking questions—questions that extend the discussion and improve the understanding of each book. He then selected the following titles for their consideration.

Togo *

Gleam and Glow *

Nim and the War Effort *

The Other Side *
Sami and the Time of Troubles
The Blue and the Gray
Visiting Day **
Dirt on Their Skirts **

The class selected the books that are marked with one star. The books marked with two stars had been chosen the previous year.

At the first meeting, each of the four groups met and began their literature circle. Because these were picture books, the discussions lasted only two or three days and each student did not experience each role. When the class chose longer books, the discussions lasted for two to three weeks.

There are many benefits to using literature circles. Most importantly, the book discussions are student-directed. The children develop the skills to analyze and evaluate literature. They take a leadership role in their learning. Because the roles are rotated, each child has a variety of experiences using different learning modalities. They focus on different aspects of a book including plot, vocabulary, and art.

Books Mentioned in the Overview

445 Blake, Robert J. ∗ *Togo*
Illus. by the author ∗ Philomel, 2002 ∗ 0-399-23381-4
EUROPEAN—NORWAY; ALASKAN ∗ GRADES 2–4

In Alaska, Leonhard Seppala runs a kennel. He also trains dogs to participate in sled races. One dog, Togo, does not seem a likely choice for a sled dog team. However, when Seppala tries to leave Togo off the team, Togo finds a way to join them. Seppala realizes that Togo was strong and a natural leader for the team. When Seppala begins to enter his team in races, they win! He realizes that Togo's leadership helped his team. One night, Seppala is asked to help take diphtheria serum 300 miles to Nome, Alaska. They begin on January 28, 1925. To save time, they go across the frozen Golovin Bay, with Togo leading the way. Then they cross Norton Bay, even as the wind shifts and the ice begins to break apart. Just as they are finishing their journey, the plans are changed. They have to backtrack to another team and cross Norton Bay again. Seppala and the team are exhausted, but Togo leads them and they reach Golovin Village. Another team continues the relay and the serum reaches Nome. An Epilogue describes the relay that brought the serum and how the Iditarod Race commemorates the events of Togo and other dog teams.

446 Bunting, Eve ∗ *The Blue and the Gray*
Illus. by Ned Bittinger ∗ Scholastic, 1996 ∗ 0-590-60197-0
AFRICAN AMERICAN ∗ GRADES 2–5

New houses are being built on the site of a Civil War battle. A boy and his father and the boy's friend J.J. talk about battles that were fought and the lives that were lost. The white father and son and J.J., who is African American, walk across a field and remember those who fought and died. The houses that are being built will hire families from diverse backgrounds, including those of the two boys in this story. The text of the book moves back and forth between the modern times and the battles of the Civil War. The text is poetic and is accompanied by oil paintings that depict the past and the present.

447 Bunting, Eve ∗ *Gleam and Glow*
Illus. by Peter Sylvada ∗ Harcourt, 2001 ∗ 0-15-202596-0
EUROPEAN—BOSNIA-HERZEGOVINA ∗ GRADES 3–6

Viktor, his little sister Marina, and their mother must leave their home to escape the approaching enemy. As they leave, they release two pet fish into the pond. Marina has named them Gleam and Glow. The family walks to the border and lives in a refugee camp, where they are joined by Papa, who has been in the underground. After many months, they return to their village, where all of the homes have been destroyed. The children run to the pond, which they find teeming with golden fish. This book was inspired by a true story from a small village in Bosnia-Herzegovina, where a family left their home in 1990, releasing two golden fish into a lake. Returning in 1995, they found lake full of golden fish.

448 Heide, Florence Parry, and Judith Heide Gilliland * *Sami and the Time of the Troubles*
Illus. by Ted Lewin * Houghton Mifflin, 1992 * 0-395-55964-2
Middle Eastern—Lebanon * Grades 2–4

Sami, 10, lives in Beirut. He enjoys everyday activities with his family but his daily life also includes guns, bombs, and living in the basement of his uncle's house. Sami remembers a time when he played war with his friend Amir. Now, with the real war all around him, Sami reflects on his feelings about fighting and violence.

449 Lee, Milly * *Nim and the War Effort*
Illus. by Yangsook Choi * Farrar, Straus and Giroux, 1997 * 0-374-35523-1
Chinese American * Grades 3–5

Nim lives with her parents, siblings, and grandparents in San Francisco. It is 1943 and the United States is involved in World War II. Nim and her family are careful to demonstrate that they are loyal Americans. Grandfather even wears a special pin with the American flag and the Chinese flag to show his heritage. Nim collects all the newspapers she can, hoping to win the paper drive at her school. A classmate, Garland Stephenson, always seems to be just ahead of her. Nim decides to go out of Chinatown to look for more papers and she finds an apartment building on Nob Hill that has a room filled with papers. Nim finds a creative way to get the papers to her school and she wins the contest. Later, she must face the disapproval of her grandfather and explain her disobedient behavior.

450 Rappaport, Doreen, and Lyndall Callan * *Dirt on Their Skirts: The Story of the Young Women Who Won the World Championship*
Illus. by E. B. Lewis * Dial, 2000 * 0-8037-2042-4
European American * Grades 2–4

It is 1946 and Margaret is at the championship game for the All-American Girls Professional Baseball League. The league was formed during World War II. With so many men fighting in the war, women took on jobs and responsibilities that used to be done by men, including playing baseball. This book features a fictional child and her family watching their team, the Racine Belles, win the championship against the Rockford Peaches. A Box Score of the game and an Author's Note about the league are included.

451 Woodson, Jacqueline ∗ *The Other Side*
Illus. by E. B. Lewis ∗ Putnam, 2001 ∗ 0-399-23116-1
African American ∗ Grades 3–6

A fence divides Clover's town: on her side are the black people and on the other side are the whites. Clover has been told to stay on her side of the fence. Clover can see a white girl on the other side and she keeps her distance, but she begins to wonder why. Clover watches the girl until one day, they introduce themselves through the fence. The two girls decide to sit on the fence together and talk. One day, they leave the fence and join a group of Clover's friends jumping rope. Then all the girls sit on the fence and think about how one day the fence will come down. E. B. Lewis's watercolor illustrations are an outstanding complement to Jacqueline Woodson's poetic text.

452 Woodson, Jacqueline ∗ *Visiting Day*
Illus. by James E. Ransome ∗ Scholastic, 2002 ∗ 0-590-40005-3
African American ∗ Grades 3–5

A little girl is excited about visiting her father. Grandma is going, too, preparing a basket of food for the long bus trip. The bus arrives at the penitentiary, where "Daddy is doing a little time." The text is brief, told from the perspective of the little girl. The illustrations depict the love of the family members and the sadness at being separated. Both the author and illustrator include Notes about their work on this book and both reveal their own experiences with relatives being incarcerated. This is a thought-provoking picture book that encourages discussion.

Additional Books to Consider

These titles present diverse experiences and are suitable for literature circles.

453 Bruchac, Joseph * *Squanto's Journey: The Story of the First Thanksgiving*
Illus. by Greg Shed * Harcourt, 2000 * 0-15-201817-4
NATIVE AMERICAN—PATUXET   *   GRADES 2–5

Unlike many books about the first Thanksgiving, this book focuses on the experiences of Squanto, the Patuxet Indian who helped the Pilgrims. The first-person narration is fictionalized but the result is a dramatic retelling of familiar events from a different perspective. Readers learn about Squanto's first encounter with Captain John Smith and Captain Thomas Hunt. Captain Hunt captured Squanto and others from his people and took them to Spain, where they became slaves. Spanish friars helped Squanto regain his freedom and travel to England. From England, Squanto traveled back to New England, where he found that many of his people had died from illness. In New England, Squanto worked with other native people and, as he spoke English, provided assistance to the English settlers. An Author's Note adds additional history and there is a glossary.

454 Cameron, Ann * *Gloria Rising*
Illus. by Lis Toft * Farrar, Straus and Giroux, 2002 * 0-374-32675-4
AFRICAN AMERICAN   *   GRADES 2–4

Right before the start of fourth grade, Gloria Jones meets Dr. Grace Street in the grocery store. Dr. Street is an African American astronaut and she encourages Gloria to do her best and work to achieve her goals. At school, Gloria's fourth-grade teacher, Mrs. Yardley, who is nicknamed "the Dragon of Doom," misinterprets classroom situations and makes negative judgments about Gloria and her friends (including Julian and Latisha, from other books). A visit to the class from Dr. Street clears up the confusion and as a result, Mrs. Yardley becomes more tolerant of the students in her classroom. An Author's Note provides Internet sites about space and astronauts.

455 Clements, Andrew ✳ *The Jacket*
Illus. by McDavid Henderson ✳ Simon & Schuster, 2002 ✳ 0-689-82595-1
AFRICAN AMERICAN ✳ GRADES 3–6

Phil Morelli is in sixth grade and attends an integrated school. Although he does not have any close friends who are black, he does not think he is prejudiced. At school one day, Phil sees a boy—a black kid—wearing his brother's jacket. Phil accosts the boy and demands to know how he got the jacket and where his brother is. When the two are taken to the principal's office, Phil accuses the boy, whose name is Daniel Taylor, of stealing the jacket. What really happened is that Daniel's grandmother, Lucy Taylor, is the cleaning lady for Phil's family. Phil realizes that his mother had given the jacket away and that he was wrong to accuse Daniel of being a thief. Daniel, however, is embarrassed that he has received "charity" from Phil's family and he refuses to keep the jacket. This book examines issues of racism and prejudice.

456 Erdrich, Louise ✳ *The Birchbark House*
Illus. by the author ✳ Hyperion, 1999 ✳ 0-7868-0300-2
NATIVE AMERICAN—OJIBWA ✳ GRADES 4–6+

Omakayas, 7, lives with her parents, her sister Angeline, her little brother Pinch, her baby brother Neewo, and her grandmother Nokomis. Omakayas and her family are Anishinabeg, part of the Ojibwa tribe. During the winter, the family lives in a cedar cabin on an island in Lake Superior. As this book begins it is summer and they have built a new home from birchbark. Omakayas has many responsibilities including helping to clean and tan a moose hide. The family survives by using every resource available to them. Omakayas gathers wood for the fire, scrapes and softens a moose hide, and works in the summer garden. Along with the details about everyday life, there are exciting moments; for example, when Omakayas encounters two bear cubs and their mother. There are also descriptions of hardship, including the death of a visitor from smallpox, which then infects Omakayas's family, killing her beloved baby brother. As Omakayas tries to cope with the loss, she learns a secret about her own past. The book is filled with rich details about a Native American family during a year in the 1840s. The author includes many Ojibwa words, which are listed in a glossary and pronunciation guide. Readers may also enjoy the sequel, *The Game of Silence* (HarperCollins, 2005).

457 Lombard, Jenny * *Drita, My Homegirl*
Putnam, 2006 * 0-399-24380-1
MULTICULTURAL * GRADES 4–6

Drita, 10, and her family are refugees from Kosovo. It is difficult to adjust to life in New York City. Drita is trying to learn English and make friends but she is clearly an outsider. Maxie is a street-smart African American girl in Drita's class. Their teacher, Miss Salvato, gives Maxie an unusual social studies assignment. She will study Drita and learn about Kosovo. At first, Maxie rebels. She is a popular fourth-grader and feels that Drita is a drag. As she learns more about Drita and her family, Maxie becomes her friend. Maxie comes to understand Drita's sense of loss and it helps her cope with the loss of her own mother who has been dead for three years. Drita and Maxie tell their stories in alternating chapters. Drita uses halting English while Maxie uses slang. Readers will want to learn more about the circumstances in Kosovo and the struggles faced by refugees.

458 Look, Lenore * *Ruby Lu, Brave and True*
Illus. by Anne Wilsdorf * Atheneum, 2004 * 0-689-84907-9
CHINESE AMERICAN * GRADES 2–4

Ruby Lu is almost 8 years old. She likes her house, her school, her family (especially her baby brother Oscar), and her friends. She likes learning magic tricks and visiting her grandparents in Chinatown. She likes everything—except when her life does not go according to her plans. For example, Oscar is not talking as well as her friend Emma's brother Sam. Finally Oscar does begin to talk! The problem is, he interrupts her magic show. Ruby frets about this for a while until she decides to make Oscar's talking a part of her magic show.

Ruby faces another problem when her mother enrolls her in Chinese school because it meets on Saturdays. Ugh. But there are fun kids in the class—including another girl named Ruby. And there are Chinese snacks and a cool teacher. Ruby loves Chinese school.

When a new girl moves into the neighborhood, there are more problems. Ruby has an adventure driving her parents' car and she helps prepare for relatives who are emigrating from China.

Through it all, Ruby is spirited and caring. The chapters in this book are short and episodic. They would provide natural breaks in the discussion process.

459 McCall Smith, Alexander ✶ *Akimbo and the Elephants*
Illus. by LeUyen Pham ✶ Bloomsbury, 2005 ✶ 1-58234-686-0
AFRICAN ✶ GRADES 3–5

Akimbo lives with his parents in Africa. His father works on a wildlife reserve. Akimbo loves watching elephants. When poachers begin killing elephants for their tusks, Akimbo is determined to try to catch them. His dangerous, even foolhardy plan involves taking a piece of ivory that has been confiscated, lying to his parents, and making a deal with the leader of the gang of poachers. Akimbo joins the poachers on a hunt and faces a charging elephant. Later he sneaks away from the poachers and contacts the rangers, who catch the poachers. Akimbo is brave, and also very lucky. Readers will appreciate the fast-paced action and Akimbo's active role as the problem solver. Research on African animals focusing on endangered and protected species would extend a discussion of this book.

Akimbo and the Lions (Bloomsbury, 2005) would also be a good choice for a literature circle discussion. There are seven chapters and lots of action. In this book, Akimbo's father is now the head ranger of the game park and he is dealing with a lion that has been attacking cattle on a ranch. Akimbo joins his father and a team of rangers as they try to trap and relocate the lion.

These books were first published in England in the early 1990s. There are two additional titles in the series: *Akimbo and the Croco-*

dile Man (Bloomsbury, 2006) and *Akimbo and the Snakes* (Bloomsbury, 2006).

460 Marsden, Carolyn, and Virginia Shin-Mui Loh * *The Jade Dragon*
Candlewick Press, 2006 * 0-7636-3012-6
Chinese American * Grades 3–5

Ginny Liao is in second grade and feels like an outsider. She is the only Chinese American girl in her class until Stephanie joins the class. Although Stephanie looks like Ginny, she acts like all the other American kids. Ginny tries to become Stephanie's friend by building on their Asian heritage. On a visit to Stephanie's home, Ginny discovers that Stephanie is adopted and knows nothing about her homeland. In an attempt to demonstrate her friendship, Ginny gives a prized jade dragon to Stephanie, leading to problems at home for Ginny. Ginny is an endearing character who tries to adjust to two worlds. This book is a great choice for discussion of friendship, belonging, and adoption.

461 Namioka, Lensey * *Half and Half*
Delacorte, 2003 * 0-385-73038-1
Multicultural * Grades 4–6

As this book begins, Fiona Cheng, 11, wants to sign up for a folk dancing class at the recreation center. She does not want to check the box on the form that indicates her race. Fiona's father is Chinese and her mother is Scottish. Fiona struggles to cope with the different influences of her heritage and the societal desire to label her. Fiona talks to her parents and her friends about her dilemma. She also worries about an upcoming visit from her Grandma and Grandpa MacMurray and about her father's respectful relationship with his Chinese mother. Fiona thinks her father's personality changes when he is around his mother and Fiona is embarrassed by it. Fiona's participation in the folk festival where she represents both of her cultures helps her appreciate her diverse heritage.

462 Smith, Cynthia Leitich ✳ *Indian Shoes*
Illus. by Jim Madsen ✳ HarperCollins, 2002 ✳ 0-06-029531-7
Native American—Cherokee, Seminole ✳ Grades 3–6

Ray Halfmoon and his grandfather live in Chicago and enjoy many activities in the city, including going to Wrigley Field to watch the Chicago Cubs play baseball and going downtown to buy a hot dog. Their heritage is Cherokee and Seminole and occasionally they visit their family in Oklahoma and celebrate native traditions as well as enjoying everyday activities such as fishing.

Each of the six chapters in this book is a story that could stand alone as a read-aloud or for a discussion group. In the first story, Ray trades his orange hightop sneakers for a pair of moccasins for Grampa. In another chapter, Ray is supposed to wear a tuxedo to carry the ring in a friend's wedding but there are no pants. Ray and Grampa come up with a creative and humorous solution. During one Christmas, the weather is too treacherous to make the trip to Oklahoma so Ray and Grampa stay in Chicago and watch all the pets in their neighborhood. The final story is about a trip to Oklahoma where a nighttime fishing expedition makes a special connection for Ray because Grampa used to fish like this with Ray's father.

463 Soto, Gary ✳ *Boys at Work*
Illus. by Robert Casilla ✳ Delacorte, 1995 ✳ 0-385-32048-5
Mexican American ✳ Grades 4–6

Rudy Herrera, 10, has a big problem. He was playing baseball with his friends and accidentally fell on a pile of equipment. In the pile was Slinky's Discman, and it is smashed. Rudy and his friend Alex know that Slinky will destroy them if they do not replace the Discman. They begin doing odd jobs around their neighborhood, including cleaning cats and catching fish to sell. None of their schemes really work, but the boys keep trying. Then they find out that the Discman didn't really belong to Slinky. It belonged to Trucha Mendoza, "an honest-to-goodness gangster." Now the boys are desperate. Trucha has been out of town, but he's coming back. On the day he returns home they still do not have enough money. There is one last scheme—returning a lost cat and claiming the reward. Trucha accompanies Rudy, Alex, and Slinky, and he takes the reward and all the money the boys have earned. Spanish phrases add to the authenticity of the barrio setting. The chapters would divide easily for reading and discussion activities.

464 Whelan, Gloria * *Homeless Bird*
HarperCollins, 2000 * 0-06-028454-4
ASIAN—INDIA * GRADES 4–6+

In India, Koly, 13, faces a difficult life. As a female, she is restricted by the expectations of her culture, society, and family. Koly longs for an education and wants to go to school like her brothers do, but she is not permitted to go. Instead, Koly stays home and prepares to be married and run a household. She helps build her dowry by working with her mother embroidering saris to sell in the marketplace. Soon, a marriage is arranged for Koly. Hari Mehta is 16 and, like Koly, his father is a Brahman, the highest Hindu class.

With her parents, Koly travels to Hari's home in another town and Koly and Hari are married. The marriage is a sham. Hari's parents arranged for the marriage to take Koly's dowry and use it to take Hari, who is terminally ill, to bathe in the Ganges. The visit to the sacred river is not successful and Hari dies.

Now, Koly's life is even more restricted. As a widow, she is the responsibility of Hari's family. In fact, they consider her a burden—especially Hari's mother, whom Koly calls Sass ("mother-in-law"). With her dowry gone and no chance for another marriage or home of her own, Koly is treated as a servant. She watches as Hari's sister, Chandra, prepares for her marriage and Koly feels hopeless about her own future. Her Sassur ("father-in-law") befriends her and teaches her to read, but he becomes ill and dies.

Koly is now alone with Sass, who has a plan to abandon Koly. The two travel to Delhi, stopping in Vrindavan on the way. Once there, Sass leaves Koly and continues the journey. Alone with only forty-seven rupees, Koly feels lost. She lives on the street, sleeping in doorways. A young rickshaw driver, Raji, befriends her and takes her to the home of Maa Kamala, who gives Koly a place to stay and helps her find work. Koly works in the bazaar stringing marigolds into garlands, but when a rich woman sees her embroidery, Koly finds a better job working on beautiful saris. Now, Koly has her independence and she feels safe and secure. Her friendship with Raji has been growing and she chooses to marry him, move to his village, and continue to embroider beautiful designs.

465 Yolen, Jane ✳ *Encounter*
Illus. by David Shannon ✳ Harcourt, 1992 ✳ 0-15-225962-7
INDIANS OF THE WEST INDIES—TAINO ✳ GRADES 3–5

This fictionalized account of the arrival of Christopher Columbus on San Salvador in 1492 is told from the point of view of a young boy. The boy and his people are fascinated by the strangers—their appearance and their gifts. The boy begins to be wary of the strangers. He has dreamed about an approaching danger and he believes the strangers are evil. He tries to warn his people but they do not listen. The boy is taken away by the strangers, but he escapes and again he tries to warn others. Because he is a child, they still do not listen. At the end of the book, the boy is now an old man, remembering the loss of his people and his culture.

Awards for Multicultural Literature

AMÉRICAS BOOK AWARD FOR CHILDREN'S AND YOUNG ADULT LITERATURE

THE AMÉRICAS AWARD is given in recognition of U.S. works of fiction, poetry, folklore, or selected nonfiction (from picture books to works for young adults) published in the previous year in English or Spanish that authentically and engagingly portray Latin America, the Caribbean, or Latinos in the United States. By combining both and linking the Americas, the award reaches beyond geographic borders, as well as multicultural-international boundaries, focusing instead upon cultural heritages within the hemisphere. The award is sponsored by the national Consortium of Latin American Studies Programs (CLASP).

The award winners and commended titles are selected for their 1) distinctive literary quality; 2) cultural contextualization; 3) exceptional integration of text, illustration, and design; and 4) potential for classroom use.

The winning titles are listed below. For a list of the commended titles and more information about the award, visit the Web site at www.uwm.edu/Dept/CLACS/outreach/americas.html.

2005

Herrera, Juan Felipe. *Cinnamon Girl: Letters Found Inside a Cereal Box* HarperCollins, 2005.

2004

Brown, Monica. *My Name Is Celia:The Life of Celia Cruz/Me llamo Celia:La vida de Celia Cruz.* Rising Moon, 2004.

Sáenz, Benjamin Alire. *Sammy and Juliana in Hollywood.* Cinco Puntos Press, 2004.

2003

Morales, Yuyi. *Just a Minute: A Trickster Tale and Counting Book.* Chronicle Books, 2003.

Ortiz Cofer, Judith. *The Meaning of Consuel.* Farrar, Straus & Giroux, 2003.

2002

Alvarez, Julia. *Before We Were Free.* Knopf, 2002.

2001

Argueta, Jorge. *A Movie in My Pillow.* Illus. by Elizabeth Gómez. Children's Book Press, 2001.

Jiménez, Francisco. *Breaking Through.* Houghton Mifflin, 2001.

2000

Skármeta, Antonio. *The Composition.* Illus. by Alfonso Ruano. Groundwood, 2000.

Joseph, Lynn. *The Color of My Words.* HarperCollins, 2000.

1999

Herrera, Juan Felipe. *Crashboomlove.* University of New Mexico Press, 1999.

1998

Ancona, George. *Barrio: José's Neighborhood.* Harcourt Brace, 1998.

Carling, Amelia Lau. *Mama and Papa Have a Store.* Illus. by the author. Dial, 1998.

1997

Jiménez, Francisco. *The Circuit: Stories from the Life of a Migrant Child.* Houghton Mifflin, 1999, c1997.

Hanson, Regina. *The Face at the Window.* Illus. by Linda Saport. Clarion, 1997.

1996

Lomas Garza, Carmen. *In My Family/En mi familia.* Illus. by the author. Children's Book Press, 1996.

Martínez, Victor. *Parrot in the Oven/Mi vida.* HarperCollins, 1996.

1995

Temple, Frances. *Tonight, by Sea.* Orchard, 1995.

1994

Joseph, Lynn. *The Mermaid's Twin Sister: More Stories from Trinidad.* Illus. by Donna Perrone. Clarion, 1994.

1993

Delacre, Lulu. *Vejigante Masquerader.* Illus. by the author. Scholastic, 1993.

ASIAN/PACIFIC AMERICAN AWARDS FOR LITERATURE

EVERY TWO YEARS, THE ASIAN/PACIFIC AMERICAN Librarians Association selects winners and honor books in two categories of children's literature by or about Asian Pacific Americans. The winning titles are listed below. For a list of the commended titles and more information about the award, visit www.apalaweb.org/awards/awards.htm.

2006

Illustration in Children's Literature

Park, Linda Sue. *The Firekeeper's Son*. Illus. by Julie Downing. Clarion, 2004.

Text in Children's and Young Adult Literature

Kadohata, Cynthia. *Kira Kira*. Atheneum Books for Young Readers, 2004.

2004

Illustration in Children's Literature

Wong, Janet S., and Margaret Chodos-Irvine (illus). *Apple Pie 4th of July*. Harcourt, 2002.

Text in Children's and Young Adult Literature

Na, An. *A Step From Heaven*. Front Street, 2001.

MILDRED L. BATCHELDER AWARD

THIS AWARD HONORS MILDRED L. BATCHELDER, a former executive director of the Association for Library Service to Children (ALSC) and a believer in the importance of good books for children in translation from all parts of the world.

Established in 1966, the award is presented to an American publisher for an outstanding children's book originally published in a foreign language in a foreign country, and subsequently translated into English and published in the United States. ALSC gives the award to encourage American publishers to seek out superior children's books abroad and to promote communication among the peoples of the world. The winners are listed below; for more information and to find the honor awards, visit www.ala.org/ala/alsc/awardsscholarships/literaryawds/batchelderaward/batchelderaward.htm.

2007

Delacorte Press for *The Pull of the Ocean* written by Jean-Claude Mourlevat and translated from French by Y. Maudet.

2006

Arthur A. Levine Books for *An Innocent Soldier* written by Josef Holub and translated from German by Michael Hofmann.

2005

Delacorte Press/Random House Children's Books for *The Shadows of Ghadames* by Joëlle Stolz, translated from French by Catherine Temerson.

2004

Walter Lorraine Books/Houghton Mifflin Company for *Run, Boy, Run* by Uri Orlev, translated from Hebrew by Hillel Halkin.

2003

The Chicken House/Scholastic Publishing for *The Thief Lord* by Cornelia Funke, translated from German by Oliver Latsch.

2002

Cricket Books/Carus Publishing for *How I Became an American* by Karin Gündisch, translated from German by James Skofield.

2001

Arthur A. Levine/Scholastic Press for *Samir and Yonatan* by Daniella Carmi, translated from Hebrew by Yael Lotan.

2000

Walker and Co. for *The Baboon King* by Anton Quintana, translated from Dutch by John Nieuwenhuizen.

1999

Dial for *Thanks to My Mother* by Schoschana Rabinovici, translated from German by James Skofield.

1998

Henry Holt for *The Robber and Me* by Josef Holub, edited by Mark Aronson and translated from German by Elizabeth D. Crawford.

1997

Farrar, Straus & Giroux for *The Friends* by Kazumi Yumoto, translated from Japanese by Cathy Hirano.

1996

Houghton Mifflin for *The Lady with the Hat* by Uri Orlev, translated from Hebrew by Hillel Halkin.

1995

Dutton for *The Boys from St. Petri* by Bjarne Reuter, translated from Danish by Anthea Bell.

1994

Farrar, Straus & Giroux for *The Apprentice* by Pilar Molina Llorente, translated from Spanish by Robin Longshaw.

1993

No award.

1992

Houghton Mifflin Company for *The Man from the Other Side* by Uri Orlev, translated from Hebrew by Hillel Halkin.

1991

Dutton for *A Hand Full of Stars* by Rafik Schami, translated from German by Rika Lesser.

1990

Dutton for *Buster's World* by Bjarne Reuter, translated from Danish by Anthea Bell.

1989

Lothrop, Lee & Shepard for *Crutches* by Peter Härtling, translated from German by Elizabeth D. Crawford.

1988

McElderry Books for *If You Didn't Have Me* by Ulf Nilsson, translated from Swedish by Lone Thygesen Clecher and George Blecher.

1987

Lothrop, Lee & Shepard for *No Hero for the Kaiser* by Rudolph Frank, translated from German by Patricia Crampton.

1986

Creative Education for *Rose Blanche* by Christophe Gallaz and Robert Innocenti, translated from Italian by Martha Coventry and Richard Craglia.

1985

Houghton Mifflin for *The Island on Bird Street* by Uri Orlev, translated from Hebrew by Hillel Halkin.

1984

Viking Press for *Ronia, the Robber's Daughter* by Astrid Lindgren, translated from Swedish by Patricia Crampton.

1983

Lothrop, Lee & Shepard for *Hiroshima No Pika* by Toshi Maruki, translated from Japanese through Kurita-Bando Literary Agency.

1982

Bradbury Press for *The Battle Horse* by Harry Kullman, translated from Swedish by George Blecher and Lone Thygesen Blecher.

1981

William Morrow for *The Winter When Time Was Frozen* by Els Pelgrom, translated from Dutch by Maryka and Raphael Rudnik.

1980

Dutton for *The Sound of the Dragon's Feet* by Aliki Zei, translated from Greek by Edward Fenton.

1979

Harcourt Brace Jovanovich for *Rabbit Island* by Jörg Steiner, translated from German by Ann Conrad Lammers.

Franklin Watts for *Konrad* by Christine Nöstlinger, translated from German by Anthea Bell.

1978

No award.

1977

Atheneum for *The Leopard* by Cecil Bødker, translated from Danish by Gunnar Poulsen.

1976

Henry Z. Walck for *The Cat and Mouse Who Shared a House* by Ruth Hürlimann, translated from German by Anthea Bell.

1975

Crown for *An Old Tale Carved Out of Stone* by A. Linevskii, translated from Russian by Maria Polushkin.

1974

Dutton for *Petros' War* by Aliki Zei, translated from Greek by Edward Fenton.

1973

William Morrow for *Pulga* by S. R. Van Iterson, translated from Dutch by Alexander and Alison Gode.

1972

Holt, Rinehart & Winston for *Friedrich* by Hans Peter Richter, translated from German by Edite Kroll.

1971

Pantheon Books for *In the Land of Ur, the Discovery of Ancient Mesopotamia* by Hans Baumann, translated from German by Stella Humphries.

1970

Holt, Rinehart & Winston for *Wildcat Under Glass* by Aliki Zei, translated from Greek by Edward Fenton.

1969

Charles Scribner's Sons for *Don't Take Teddy* by Babbis Friis-Baastad, translated from Norwegian by Lise Sømme McKinnon.

1968

Alfred A. Knopf Inc. for *The Little Man* by Erich Kästner, translated from German by James Kirkup.

PURA BELPRÉ AWARD

THE PURA BELPRÉ AWARD, ESTABLISHED IN 1996, is presented every two years to honor Pura Belpré, who was the first Latina librarian at the New York Public Library and is known for her work in preserving and disseminating Puerto Rican folklore. The award is presented to a Latino/Latina writer and illustrator who best portrays, affirms, and celebrates the Latino cultural experience in an outstanding work of literature for children and youth. It is co-sponsored by the Association for Library Service to Children (ALSC), a division of the American Library Association, and REFORMA, the Association to Promote Library and Information Services to Latinos and the Spanish Speaking.

The winning titles are listed below. For a list of the commended titles and more information about the award, visit www.ala.org/ala/alsc/awardsscholarships/literaryawds/belpremedal/belprmedal.htm.

2006

For Narrative
Canales, Viola. *The Tequila Worm*. Random House, 2005.

For Illustration
Colón, Raul. *Doña Flor: A Tall Tale About a Giant Woman with a Great Big Heart* by Pat Mora. Knopf, 2005.

2004

For Narrative
Alvarez, Julia. *Before We Were Free*. Knopf, 2002.

For Illustration
Morales, Yuyi. *Just a Minute: A Trickster Tale and Counting Book*. Chronicle Books, 2003.

2002

For Narrative

Ryan, Pam Muñoz. *Esperanza Rising.* Scholastic Press, 2000.

For Illustration

Guevara, Susan. *Chato and the Party Animals* by Gary Soto. Putnam, 2000.

2000

For Narrative

Ada, Alma Flor. *Under the Royal Palms: A Childhood in Cuba.* Atheneum, 1998.

For Illustration

Lomas Garza, Carmen. *Magic Windows.* Children's Book Press, 1999.

1998

For Narrative

Martinez, Victor. *Parrot in the Oven: Mi vida.* HarperCollins, 1996.

For Illustration

Garcia, Stephanie. *Snapshots from the Wedding* by Gary Soto. Putnam, 1997.

1996

For Narrative

Ortiz Cofer, Judith. *An Island Like You: Stories of the Barrio.* Orchard Books, 1995.

For Illustration

Guevara, Susan. *Chato's Kitchen* by Gary Soto. Putnam, 1995.

VIRGINIA HAMILTON
LITERARY AWARD

THIS AWARD WAS ESTABLISHED IN 1998 by the Advisory Board of Kent State University's Virginia Hamilton Conference. The award recognizes an American author or illustrator whose books demonstrate artistic excellence and make a significant contribution to the field of multicultural literature for children and adolescents. The award is conferred annually at the Virginia Hamilton Conference. For more information about the conference, visit the Web site at http://dept.kent.edu/virginiahamiltonconf/.

2006 Allen Say
2005 Joseph Bruchac
2004 Arnold Adoff
2003 Ashley Bryan

2002 Leo and Diane Dillon
2001 Patricia McKissack
2000 Jerry Pinkney
1999 Walter Dean Myers

CORETTA SCOTT KING AWARDS

GIVEN TO AFRICAN AMERICAN AUTHORS AND ILLUSTRATORS for outstanding inspirational and educational contributions, the Coretta Scott King Book Award titles promote understanding and appreciation of the culture of all peoples and their contribution to the realization of the American dream.

The award is designed to commemorate the life and works of Dr. Martin Luther King Jr. and to honor Mrs. Coretta Scott King for her courage and determination to continue the work for peace and world brotherhood.

Winning titles must portray some aspect of the African American experience, past, present, or future; must be written/illustrated by an African American; and must be published in the U.S. in the year preceding presentation of the award. The winning titles are listed below. For a list of the commended titles and more information about the award, visit www.ala.org/ala/emiert/corettascottkingbookaward/corettascott.htm.

2007
Author
Draper, Sharon. *Copper Sun*. Atheneum.

Illustrator
Nelson, Kadir A. *Moses: When Harriet Tubman Led Her People to Freedom* by Carole Boston Weatherford. Jump at the Sun/Hyperion.

2006
Author
Lester, Julius. *Day of Tears: A Novel in Dialogue*. Jump at the Sun/Hyperion.

Illustrator
Collier, Bryan. *Rosa* by Nikki Giovanni. Holt.

2005
Author
Morrison, Toni. *Remember: The Journey to School Integration*. Houghton Mifflin.

Illustrator
Nelson, Kadir A. *Ellington Was Not a Street*. Simon & Schuster.

2004
Author
Johnson, Angela. *The First Part Last*. Simon & Schuster.

Illustrator
Bryan, Ashley. *Beautiful Blackbird*. Atheneum.

2003
Author
Grimes, Nikki. *Bronx Masquerade*. Dial.

Illustrator
Lewis, E. B. *Talkin' About Bessie: The Story of Aviator Elizabeth Coleman* by Nikki Grimes. Orchard.

2002

Author

Taylor, Mildred D. *The Land*. Putnam.

Illustrator

Pinkney, Jerry. *Goin' Someplace Special* by Patricia McKissack. Atheneum.

2001

Author

Woodson, Jacqueline. *Miracle's Boys*. Putnam.

Illustrator

Collier, Bryan. *Uptown*. Holt.

2000

Author

Curtis, Christopher Paul. *Bud, Not Buddy*. Delacorte.

Illustrator

Pinkney, Brian. *In the Time of the Drums* by Kim L. Siegelson. Jump at the Sun/Hyperion.

1999

Author

Johnson, Angela. *Heaven*. Simon & Schuster.

Illustrator

Wood, Michele. *i see the rhythm* by Toyomi Igus. Children's Book Press.

1998

Author

Draper, Sharon M. *Forged by Fire*. Atheneum.

Illustrator

Steptoe, Javaka. *In Daddy's Arms I Am Tall: African Americans Celebrating Fathers* by Alan Schroeder. Lee & Low.

1997

Author

Myers, Walter Dean. *Slam!* Scholastic.

Illustrator

Pinkney, Jerry. *Minty: A Story of Young Harriet Tubman* by Alan Schroeder. Dial.

1996

Author

Hamilton, Virginia. *Her Stories*. Scholastic.

Illustrator

Feelings, Tom. *The Middle Passage: White Ships Black Cargo*. Dial.

1995

Author

McKissack, Patricia C., and Fredrick McKissack. *Christmas in the Big House, Christmas in the Quarters*. Scholastic.

Illustrator

Ransome, James. *The Creation* by James Weldon Johnson. Holiday House.

1994

Author

Johnson, Angela. *Toning the Sweep*. Orchard.

Illustrator

Feelings, Tom. *Soul Looks Back in Wonder* ed. by Phyllis Fogelman. Dial.

1993

Author

McKissack, Patricia C. *The Dark-Thirty: Southern Tales of the Supernatural*. Knopf.

Illustrator

Wilson, Kathleen Atkins. *The Origin of Life on Earth: An African Creation Myth* retold by David A. Anderson/Sankofa. Sights Productions.

1992

Author

Myers, Walter Dean. *Now Is Your Time!* HarperCollins.

Illustrator

Ringgold, Faith. *Tar Beach*. Crown.

1991

Author

Taylor, Mildred D. *The Road to Memphis.* Dial.

Illustrator

Dillon, Leo, and Diane Dillon. *Aida* by Leontyne Price. Harcourt.

1990

Author

McKissack, Patricia C. *A Long Hard Journey.* Walker.

Illustrator

Gilchrist, Jan Spivey. *Nathaniel Talking* by Eloise Greenfield. Black Butterfly.

1989

Author

Myers, Walter Dean. *Fallen Angels.* Scholastic.

Illustrator

Pinkney, Jerry. *Mirandy and Brother Wind* by Patricia C. McKissack. Knopf.

1988

Author

Taylor, Mildred D. *The Friendship.* Dial.

Illustrator

Steptoe, John. *Mufaro's Beautiful Daughters: An African Tale.* Lothrop.

1987

Author

Walter, Mildred Pitts. *Justin and the Best Biscuits in the World.* Lothrop.

Illustrator

Pinkney, Jerry. *Half a Moon and One Whole Star* by Crescent Dragonwagon. Macmillan.

1986

Author

Hamilton, Virginia. *The People Could Fly: American Black Folktales.* Illus. by Leo and Diane Dillon. Knopf.

Illustrator

Pinkney, Jerry. *The Patchwork Quilt* by Valerie Flournoy. Dial.

1985

Author

Myers, Walter Dean. *Motown and Didi.* Viking.

Illustrator

No award.

1984

Author

Clifton, Lucille. *Everett Anderson's Goodbye.* Holt.

Illustrator

Cummings, Pat. *My Mama Needs Me* by Mildred Pitts Walter. Lothrop.

1983

Author

Hamilton, Virginia. *Sweet Whispers, Brother Rush.* Philomel.

Illustrator

Magubane, Peter. *Black Child.* Knopf.

1982

Author

Taylor, Mildred D. *Let the Circle Be Unbroken.* Dial.

Illustrator

Steptoe, John. *Mother Crocodile: An Uncle Amadou Tale from Senegal* by Rosa Guy. Delacorte.

1981

Author
Poitier, Sidney. *This Life*. Knopf.

Illustrator
Bryan, Ashley. *Beat the Story Drum, Pum-Pum*. Atheneum.

1980

Author
Myers, Walter Dean. *The Young Landlords*. Viking.

Illustrator
Bayard, Carole. *Cornrows* by Camille Yarborough. Coward-McCann.

1979

Author
Davis, Ossie. *Escape to Freedom*. Viking.

Illustrator
Feelings, Tom. *Something on My Mind* by Nikki Grimes. Dial.

1978

Author
Greenfield, Eloise. *Africa Dream*. Illus. by Carole Bayard. Crowell.

Illustrator
Bayard, Carole. *Africa Dream* by Eloise Greenfield. Crowell.

1977

Author
Haskins, James *The Story of Stevie Wonder*. Lothrop.

Illustrator
No award.

1976

Author
Bailey, Pearl. *Duey's Tale*. Harcourt.

Illustrator
No award.

1975

Author
Robinson, Dorothy W. *The Legend of Africania*. Johnson.

Illustrator
No award.

1974

Author
Mathis, Sharon Bell. *Ray Charles*. Illus. by George Ford. Crowell.

Illustrator
Ford, George. *Ray Charles* by Sharon Bell Mathis. Crowell.

1973

Author
Robinson, Jackie. *I Never Had It Made: An Autobiography of Jackie Robinson*. Putnam, 1972.

Illustrator
No award.

1972

Author
Fax, Elton C. *17 Black Artists*. Dodd.

Illustrator
No award.

1971

Author
Rollins, Charlemae. *Black Troubador: Langston Hughes*. Rand McNally.

Illustrator
No award.

1970

Author
Patterson, Lillie. *Martin Luther King, Jr.: Man of Peace*. Garrard.

Illustrator
No award.

TOMÁS RIVERA MEXICAN AMERICAN CHILDREN'S BOOK AWARD

THE AWARD WAS ESTABLISHED IN 1995 by the College of Education at Texas State University–San Marcos to encourage authors, illustrators, and publishers of books that authentically reflect the lives of Mexican American children and young adults in the United States. For more information, visit www.education.txstate.edu/subpages/tomas rivera/.

2005
Reich, Susanna. *José: Born to Dance*. Illus. by Raúl Colón. Simon & Schuster, 2005.

2004
Ryan, Pam Muñoz. *Becoming Naomi León*. Scholastic, 2004.

2003
Morales, Yuyi. *Just A Minute: A Trickster Tale and Counting Book*. Illus. by the author. Chronicle Books, 2003.

2002
Mora, Pat. *A Library for Juana*. Illus. by Beatriz Vidal. Knopf, 2002.

2001
Jiménez, Francisco. *Breaking Through*. Houghton Mifflin, 2001.

2000
Pérez, Amada Irma. *My Very Own Room/Mi propio cuartito*. Illus. by Maya Christina Gonzalez. Children's Book Press, 2000.

1999
Anaya, Rudolfo. *My Land Sings: Stories from the Rio Grande*. Illus. by Amy Cordova. Rayo, 1999.

1998
Salinas, Bobbi. *The Three Pigs/Los tres credos: Nacho, Tito y Miguel*. Illus. by the author. Pinata Books, 1998.

1997
Mora, Pat. *Tómas and the Library Lady*. Illus. by Raúl Colón. Knopf, 1997.

1996
Lomas Garza, Carmen. *In My Family/En mi familia*. Illus. by the author. Children's Book Press, 1996.

1995
Soto, Gary. *Chato's Kitchen*. Illus. by Susan Guevara. Putnam, 1995.

Anaya, Rudolfo. *The Farolitos of Christmas*. Illus. by Edward Gonzales. Hyperion, 1995.

SYDNEY TAYLOR BOOK AWARDS

THE SYDNEY TAYLOR BOOK AWARD was established in honor of the author of the classic All-of-a-Kind Family series to encourage the publication of outstanding books of positive Jewish content for children. The seal of the Association of Jewish Libraries is awarded annually to the authors of the most distinguished contributions to Jewish children's literature published in the preceding year. The first Sydney Taylor Book Award was given in 1968. In most years since then, two awards have been given, one for younger readers and one for older readers. Sydney Taylor Body-of-Work Awards have been granted periodically since 1971. A list of Notable Children's Books of Jewish Content is published annually by the Sydney Taylor Book Award Committee. For honor titles and more information, visit www.jewishlibraries.org/ajlweb/awards/st_books.htm.

2005

For Older Readers
Littman, Sarah. *Confessions of a Closet Catholic*. Dutton.

For Younger Readers
Silverman, Erica. *Sholom's Treasure: How Sholom Aleichem Became a Writer*. Illus. by Mordicai Gerstein. Farrar, Straus and Giroux.

2004

For Older Readers
Kass, Pnina Moed. *Real Time*. Clarion Books.

For Younger Readers
No award.

2003

For Older Readers
Patz, Nancy. *Who Was The Woman Who Wore The Hat?* Dutton.

For Younger Readers
Davis, Aubrey. *Bagels from Benny*. Illus. by Dusan Petricic. Kids Can Press.

2002

For Older Readers
Levine, Karen. *Hana's Suitcase: A True Story*. Second Story Press.

For Younger Readers
Hershenhorn, Esther. *Chicken Soup by Heart*. Illus. by Rosanne Litzinger. Simon & Schuster.

2001

For Older Readers
Reef, Catherine. *Sigmund Freud: Pioneer of the Mind*. Clarion Books.

For Younger Readers
Rael, Elsa Okon. *Rivka's First Thanksgiving*. Illus. by Maryann Kovalski. Simon & Schuster.

2000

For Older Readers
Vos, Ida. *The Key Is Lost*. Translated by Terese Edelstein. HarperCollins.

For Younger Readers
Kimmel, Eric A. *Gershon's Monster: A Story for the Jewish New Year.* Illus. by Jon J Muth. Scholastic.

1999
For Older Readers
Rosen, Sybil. *Speed of Light.* Atheneum.

For Younger Readers
Schur, Maxine Rose. *The Peddler's Gift.* Illus. by Kimberly Bulcken Root. Dial.

1998
For Older Readers
Napoli, Donna Jo. *Stones in Water.* Dutton.

For Younger Readers
Stillerman, Marci. *Nine Spoons.* Illus. by Pesach Gerber. HaChai Publishers.

1997
For Older Readers
Elijah. Illus. by Elivia Savadier. Scholastic.

For Younger Readers
Rael, Elsa Okon. *When Zaydeh Danced on Eldridge Street.* Illus. by Marjorie Priceman. Simon & Schuster.

1996
For Older Readers
Schur, Maxine Rose Schur. *When I Left My Village.* Illus. by Brian Pinkney. Dial.

For Younger Readers
Sofer, Barbara. *Shalom, Haver: Goodbye, Friend.* Kar-Ben.

1995
For Older Readers
Vos, Ida. *Dancing on the Bridge of Avignon.* Translated from Dutch. Houghton Mifflin.

For Younger Readers
Hoestlandt, Jo. *Star of Fear, Star of Hope.* Illus. by Johanna Kang. Translated from French. Walker and Co.

1994
For Older Readers
Schnur, Steven. *The Shadow Children.* Illus. by Herbert Tauss. Morrow.

For Younger Readers
Oberman, Sheldon. *The Always Prayer Shawl.* Illus. by Ted Lewin. Boyds Mill.

1993
For Older Readers
Matas, Carol. *Sworn Enemies.* Bantam Doubleday Dell.

For Younger Readers
Jaffe, Nina. *The Uninvited Guest.* Illus. by Elivia Savadier. Scholastic.

1992
For Older Readers
Hesse, Karen. *Letters from Rifka.* Henry Holt.

For Younger Readers
Gilman, Phoebe. *Something from Nothing.* Scholastic.

1991
For Older Readers
Schwartz, Howard, and Barbara Rush. *The Diamond Tree: Jewish Tales from Around the World.* Illus. by Uri Shulevitz. HarperCollins.

For Younger Readers
Goldin, Barbara Diamond. *Cakes and Miracles: A Purim Tale.* Illus. by Erika Weihs. Viking.

1990
For Older Readers
Geras, Adèle. *My Grandmother's Stories.* Illus. by Jael Jordan. Knopf.

For Younger Readers
Kimmel, Eric. *The Chanukkah Guest.* Illus. by Giora Carmi. Holiday House.

1989

For Older Readers

Lowry, Lois. *Number the Stars*. Houghton Mifflin.

For Younger Readers

Blanc, Esther Silverstein. *Berchick*. Illus. by Tennessee Dixon. Volcano Press.

1988

For Older Readers

Yolen, Jane. *The Devil's Arithmetic*. Viking.

For Younger Readers

Polacco, Patricia. *The Keeping Quilt*. Simon & Schuster.

1987

For Older Readers

Levitin, Sonia. *The Return*. Atheneum.

For Younger Readers

Adler, David. *The Number on My Grandfather's Arm*. Photos by Rose Eichenbaum. UAHC Press, 1987.

1986

For Older Readers

Pitt, Nancy. *Beyond the High White Wall*. Scribner.

For Younger Readers

Hirsh, Marilyn. *Joseph Who Loved the Sabbath*. Illus. by Devis Grebu. Viking Kestrel.

1985

For Older Readers

Snyder, Carol. *Ike and Mama and the Seven Surprises*. Lothrop, Lee and Shepard.

For Younger Readers

Freedman, Florence B. *Brothers*. Illus. by Robert Andrew Parker. Harper & Row.

1984

For Older Readers

Orlev, Uri. *The Island on Bird Street*. Houghton Mifflin.

For Younger Readers

Schwartz, Amy. *Mrs. Moskowitz and the Sabbath Candlesticks*. Jewish Publication Society.

1983

For Older Readers

Zar, Rose. *In the Mouth of the Wolf*. Jewish Publication Society.

For Younger Readers

Pomerantz, Barbara. *Bubby, Me, and Memories*. UAHC Press.

1982

For Older Readers

Sachs, Marilyn. *Call Me Ruth*. Bantam Doubleday Dell.

For Younger Readers

Heller, Linda. *The Castle on Hester Street*. Jewish Publication Society.

1981

For Older Readers

Lasky, Kathryn. *The Night Journey*. Penguin.

For Younger Readers

Cohen, Barbara. *Yussel's Prayer*. Illus. by Michael J. Deraney. Lothrop, Lee and Shepard.

1980

Everett Fisher, Leonard. *A Russian Farewell*. Four Winds Press.

1979

Snyder, Carol. *Ike and Mama and the Block Wedding*. Coward, McCann.

1978

Orgel, Doris. *The Devil in Vienna*. Penguin.

1977

Heyman, Anita. *Exit From Home*. Random House.

1976

Meltzer, Milton. *Never to Forget*. HarperCollins.

1975

Moskin, Marietta. *Waiting for Mama*. Coward, McCann.

1974

No award.

1973

Suhl, Yuri. *Uncle Misha's Partisans*. Four Winds.

1972

No award.

1971

No award.

1970

Lange, Suzanne. *The Year*. S. G. Phillips.

1969

Ish-Kishor, Sulamith. *Our Eddie*. Pantheon.

1968

Hautzig, Esther. *The Endless Steppe*. Harper-Collins.

Culture/Grade Level Index

References are to entry numbers, not page numbers.
Grade levels follow entry numbers.

Lewin, Ted, *Big Jimmy's Kum Kau Chinese Take Out*, 154 (1–3)

Lin, Grace, *Dim Sum for Everyone!* 155 (K–2)

Fortune Cookie Fortunes, 161 (PS–2)

The Year of the Dog, 435 (3–6)

Look, Lenore, *Henry's First-Moon Birthday*, 164 (1–3)

Love As Strong As Ginger, 95 (2–4)

Ruby Lu, Brave and True, 458 (2–4)

Uncle Peter's Amazing Chinese Wedding, 184 (1–3)

Lord, Bette Bao, *In the Year of the Boar and Jackie Robinson*, 316, 436 (4–6)

Marsden, Carolyn, and Virginia Shin-Mui Loh, *The Jade Dragon*, 460 (3–5)

Morris, Ann, *Grandma Lai Goon Remembers*, 272 (2–5)

Namioka, Lensey, *Yang the Eldest and His Odd Jobs*, 101 (4–6)

Stone, Amy, *Maya Lin*, 350 (3–6)

Thong, Roseanne, *One Is a Drummer*, 35 (PS–1)

Yee, Lisa, *Millicent Min*, 67 (4–6+)

Stanford Wong Flunks Big-Time, 68 (4–6+)

Yep, Laurence, *Skunk Scout*, 102 (3–6)

Yin, *Coolies*, 372 (4–6)

Young, Ed, *My Mei Mei*, 79 (K–3)

Cuban American

Chapra, Mimi, *Amelia's Show-and-Tell Fiesta / Amelia y la fiesta de "muestra y cuenta,"* 181 (PS–1)

Egyptian, Ancient

Bower, Tamara, *How the Amazon Queen Fought the Prince of Egypt*, 122 (4–6+)

Lattimore, Deborah Nourse, *The Winged Cat*, 124 (4–6+)

Love, D. Anne, *Of Numbers and Stars*, 125 (3–6)

Trumble, Kelly, *The Library of Alexandria*, 126 (5–6+)

Eurasian–Turkey

Demi, *The Hungry Coat*, 249 (2–6)

Johnson-Davies, Denys, *Goha the Wise Fool*, 251 (3–6)

European see also Greek, Ancient; Jewish–European

Aylesworth, Jim, reteller, *The Gingerbread Man*, 224 (PS–2)

European–Austria

Rubin, Susan Goldman, *The Flag with Fifty-Six Stars*, 340 (5–6+)

European–Bosnia-Herzegovina

Bunting, Eve, *Gleam and Glow*, 420, 447 (3–6)

European–Czech

Kushner, Tony, *Brundibar*, 342 (3–6)

European–England

Aliki, *William Shakespeare and the Globe*, 277 (3–6)

Davidson, Rebecca Piatt, *All the World's a Stage*, 279 (4–6)

Mayer, Marianna, *William Shakespeare's The Tempest*, 280 (All Ages)

European–France

McClintock, Barbara, reteller, *Cinderella*, 221 (2–4)

Morgenstern, Susie, *A Book of Coupons*, 406 (3–5)

European–Ireland

Bunting, Eve, *Market Day*, 388 (1–3)

European–Netherlands

Fleming, Candace, *Boxes for Katje*, 348 (3–5)

European–Norway

Batt, Tanya Robyn, *The Princess and the White Bear King*, 242 (2–5)

Blake, Robert J., *Togo*, 445 (2–4)

Lunge-Larsen, Lise, *The Race of the Birkebeiners*, 238 (3–6)

The Troll with No Heart in His Body and Other Tales of Trolls, from Norway, 243 (2–5)

European–Russia

Horn, Sandra Ann, *Babushka*, 176 (PS–2)

European–Switzerland

Brett, Jan, *The Gingerbread Baby*, 225 (PS–2)

European American see also specific groups, such as German American, Irish American, Italian American, Polish American

Adler, David A., *America's Champion Swimmer*, 134 (2–5)

A Picture Book of Amelia Earhart, 326 (1–3)

Best, Cari, *Shrinking Violet*, 45 (1–3)

Bunting, Eve, *Riding the Tiger*, 104 (4–6)

The Wall, 349 (2–6)

Muslim

Muslim American

Native American

Author Index

References are to entry numbers, not page numbers.

Title Index

References are to entry numbers, not page numbers.

Illustrator Index

References are to entry numbers, not page numbers.

Subject/Grade Level Index

References are to entry numbers, not page numbers.
Grade levels follow entry numbers.

Shea, Pegi Deitz, *The Whispering Cloth*, 307 (3–6)

Families
Morris, Ann, *Families*, 4 (PS–1)

Family life
Hausherr, Rosmarie, *Celebrating Families*, 110 (All ages)

Morris, Ann, *Grandma Hekmatt Remembers*, 419 (2–5)

Grandma Lai Goon Remembers, 272 (2–5

Grandma Maxine Remembers, 273 (2–5)

Family life–Fiction
Ada, Alma Flor, *I Love Saturdays y domingos*, 107 (PS–2)

Cameron, Ann, *Gloria's Way*, 100 (2–4)

Curtis, Christopher Paul, *The Watsons Go to Birmingham, 1963*, 358 (4–6+)

Erdrich, Louise, *The Birchbark House*, 456 (4–6+)

Friedman, Ina R., *How My Parents Learned to Eat*, 108 (1–3)

Giovanni, Nikki, *Knoxville, Tennessee*, 150 (PS–2)

Hamanaka, Sheila, *Grandparents Song*, 109 (K–3)

Havill, Juanita, *Jamaica Tag-Along*, 21 (K–2)

Johnson, Angela, *Heaven*, 432 (5–6+)

Johnston, Tony, *Any Small Goodness*, 433 (3–6)

Joosse, Barbara M., *Mama, Do You Love Me?* 92 (PS–1)

Papa, Do You Love Me? 93 (PS–1)

Juster, Norton, *The Hello, Goodbye Window*, 94 (PS–1)

Lee, Milly, *Landed*, 311 (4–6)

Nim and the War Effort, 449 (3–5)

Levinson, Riki, *Soon, Annala*, 312 (K–3)

Watch the Stars Come Out, 313 (K–3)

Lin, Grace, *The Year of the Dog*, 435 (3–6)

Look, Lenore, *Ruby Lu, Brave and True*, 458 (2–4)

Marsden, Carolyn, and Virginia Shin-Mui Loh, *The Jade Dragon*, 460 (3–5)

Mitchell, Rhonda, *The Talking Cloth*, 305 (2–4)

Namioka, Lensey, *Yang the Eldest and His Odd Jobs*, 101 (4–6)

Polacco, Patricia, *When Lightning Comes in a Jar*, 151 (2–4)

Schertle, Alice, *Down the Road*, 97 (K–2)

Smith, Cynthia Leitich, *Indian Shoes*, 66, 462 (3–6)

Steptoe, Javaka, *The Jones Family Express*, 148 (2–4)

Van Leeuwen, Jean, *Going West*, 289 (1–3)

Woodson, Jacqueline, *Visiting Day*, 452 (3–5)

We Had a Picnic This Sunday Past, 152 (1–3)

Yep, Laurence, *Skunk Scout*, 102 (3–6)

Fathers–Fiction
Curtis, Christopher Paul, *Bud, Not Buddy*, 430 (4–6+)

Fear–Fiction
Polacco, Patricia, *Thunder Cake*, 96 (K–2)

Fiestas
Elya, Susan Middleton, *F Is for Fiesta*, 41, 182 (PS–3)

Orozco, José-Luis, selector, arranger,and translator, *Fiestas*, 183 (PS–3)

Fiestas–Fiction
Chapra, Mimi, *Amelia's Show-and-Tell Fiesta / Amelia y la fiesta de "muestra y cuenta,"* 181 (PS–1)

Folklore *see also* Fables
Aylesworth, Jim, reteller, *The Gingerbread Man*, 224 (PS–2)

Hurston, Zora Neale, collector, *The Six Fools*, 250 (2–6)

Kimmel, Eric A., *The Runaway Tortilla*, 228 (PS–2)

MacDonald, Margaret Read, *Tuck-Me-In Tales*, 90 (PS–1)

Morales, Yuyi, *Just a Minute*, 264 (1–3)

Muten, Burleigh, *Grandmothers' Stories*, 274 (1–5)

Salley, Colleen, *Epossumondas*, 253 (K–3)

Folklore–Africa
Aardema, Verna, *Rabbit Makes a Monkey of Lion*, 260 (2–4)

Bryan, Ashley, *Beautiful Blackbird*, 236 (2–4)

McDermott, Gerald, adapter, *Anansi the Spider*, 232 (1–4)

Folklore–Australia
Czernecki, Stefan, and Timothy Rhodes, *The Singing Snake*, 245 (2–4)

Roth, Susan L., *The Biggest Frog in Australia*, 240 (1–3)

Folklore–Caribbean
San Souci, Robert D., *Cendrillon*, 222 (2–4)

Folklore–China
Demi, *The Dragon's Tale*, 230 (2–4)

The Greatest Power, 256 (2–6)

Young, Ed, *The Lost Horse*, 241 (2–4)

Montparker, Carol, *Polly and the Piano*, 212 (3–6)

Namioka, Lensey, *Yang the Eldest and His Odd Jobs*, 101 (4–6)

Mystery stories

Cushman, Doug, *The Mystery of King Karfu*, 123 (PS–2)

Mythology—Greek

Yolen, Jane, *Wings*, 106 (2–6)

Names—Fiction

Choi, Yangsook, *The Name Jar*, 46 (2–4)

Recorvits, Helen, *My Name Is Yoon*, 50 (1–3)

Nature

Swinburne, Stephen R., *The Woods Scientist*, 103 (3–6)

Nature—Fiction

Yep, Laurence, *Skunk Scout*, 102 (3–6)

Neighborhoods—Fiction

Cole, Kenneth, *No Bad News*, 111 (1–4)

Shin, Sun Yung, *Cooper's Lesson*, 112 (2–4)

Smith, Patricia, *Janna and the Kings*, 113 (1–3)

Steptoe, John, *Creativity*, 114 (3–6)

Tauss, Marc, *Superhero*, 115 (1–4)

Nepal—Fiction

Young, Ed, *I, Doko*, 195 (2–6)

Netherlands—Fiction

Borden, Louise, *The Greatest Skating Race*, 332 (3–6)

Fleming, Candace, *Boxes for Katje*, 348 (3–5)

Nigeria—Fiction

Olaleye, Isaac, *Bikes for Rent!* 384 (3–6)

Onyefulu, Ifeoma, *Here Comes Our Bride! An African Wedding Story*, 185 (1–3)

Norway—Folklore

Batt, Tanya Robyn, *The Princess and the White Bear King*, 242 (2–5)

Lunge-Larsen, Lise, *The Race of the Birkebeiners*, 238 (3–6)

The Troll with No Heart in His Body and Other Tales of Trolls, from Norway, 243 (2–5)

Nursery rhymes

Benjamin, Floella, collector, *Skip Across the Ocean*, 158 (PS–2)

Unobagha, Uzo, *Off to the Sweet Shores of Africa, and Other Talking Drum Rhymes*, 162 (PS–2)

Operas

Kushner, Tony, *Brundibar*, 342 (3–6)

Origami—Fiction

Falwell, Cathryn, *Butterflies for Kiri*, 189 (1–3)

Wells, Rosemary, *Yoko's Paper Cranes*, 190 (PS–2)

Parker, Charlie

Raschka, Chris, *Charlie Parker Played Be Bop*, 199 (1–3)

Parker, John P.

Rappaport, Doreen, *Freedom River*, 293 (3–5)

Parks, Rosa

Giovanni, Nikki, *Rosa*, 369 (2–6)

Peru—Folklore

Ehlert, Lois, *Moon Rope*, 237 (2–4)

Pets—Fiction

Fleming, Candace, *Lowji Discovers America*, 65 (3–6)

Philosophy

Muth, Jon J, *The Three Questions*, 258 (3–6)

Zen Shorts, 259 (3–6)

Pickett, Bill

Pinkney, Andrea D., *Bill Pickett*, 285 (1–4)

Pilots

Adler, David A., *A Picture Book of Amelia Earhart*, 326 (1–3)

Brooks, Philip, *The Tuskegee Airmen*, 327 (3–5)

Cummins, Julie, *Tomboy of the Air*, 328 (3–6)

Demarest, Chris L., *Lindbergh*, 329 (2–4)

Grimes, Nikki, *Talkin' About Bessie*, 330 (2–5)

Pilots—Fiction

Johnson, Angela, *Wind Flyers*, 331 (1–4)

Plays *see also* **Reader's Theater, Theater**

Bruchac, Joseph, *Pushing Up the Sky*, 278 (2–6)

Davidson, Rebecca Piatt, *All the World's a Stage*, 279 (4–6)

Mayer, Marianna, *William Shakespeare's The Tempest*, 280 (All Ages)

Poetry

Ada, Alma Flor, *Gathering the Sun*, 368 (2–6)

Alarcón, Francisco X., *Poems to Dream Together / Poemas para soñar juntos*, 213 (4–6+)

Slavery *see also* **Underground Railroad**

Slavery—Fiction
Hopkinson, Deborah, *Sweet Clara and the Freedom Quilt*, 303 (2–4)
Woodson, Jacqueline, *Show Way*, 308 (3–5)
Wyss, Thelma Hatch, *Bear Dancer*, 444 (3–6)

Slaves—Biography
Pringle, Laurence, *American Slave, American Hero*, 286 (3–5)

Sled dogs—Fiction
Blake, Robert J., *Togo*, 445 (2–4)

Songs and lullabies
Delacre, Lulu, selector, *Arrorró mi niño*, 88 (PS–1)
Ho, Minfong, *Hush! A Thai Lullaby*, 89 (PS–1)
Orozco, José-Luis, selector, arranger,and translator, *Fiestas*, 183 (PS–3)

South Africa
Angelou, Maya, *My Painted House, My Friendly Chicken, and Me*, 394 (1–4)
Cave, Kathryn, *One Child, One Seed*, 30 (K–2)

South Africa—Biography
Cooper, Floyd, *Mandela*, 360 (2–6)
McDonough, Yona Zeldis, *Peaceful Protest*, 361 (4–6)

South Africa—Fiction
Daly, Niki, *Happy Birthday, Jamela!* 16 (K–2)
Jamela's Dress, 11 (K–2)
What's Cooking, Jamela? 17 (K–2)
Where's Jamela? 18 (K–2)
Isadora, Rachel, *Over the Green Hills*, 395 (K–2)
Sisulu, Elinor Batezat, *The Day Gogo Went to Vote*, 355 (2–4)
Winter, Jeanette, *Elsina's Clouds*, 397 (K–3)

South Africa—Folklore
Stewart, Dianne, *Gift of the Sun*, 254 (2–4)

South America—Fiction
Torres, Leyla, *Saturday Sancocho*, 157, 387 (1–3)

South America—Folklore
McDermott, Gerald, reteller, *Jabutí the Tortoise*, 247 (2–4)

Spanish language
Elya, Susan Middleton, *F Is for Fiesta*, 41, 182 (PS–3)
Morales, Yuyi, *Just a Minute*, 264 (1–3)

Speeches
King, Martin Luther, Jr., *I Have a Dream*, 365 (1–6)

Sports *see also* specific sports, such as **Basketball, Boxing**

Sports—Biography *see also* specific sports such as **Baseball—Biography**
Adler, David A., *America's Champion Swimmer*, 134 (2–5)
Bruchac, Joseph, *Jim Thorpe's Bright Path*, 138 (2–4)
Krull, Kathleen, *Wilma Unlimited*, 139 (2–4)

Statue of Liberty—Fiction
Bunting, Eve, *A Picnic in October*, 309 (1–3)

Storytelling
Lewin, Ted, *The Storytellers*, 271 (1–4)
Morris, Ann, *Grandma Hekmatt Remembers*, 419 (2–5)
Grandma Lai Goon Remembers, 272 (2–5)
Grandma Maxine Remembers, 273 (2–5)

Storytelling—Fiction
Aliki, *Marianthe's Story One*, 268 (1–3)
Muth, Jon J, *Zen Shorts*, 259 (3–6)

Storytelling—Japan
Say, Allen, *Kamishibai Man*, 275 (1–5)

Superheroes—Fiction
Tauss, Marc, *Superhero*, 115 (1–4)

Tanzania—Fiction
Mollel, Tololwa M., *My Rows and Piles of Coins*, 383 (1–3)
Stuve-Bodeen, Stephanie, *Babu's Song*, 386 (3–6)

Teeth
Beeler, Selby, *Throw Your Tooth on the Roof*, 80 (K–3)

Teeth—Fiction
Diakité, Penda, *I Lost My Tooth in Africa*, 81 (1–3)
Ruelle, Karen Gray, *Dear Tooth Fairy*, 82 (K–2)

Thailand—Fiction
Shea, Pegi Deitz, *The Whispering Cloth*, 307 (3–6)

Thanksgiving—Fiction
Bruchac, Joseph, *Squanto's Journey*, 453 (2–5)

Theater *see also* **Plays, Reader's Theater**
The World of Theater, 282 (All ages)

ABOUT THE AUTHORS

KATHY EAST, assistant director and head of youth services at the Wood County District Public Library in Bowling Green, Ohio, is active in professional organizations regionally, nationally, and internationally. A former president of the Association for Library Service to Children and former chair of the Caldecott Committee, East has represented the American Library Association at the International Federation of Library Associations and Institutions in the Section on Children and Young Adults.

REBECCA L. THOMAS is an elementary school librarian, Shaker Heights City Schools, Ohio. She has served on the Caldecott Committee and Penguin Putnam Award Committee for the American Library Association. She is also an adjunct professor at Baldwin-Wallace College in Berea, Ohio, where she teaches a graduate-level course in children's and YA literature, and a recipient of the Mary Karrer Award from Ohio State University's College of Education. She is the author of numerous reference books, including the *Popular Series Fiction* set for Libraries Unlimited (2004) and *Connecting Cultures* (Bowker, 1996).